PERSPECTIVES ON ECONOMIC DEVELOPMENT:

ESSAYS IN THE HONOUR OF W. ARTHUR LEWIS

edited by

T. E. BARKER
Lecturer in Economics,
University of the West Indies.

A. S. DOWNES
Lecturer in Economics,
University of the West Indies.

J. A. SACKEY
Economist, World Bank,
formerly Lecturer in Economics,
University of the West Indies.

PUBLISHED ON BEHALF OF:
    The Department of Economics
    University of the West Indies,
    Cave Hill Campus,
    Barbados.

UNIVERSITY
PRESS OF
AMERICA

LANHAM • NEW YORK • LONDON

Copyright © 1982 by

University Press of America,™ Inc.

4720 Boston Way
Lanham, MD 20706

3 Henrietta Street
London WC2E 8LU England

Library of Congress Cataloging in Publication Data

Main entry under title:

Perspectives on economic development.

"List of the works of W. Arthur Lewis": p.
Includes index.
1. Economic development—Addresses, essays, lectures.
2. Underdeveloped areas—Addresses, essays, lectures.
3. Lewis, W. Arthur (William Arthur), 1915-   .
I. Lewis, W. Arthur (William Arthur), 1915-   .
II. Barker, T.E. III. Downes, A.S. IV. Sackey, J.A.
HD82.P447   338.9   81-43790
ISBN 0-8191-2381-1   AACR2
ISBN 0-8191-2382-X (pbk.)

PERSPECTIVES

ON

ECONOMIC DEVELOPMENT

ESSAYS IN THE HONOUR OF
W. ARTHUR LEWIS

Edited by

T. Barker, A. Downes and J. Sackey

"TO ALL WHO ARE
STRUGGLING TO OVERCOME
POVERTY IN THE
THIRD WORLD".

C O N T E N T S

C O N T E N T S

A C K N O W L E D G E M E N T S

We would like to thank all those contributors who readily responded to our call for papers. Without them, this volume would not be possible. The editor of the 'Manchester School' kindly granted us permission to reprint the article "The Lewis Model and Development Theory" by P.L. Lesson. We are grateful to those members of the Department of Economics who commented on the introduction and also rendered useful assistance during the preparation of the volume. Audine Wilkinson, the Librarian of the Institute of Social and Economic Research, University of the West Indies, Cave Hill Campus allowed us to use her bibliography of Lewis' works. Nigel Walrond also assisted throughout various stages of the project. Special thanks go to Betty Thorpe who patiently typed all the correspondence in addition to retyping some of the papers included in the volume and Cynthia Fields for her assistance in typing the final manuscript.

I N T R O D U C T I O N

The post-war awakening to the plight of the so-called "Third World" brought a renewed interest in the subject of economic development. The literature on economic development is voluminous. It ranges from analyses of the causes of under-development to a plethora of policy prescriptions relating to the achievement of development targets. One eminent economist who has contributed significantly to the study of economic development is Professor W. Arthur Lewis of Princeton University. Professor Lewis was one of the first economists to undertake indepth analyses of the problems of developing countries and also to suggest policies for overcoming these problems.

William Arthur Lewis was born on January 23, 1915 on the island of St. Lucia in the British West Indies. He received his early education at St. Mary's College in St. Lucia before proceeding to the London School of Economics and Political Science (L.S.E.) where he received a Bachelor of Commerce degree. He then went on to Manchester University, where he obtained his Masters degree. Returning to the L.S.E., he obtained his Doctorate in 1940.

Lewis was closely attached to the London School of Economics and Manchester University. Between 1938-1947 he was a lecturer in Economics at the L.S.E. In 1947, he was appointed Reader in Colonial Economics. While teaching at the L.S.E. he expressed a keen interest in micro-economic theory, but his appointment to Reader in Colonial Economics enabled him to undertake detailed research on the problems facing the British colonies. Lewis' interest in development problems was further stimulated when he moved to Manchester University where he occupied the Stanley Jevons Chair of Political Economy from 1948-1958.

During the period 1948-1958, Lewis was able to contribute a series of seminal works relating to the nature of economic growth and the process of economic development. Two of his best known contributions are "Economic Development with Unlimited Supplies of Labor" (Manchester School, May 1954) and a book entitled "The Theory of Economic Growth" (Allen and Unwin 1955). Lewis extended and applied the ideas propounded in these studies in a series of other contributions in the 1950's (Lewis 1958a, 1958b).

Lewis is known for his ingenious employment of classical methodology in his analysis of development processes and problems. His celebrated 1954 article and its later extensions (Lewis (1958a), (1973), (1979), examined the development of a dual economy within the framework of both a closed and an open economy. He analysed the process of economic transformation whereby excess labor in the subsistence sector would be gradually absorbed by the capitalist sector. Implicit in this process of resource reallocation is the industrialization of the economy, coupled with the gradual modernization of the agricultural sector. In this context, Lewis was oriented towards a balanced growth strategy, in that he analysed the process of transition from a traditional to a mature industrial economy while emphasizing the need for agricultural development to increase food productivity (Lewis, 1953). The framework utilized by Lewis has been commented upon and extended by several economists (for example Harris and Todaro (1970). Extensions have been suggested within the context of rural-urban migration, determination of shadow wage rate in project evaluation and urban unemployment.

Although his position at Manchester University was academically simulating, Lewis always felt that he had a commitment to contribute to the development of West Indies in a practical way. His keen interest in the role of education in economic development led him to accept the post of Principal at the University College of the West Indies in 1959. He was instrumental in extending the campuses of the University College, and above all, in securing autonomy for the institution from the University of London. In 1962, he was appointed to the distinguished post of Vice-Chancellor of the University of the West Indies.

In 1968, Lewis returned to the academic field, when he accepted the post of Professor of Public and International Affairs at Princeton University in the U.S.A. He held this position for five years, until he was appointed in 1968 to the distinguished post of James Madison Professor of Political

Economy at the Woodrow Wilson School of Public and
International Affairs at Princeton University. Despite his substantive position, Lewis was still able to
continue his contribution to the economic development
of the West Indies. In 1970, he was seconded from his
post at Princeton, to become the first president of
the Caribbean Development Bank. His wide knowledge of
economic affairs and his managerial expertise gained
the Bank a high international reputation. Despite his
workload, he was able to function as Chancellor of the
University of Guyana between 1966-1973. In 1973 he
returned to Princeton University.

Lewis devoted a great deal of his time to
the practical aspects of poverty eradication and the
increasing of employment opportunities through working
directly with several governments in the developing
world. He was a consultant to the Caribbean Commission
(1949), the United Nations Economic Commission for
Asia and the Far East (1952), Gold Coast (now Ghana)
Government (1953), West Nigerian Government (1955) and
also adviser to the Prime Minister of Ghana (1957-58)
and the Prime Minister of the West Indies Federation
(1961). He was also a member of the United Nations
Group of Experts on Underdeveloped Countries (1951) and
the Deputy Managing Director of the United Nations
Special Fund (1959-60). He co-authored the famous
"Partner in Progress:Pearson Commission Report" under
the auspicies of the World Bank in 1969. At the
invitation of the Premier of Trinidad and Tobago, he
drafted its first development plan (1958-63), along
with Theodore Moscoso of Puerto Rico. In recent times,
he has been advising on ways in which economic integration can be useful strategy for increasing growth and
furthering the development process in the Caribbean.

Professor Lewis' distinguished academic and
administrative careers have brought him two illustrious
commendations. In 1963, a knighthood was conferred
upon him, while in 1979, he was jointly awarded a
Nobel Prize for his contribution to economics especial-
ly in the area of economic development and planning.
In addition, Lewis has been granted a number of
honorary doctorates from various universities including
Toronto, Columbia, Dakar, Bristol, Rutgers, Manchester,
Lagos and West Indies. He has also been a Fellow of
Several Societies, including the American Economic
Association.

Lewis was visiting Professor of Economics at the University of the West Indies, Cave Hill Campus. During his sojourn 1975-1978, he taught a course in Development Planning to both under-graduate and graduate students. In recognition of his contribution to the development of the Department of Economics, this volume has been compiled in his honor.

In his writings, Lewis has exhibited the notion that economic development analysis is multi-disciplinary and pragmatic. In this regard, his interest in development planning from both theoretical and practical perspectives led to his writing of two key texts: Principles of Economic Planning (Allen and Unwin, 1963), and "Development Planning: Essential of Economic Policy (Allen and Unwin, 1966). These books drew upon his vast experiences as a practising development planner and adviser and provided a unique blend of theory and practice. To Lewis, development planning involves the formulation and implementation of appropriate policies. He placed emphasis on the fulfilment of basic social needs. According to Lewis, development plans should include the requirements for eradicating poverty, that is, the provision of "food, shelter, clothing, access to essential services, such as safe drinking water, sanitation, transport, health and education, and also that each person available for and willing to work should have an adequately remunerative job" (I.L.O, 1976, pp. 7).

The role of international economic changes on the process of economic development was also emphasized by Lewis. In his Nobel Prize acceptance speech, he noted that "for the past hundred years the rate of growth of output in the developing world has depended on the rate of growth of output in the developed world" (Lewis, 1980, pp. 555). His analysis of the world economy from a historical perspective led to his "rather deep rooted pervasive skepticism about the effectiveness of trade as an engine of growth" (Findlay, 1980, pp. 72). In fact, he has always suggested that developing countries should seek to develop their economies principally (but not without external assistance) on their own potential. He had long pointed out that "the central problem in the theory of economic growth is to understand the process by which a community which was previously saving and investing 4 or 5 per cent of its national income or less, converts itself into an economy where voluntary saving is running at about 12 to 15 per cent of national income or more" (Lewis, 1954). He did not analyze this process in solely economic terms, but relied substantially on the non-economic factors which can affect the savings capacity of the economy. In this regard, Lewis' approach is a classic example of the inter-disciplinary method of development analysis and provides an exception to the generally ahistorical examination of development problems.

Although, Lewis emphasises the dominant fundamentals of the period, he nevertheless, operates in a multidisciplinary and 'general equilibrium' framework. In this context, he sees economic development as a "multi-dimensional" process which can only be analysed within a broad perspective. This broad perspective underlies the essays in this collection to honor his contribution to development economics.

The contributions of the various development economists brought together in these essays are broad and varied. They cover Arthur Lewis' main areas of interest. The first in the volume is a review by P.F. Leeson of the Lewis model of Economic Development with Unlimited Supplies of Labor (Lewis, 1954). It is articulated within the context of the model's role in the growth of development economics. Leeson briefly outlines the Lewis model and then discusses various criticisms of it. He also extends the basic Lewis model and discusses the effects on the model of both the transformation of the subsistence sector and changes in the capitalist sector wage rate. Finally, Leeson looks at the Lewis model in a historic context and notes that it was mainly intended to shed light on historical changes. It is shown that the Lewis model is still a very illuminating framework within which to discuss the process of economic development.

Professor W. Baer uses the Lewis model to examine industrialization and development in the special context of the experiences of Latin American countries. Tracing through the historical dimensions of the industrialization process in the early 20th century, Baer focuses on the import substitution strategy in the post world war 11 period and discusses its shortcomings. In particular, he discusses the effect of neglecting exports and the creation of industrial dependency. Finally, the study investigates the current role of industry in the context of (i) employment, (ii) income distribution, (iii) regional concentration, (iv) multinationals; and (v) the role of state enterprises in the industrialization process. Essentially, the emphasis is placed on the future role of industry on the region's domestic and international growth.

F. Long's study illuminates and extends the issue of industrialization and development by discussing the question of the transfer of technology with special reference to a dual sector framework. Long notes that the Lewis model does not explicitly deal with the subject of technological transfer and argues that an open economy version of the model has important implications for the question of technology transfer. He cites evidence to suggest that the industrialization experience of many developing countries based on modern (imported) technology appears to have fallen much short of theoretical expectation. Growth has taken place in a large number of instances, but development remains questionable, partly as a result of technological distortions. He points out, however, that an international code of conduct on technology transfer is being elaborated to minimize some of the problems facing developing countries in this area.

Emanating from Long's analysis relating to distortions inherent in improper technology transfer, the role of proper policy formulation becomes eminent. It is from the perspective of proper policy formulation that Professor B. Johnston argues that programmes which advance understanding and effective action in attaining the goals of development require a combination of economic and policy analyses. In particular, he attributes the failure of many developing countries to reduce poverty (especially in the rural areas), in no small measure, to a common failure to supplement formal economic analysis with a policy analysis perspective. In this context, Johnston suggests a move away from the fad in development economics of emphasizing fundamentalism such as "capital shortage" and "basic needs". Hence, in recognizing that policy analysts have to deal with politicians, they need to learn how "to speak truth to power" clearly and persuasively enough so that development goals are readily achieved.

In addition, Johnston distinguishes between the cogitative (or thinking through) and interactive (or acting out) approaches to policy analysis. He appeals for a greater emphasis to be placed on the latter, especially in the context of rural development strategy. In general, Johnston examines three programme areas from the perspective of policy analysis: production, consumption and organization.

Johnston's three policy prongs of a strategy for rural development are, to a substantial extent, consistent with the concept of basic needs. Professor P. Streeten, however, looks beyond the simple policy characteristics of a basic needs strategy (B.N.S.) and discusses its complementarity with the new international economic order (N.I.E.O). He notes that the relationship between a B.N.S. and the N.I.E.O can be discussed at several levels, but stresses that the complementarity of the concepts derives from the view that if the N.I.E.O leads to more resources for the developing countries, this can contribute to basic needs satisfaction. Similarly, the objectives of a B.N.S. can be seen as those for which support for international cooperation can be mobilized. Streeten further elaborates on the benefits to be derived if a B.N.S. is adopted on a global scale and suggests means of attaining these benefits. Finally, he identifies and responds to the negative reactions to a B.N.S. in both rich and poor countries.

While a basic needs strategy has been identified as a potentially useful one for solving the problem of poverty in developing countries, J. Harewood takes us further by exploring the relationship between unemployment and poverty in the special context of the Commonwealth Caribbean countries. He initially discusses at length the weaknesses inherent in the scanty data on unemployment in the region. He also explores the problems of defining and quantifying poverty, especially in the context of LDCs like those in the Caribbean. Nevertheless, based on available data especially for Trinidad and Tobago, Harewood argues that the evidence does not confirm the view that there is a very close relationship between unemployment and poverty in the region. Deriving from this observation, he suggests that programmes oriented toward solving the region's poverty through reducing the level of unemployment may not be entirely successful. The paper, in addition, provides case studies on various strategies employed for solving the region's unemployment and poverty problems, and evaluates their impact in the light of the available information.

In his evaluation of the relative efficacy of various policy strategy for reducing unemployment, Professor A. Blomqvist takes a special look at the problem of unemployed graduates in LDCs. Specifically, he constructs an explicitly dynamic model of human (i.e. education) and non-human capital formation where there is wage rigidity in the market for educated manpower. This model explains how graduate unemployment arises. With the framework of the model, Blomqvist also considers the question of the second-best policy measures (such as employment subsidies or changes in the private costs of education), given that wage rigidity cannot be directly removed.

The principal derivatives of Blomqvist's analysis are that under certain conditions, the appropriate shadow price of labor may be equal to, or even exceed, its market wage when graduate unemployment exists, and that the optimal level of an employment subsidy may be either positive or negative. Similarly, he demonstrates that the wage rigidity may lead to a situation, analogous to the one considered by Bhagwati and others in their work on "immiserizing growth", in which attempts to raise the long-run level of consumption in the economy through additional capital formation will in fact reduce long-run welfare.

Professor A. Prest's paper is essentially a critical review of empirical studies on public sector expenditure and revenue ratios. His point of departure is the study by Martin and Lewis (1956) on the pattern of public revenue and expenditure in the process of economic development. Prest briefly reviews the Martin-Lewis study and examines its policy conclusions in the light of new methodological approaches and the availability of more refined and longer data sets. In general, Professor Prest calls our attention to the difficulties in interpreting the various expenditure and revenue ratios from a policy perspective. Within the realm of suggestions, he appeals for a more in-depth micro-type analysis into government expenditure and revenue on a country-by-country basis rather than the broad inter-country comparisons that are apparently limited in their policy orientation.

Professor W. Rostow looks at the historical experience of the impact of the terms of trade on the economic performance of a number of countries. He views the development of trade theory from Ricardo to the Neoclassicals as being inadequate for explaining the dynamic movements in the terms of trade. The main reason for this view is that the tools utilized are a-historical. From the policy perspective, Rostow notes that the fluctuations in the terms of trade can yield a constructive outcome if the economy has the "capacity to transform". This was evident in Latin America in the 1930s and is quite possible in the current era of high energy and agricultural prices. This capacity to transform or react to changes in the international economy can determine the extent to which developing countries can further their economic development.

The 'capacity to transform' can be enhanced by regional economic integration. W. Demas elaborates on the ways by which small developing countries can react to changes in the international economy through economic integration. This note, originally an appendix to a larger report submitted by a committee set up to analyse the difficulties and challenges of the Caribbean integration movement (CARICOM), reviews the rationale for economic integration in the Commonwealth Caribbean. In addition, to analyzing the traditional rationale for integration, Demas places emphasis on the role of functional cooperation in the context of an integration scheme involving unequal partners. He also offers clarification on issues related to the free movement of factors of production, the common independent currency, the role of public vis-a-vis private sectors in the integration scheme and the part played by ideological differences in the integration process.

AUGUST 1981

T. Barker, A. Downes, J. Sackey

REFERENCES

FINDLAY, R. - "On W. Arthur Lewis' Contributions to Economics" *Scandinavian Journal of Economics*, 1980, pp 62-79.

HARRIS J. R. & M. P. TODARO: - "Migration, Unemployment and Development: A Two Sector Analysis" *American Economic Review*, Vol. 70, No, 1, March 1970, pp 126-142.

MARTIN A. & W. A. LEWIS: - "Patterns of Public Revenue and Expenditure" *The Manchester School*, September 1956, pp 203-244.

INTERNATIONAL LABOUR ORGANISATION: - *Employment, Growth and Basic Needs: A One World Problem*, 1976.

LEWIS W. A.: - *Industrial Development in the Caribbean*, Caribbean Commission, 1949.

LEWIS W. A.: - *Aspects of Industrialization*, Cairo, National Bank of Egypt 1953.

LEWIS W. A.: - "Economic Development with Unlimited Supplies of Labour" *The Manchester School*, Vol 22, No. 2, May 1954, pp 139-161.

LEWIS W. A.: - *The Theory of Economic Growth*, London, Allen and Unwin, 1955.

LEWIS W. A.: - "Unlimited Labour: Further Notes" *The Manchester School*, Vol 26, No. 1, 1958a, pp. 1-32.

LEWIS W. A.: - "Employment Policy in an Underdeveloped Area" *Social and Economic Studies*, Vol 7, No. 3, September 1958b, pp 42-53.

LEWIS W. A.: - *The Principles of Economic Planning*, London, Allen and Unwin, 1963.

LEWIS W. A.: - *Development Planning: The Essentials of Economic Policy*, London, Allen and Unwin, 1966.

LEWIS W. A.: - "Reflections on Unlimited Labour" in
L. E. diMarco(ed) *International Economics and
Development*, New York, Academic Press, 1972.,
pp. 75-96.

LEWIS W. A.: - "The Dual Economy Revisited" *The
Manchester School* Vol. 48, No. 3 1979, pp. 211-229.

LEWIS W. A.: - "The Slowing Down of the Engine of
Growth" *American Economic Review*, Vol. 70, No. 4,
September, 1980

Who's Who: *An Annual Biographical Dictionary*, London, Adam
and Charles Black, 1981.

THE LEWIS MODEL AND DEVELOPMENT THEORY

by
P. F. Leeson*

INTRODUCTION

When, in May 1954, The Manchester School published "Economic Development with Unlimited Supplies of Labour" by Arthur Lewis, development economics was in its infancy. The twenty-five years of experience by the "less developed countries" since then have been accompanied by a massive growth of the subject, at least in volume terms. During that period the Lewis model has retained its place in the literature, in spite of the many attacks which have been made on it. A listing of the criticisms themselves would make an interesting essay in the history of economic thought, mirroring as they have done the varied standpoints of scholars critical of development economics, as well as the changing preoccupations of those working within it. They have ranged from arguments based on a neo-classical position at one extreme to those based on neo-Marxism at another. They have often exhibited the conflation of the policy-prescriptive with the historical-analytical which is widespread within development economics. However, progress in the subject has not been such that the Lewis model has ever dropped out of discussion, nor has it quite been elevated to the status of respected, but superseded, founding contribution - though it sometimes seems to have suffered the fate of such contributions in being read only in secondary and not always accurate accounts.

THE MODEL

Lewis drew on the historical experience of Western industrialized countries and on the ideas of the classical economists to derive a very general picture of the development process.[1] A "Capitalist"

(Editors' Note: This article first appeared in THE MANCHESTER SCHOOL, Vol. XLVll, No. 3 September, 1979 pp 196-210, and is being reprinted with the kind permission of the editor and the author.)

sector develops by drawing labour from a non-capital-
ist "subsistence" sector. In a variant of the model
there is trade between the two sectors as well. In
many, though not all, countries, Lewis argues, there
are, at an early stage of development, ample supplies
of labour in the subsistence economy, so that the
supply to the capitalist sector will exceed demand at
a wage which can thus remain constant during a prolonged phase of labour transfer. This wage will be
determined by the alternative available to those
entering capitalist employment, i.e., the standard of
living in the subsistence sector. In practice the
wage will be above that minimum by a margin which is
partly real, necessary to induce labour transfer, and
possible also representing the attainment of a higher
conventional standard of living by capitalist sector
workers, and partly illusory, to compensate for additional costs of living in capitalist sector employment.

        Inside the capitalist sector, as growth
proceeds, the share of profits might vary over time,
depending on the nature of technical change; given
the constant wage it will almost certainly rise. But
even if it stays constant the growth of the capitalist sector relative to the subsistence sector will
mean a growing share of profits in national income.
Since a larger part of profit income is saved and
invested than is the case with other forms of income,
the savings ratio will rise and with it the capital
accumulation on which economic development depends.
This phase comes to an end when the labour surplus
has been absorbed and wages rise. In certain circumstances, however, the wage level might rise and eat
into the capitalist surplus while surplus labour
still exists. Thus rising living standards in the
subsistence sector might exercise an effect on the
real wage minimum. Where trade between the sectors
exists and the capitalist sector buys wage-goods from
the subsistence sector, worsened terms of trade might
cause even a constant real wage to take a larger
share of the capitalist product. Again, workers in
the capitalist sector might, by trade union action or
otherwise, manage to widen the gap between their wage
and subsistence sector standards.

CRITICISMS OF THE MODEL[2]

Some of the early critics focussed on Lewis' suggestion that such could be the extent of surplus labour that the marginal product in the subsistence sector might be zero, so that labour transfer could take place without loss of output. This seemed to have unacceptable implications as to the mode of economic behaviour in the subsistence sector. And if the marginal product rose as labour transferred then so ought the wage schedule to rise too. For others, even the acceptance of Lewis' assumption that it is the average and not the marginal product in the sub-sistence sector which determines the sectoral living standard and, hence, the capitalist wage, left the model with a flaw. Even, or especially, if marginal product is zero or low, labour transfer would result in a rising average income amongst the remaining sectoral members, and hence the logic of the model ought to indicate a rising labour supply price right from the start.

It has been said that the Lewis model por-trays a smooth process of transfer of labour from underemployment in rural areas to full employment in a growing modern industrial urban sector, whereas in fact there is massive un-and underemployment in urban areas and very little surplus labour in the country-side. Moreover the facts belie the supposed link between rural incomes and industrial wages, since the gap has widened enormously. Whilst high urban wages are a major factor in attracting migrants from the countryside, the nature of technical change has been such that very little additional industrial employment is on offer.

It has further been argued that Lewis assumed that there was no problem of the creation of a capitalist class in a backward society, that capitalists would automatically re-invest all their profits, and that no problem of demand for capitalist sector output existed.

To some critics the policy implications of the Lewis model appeared to be that industrialization could, and should, be accomplished without the need to pump extra resources into agriculture, that

3

development via private capitalism is both necessary and desirable, and that rising inequalities are inevitable in the process. They urged that, on the contrary, priority should be given to agricultural and small-scale enterprise, thus leading to greater equality and the more speedy eradication of poverty. So far from the traditional sector being necessarily stagnant and economically irrational there are great possibilities of increasing rural output if farmers are given cheap inputs, better prices for output and appropriate institutional reforms.

These criticisms, based on policy considerations, have certain affinities with others stemming from different considerations. "Dual economy" models, of which Lewis' is one well-known example, are held to imply a false picture of the nature of the historical process of change in underdeveloped countries. The prospect before these countries is not to be conjured up by a picture of a modern sector rising out of a primordial, stagnant, untouched traditional economy, with the implication that all countries can pass through stages of growth which replicate those through which the present day "advanced" countries went. On the contrary, the development of the capitalist world has entailed for a very long time the disruption and restructuring of the economies of the present day underdeveloped countries. So far from the traditional economy being isolated it has for centuries been the victim of exploitative relations with the metropolitan countries.

As for the emerging, so-called "modern" sector this represents neither development of a kind similar to that of the metropoles nor true development by any normative criterion. Such is the structure of international relations that the underdeveloped countries are unable to generate a process of independent capitalist development but are restricted to a warped, dependent, comprador form of relationship benefitting only a minority in each country, and increasingly unable to provide employment for, and generate development from, the numbers of job seekers piling up in the cities. The Lewis process does not operate and the Third World masses are excluded from participation in capitalist world growth.

4

Some of these criticisms could be, and were, answered by Lewis simply by asking his critics to read his original articles more carefully.[3] His two sectors were the "capitalist" and the "subsistence" sectors, not the industrial and the agricultural, nor the urban and the rural. The urban poor were not assumed away but were specifically listed amongst the groupings from which the labour supply comes. Thus the model must be construed to mean that rural to urban migration which does not result in capitalist sector employment is merely a process of moving around inside the composite subsistence sector. Lewis was not assuming that the process of capitalist sector growth is in private capitalist hands. Accumulation in state hands as in the U.S.S.R. would fit just as well. And the process applies just as much to capitalist agriculture, mining or plantations as to industry. The model does not necessarily involve a widening of the existing distribution of income since rising capitalist incomes can go alongside a declining share going to the landowning class. And, as Lewis argues, the model is not normative, it describes what has happened. He himself is fully in favour of devoting resources to improving the lot of the peasants and has written extensively about the need for this, and about the fact that industrial revolutions have often depended on a simultaneous or prior agrarian revolution. It must nevertheless be said that, in spite of Lewis' qualifications, the persuasive force of the model, so far as policy is concerned, is along the lines asserted by the critics.

As for the marginal product in agriculture or in other subsistence sector occupations, Lewis had in mind that the marginal product per man could be zero whilst that per man-hour is positive. When a member leaves the family farm the remaining farmers could maintain output by working harder or longer, and there were, in his judgement, many situations in which they would do this for no greater reward than the addition to their individual incomes of a share in the departing member's consumption. But in any case the model does not depend on the marginal product being zero, merely that it should be less than the industrial wage. To those who pointed to the model's requirement that there should be a link between rising average subsistence sector incomes and the wage, as labour transfer proceeds, Lewis replied, firstly, that population growth in the subsistence sector helps to negate the rise in incomes, and, secondly, that the link between subsistence income and the capitalist sector wage is flexible, so that a small rise in the former need not automatically cause an upward movement in the latter.

Thus Lewis declares himself in favour of realism as against precision in the formulation of his model. If the wage link is weakened too drastically, however, there might not be much of the model left. If the insensitivity of the wage to changes in rural income arises because the gap is very large, then it will be trite to say that there will always be a ready supply of labour at the going wage rate, over a wide range of variation in the average (or marginal) product in the subsistence sector.

Although, as Lewis says, the marginal product in the subsistence sector may not be of importance for the wage function when the sectors do not trade with one another, it certainly is of significance when trade does take place. If the subsistence sector sells wage-goods, especially food, to the capitalist sector, then a fall in subsistence sector output consequent upon labour transfer will be one factor tending to worsen the capitalist terms of trade and tending to enforce a rise in the wage as a fraction of output per man, and thus to reduce accumulation. Put in other words, it forces the capitalist sector to devote more resources to consumption goods to sell subsistence sector members (they are assumed not to buy investment goods) in order to obtain the necessary food for the workers, and hence reduces the resources available for production of capital goods.

Lewis might here have made more use of the composite nature of his subsistence sector. If the entrants to industry come from the urban section of the subsistence sector then, although other kinds of (not necessarily traded) output may be reduced, food output will not suffer. The population growth which tends to offset any rise in subsistence sector incomes will also tend to maintain the work force and thus prevent output from falling - though it may also

6

maintain sectoral consumption, and thus militate against the release of a marketed surplus of wage-goods to accompany the labour transfer.

TRANSFORMATION OF THE SUBSISTENCE SECTOR

But the question arises: why leave the matter there? The Lewis model is concerned with the broad sweep of historical change over a prolonged period. During such a period many changes, all of which have been discussed by writers in this field, will occur in the subsistence sector besides population growth. Many of those changes will be causally related to the process of labour transfer. Whether output is, or is not, maintained when labour transfer occurs depends on so many factors as to render the definition and measurement of marginal product very problematic. In the rural part of the subsistence sector these factors include the balance between migration and population growth and its effect on the age-sex composition; whether non-farming subsistence sector members leave their other tasks, involving non-traded products or products of less significance then food, to help in the harvest; whether labour transfer leads to neglect of long-term maintenance; whether migration is accompanied by reorganization of work as well as longer hours; whether links with the capital-ist sector increase receptivity to new ideas; whether the arrival of capitalist sector consumption goods gives an incentive to increase output for the market. Any outcome is possible when labour leaves the sector, including a rise in output, i.e., the output curve might appear to demonstrate negative marginal product, a possibility mentioned by Lewis. In due course what is here termed the subsistence sector is transformed by capital accumulation (not all of it utilizing investment goods purchased from industry but partially self-generated), accompanied by technical change. The scope for labour-shedding without loss of output becomes very large.

As for the question of subsistence sector living standards and their relationship to the capitalist wage, not only does population growth tend to offset any rise but the process of labour transfer is intimately connected with forces tending to lead

7

to social differentiation within the sector. Even if the model is confined to the assumption that the subsistence sector is made up solely of peasant family farms, the migration process, not being uniform across families, may involve a widening gap between the richer and the poorer. Luck and the varying effects of population growth may have the same effect. The concept of the average is in this case, as in others, misleading. Average income may rise but there may still be a lower stratum for whom the constant minimum wage is sufficient incentive to transfer.

Differentiation also often involves the polarization of the rural population into employers and labourers, or landlords and tenants. In the former case, by analogy with Lewis' over-populated peasant farming regime, it is possible to envisage employers relying on a mixture of full-time (family) labour and a reservoir of casual labour, so that as some workers migrate the others are offered longer hours of employment. But the additional work need not be offered proportionately to all workers. There might be a move towards greater reliance on full-time workers (especially if technology is becoming more capital-using) and the casuals might not benefit. The employer has a perfectly rational reason for the retention in the village of this reservoir of part-time labour since there are periods of peak demand. But we may still finish up with some farm workers living better than some independent peasants; and others, for whom casual work can no longer support life, heading for the town.

The landlord-tenant regime may differ little from the independent peasant regime at one extreme where rents are fixed by custom. But where the landlord is in a position to increase rents when incomes rise (if industrial workers can notice this so can he) then the tenants' incomes need not rise. The proceeds will be intimately linked with migration if it occurs as a result of the re-negotiation of rents when plots are vacated by eviction or otherwise.

Under any of these regimes - peasant ownership, employer-labourer, or landlord-tenant - a situation could exists in which, even with unchanging techniques, labour could migrate without loss of output, and in which, even if average village incomes rose, there would be a ready supply of labour to the capitalist sector at a constant wage. These phenomena can be ecplained all the more readily if there is in progress a transition from a peasant regime to a mixture of the other two – though there may be different implications for, say, total output, depending on which one comes to predominate. Moreover the situation portrayed by Krishna Bharadwaj** in this issue, in which one man may be employer, landlord, moneylender, merchant (and one might add magistrate as well), is a likely state of affairs. In all his role he gains economic bargaining power and political control (important in legal questions to do with land tenure, and in labour discipline) from an over populated village. There must be many cases where we hardly need "the code of ethical behaviour" by which Lewis explains the employer's practice of employing more labourers than the minimum needed. In practice, of course, the transition would not tkae place with unchanging techniques, but would be accompanied by capital accumulation and technical change, often of a labour-saving character, making the maintenance and even increase of output the more likely, and the position of the landless labourers the more precarious.

The differentiation of the rural subsistence economy along these lines helps also to explain why a rise in average rural incomes, if it occurred, need not generate such a rise in rural food consumption as to impede capitalist sector expansion. Probably Lewis' qualification that population growth negates the rise in average incomes in many areas is correct and labour transfer simply prevents incomes from falling as fast as they otherwise might. The differentiation process is relevant in this case in explaining how a rise in rural food consumption consequent on population growth does not occur, and thus threaten the marketed surplus. For poor families population growth means less food per head – accompanied again no doubt by differentiation within the family. It might be noted that the increase in the marketed surplus, consequent upon the changes of regime just described, need not necessarily mean

**Editors' Note: K. Bharadwaj (1979) "Towards a Macroeconomic Framework for a Developing Economy: The Indian Case" Manchester School Vol. 48, no. 3 pp. 270-302.

better terms of trade for industry if the change of regime involves a change from sales by peasants to sales by employer-landlord-merchants with their greater bargaining power.

What of the situation outside agriculture but still inside the subsistence sector? One aspect of the differentiation process is the location of increasing numbers of subsistence sector personnel in urban rather than rural areas. This distinction touches on so many matters of vital importance for a study of Third World economies that there is general agreement that it is quite inadequate to proceed with analysis based simply on one composite subsistence sector. The urban members are nowadays commonly accorded the privilege of having a sector of their own - the Urban "Informal" Sector. But, as Martin Godfrey argues in this issue,[4]** discussion of the Informal Sector does not entail the abandonment of the Lewis model. Analysis of the role of the subsistence sector can be carried out very satisfactorily within the Lewis framework. The Informal Sector contains the labour reservoir willing to work for low pay. It provides cheap non-food wage goods and services for the modern sector. Its capacity to maintain output of services, when members leave to enter capitalist sector employment is even more marked than is that of agriculture. Amongst the sector's relationships with the capitalist and the rural agricultural sectors which are of importance is the question of the balance between the number of migrants from agriculture to informal sector status and the numbers entering capitalist sector jobs. If the former exceeds the latter then a food surplus, adequate for capitalist sector needs, would open up, even if workers consume more food than peasants, provided that the urban poor consume less food than they would have done as peasants.

THE CAPITALIST WAGE

The problem of the link, and the gap, between the industrial wage and subsistence sector

**Editors' Note: The reference here is Godfrey M. (1979): "Rural-Urban Migration in a 'Lewis Model' context" Manchester School Vol 48, no. 3, pp 230-247.

incomes has always been a major difficulty for the Lewis model. The great size of the gap in some countries in the face of large numbers of job seekers - one of the "pull" factors encouraging migration, in addition to the "push" factors discussed above - is a phenomenon on which Lewis (in this issue)** agrees that his model shed little light. Yet the model did make an important contribution in its time to the classical notion of the conventional wage - that it was not based directly on subsistence needs but rather on the alternative standard of living available in the subsistence sector. To see the whole process in historical perspective we ought perhaps to note not only the present day tendency for the wage to be well above subsistence sector standards, but also the occasions when the reverse might have been true, when workers in mines and plantations continued to live in their subsistence sector homes and to derive many of their "wage goods" from the family provision. In this situation wages did not need to provide for the full maintenance of the labourer and yet might, though low, be acceptable as a net addition to the family income. Even when the worker is located in an urban area his family might still be living in the village and be maintained out of subsistence sector output. One whole dimension of the development process is the way in which, by migration and urbanization, the worker and his family become incorporated into modern sector living. They become separated from their sub-sistence sector origins and become dependent on modern sector consumption goods. Indeed the subsistence sector alternative to modern consumer goods may cease to exist. In Lewis' words the workers "may imitate the capitalist way of life" - nowadays increasingly an internationally diffused way of life. The process, still under way even in advanced industrial countries, involves a rise over time in the wage schedule.

It may be that, just as it is relevant to study the structure of rural incomes created by the differentiation process (of which one scheme is out-lined by Martin Godfrey in his paper), so a study of the segmented labour markets in the cities and the concept of non-competing groups discussed by Lewis here is the way to a resolution of the problem of the

**Editors' Note: The reference here is Lewis W. A. (1979): "The Dual Economy Revised "The Manchester School Vol. 48, No. 3 pp. 211-229.

gap. The original model was intended to apply to the wages of unskilled workers for whom subsistence sector occupations were the alternatives. What are the alternatives for other sections? In some cases the great growth of government employment has provided the alternative. Maybe the minority who have attained an international standard of living have established a gulf between themselves and the subsistence economy which is inexplicable in a Lewis model context. But it may also be the case that the Lewis model in its original form applies perfectly well to the incipient capitalist development going on in the Informal Sector.

DUAL ECONOMY MODELS

          Lewis defined his "subsistence sector" as "all that part of the economy which is not using reproducible capital". The term is not very satisfactory, even if we only consider that one variant of the model includes trade between the sectors. Its meaning is strained even further if we go on to envisage the sector as being in a state of transformation, and encompassing peasants, labourers, landlords, employers, merchants. The temptation is great to adopt the alternative, agricultural-industrial, sector distinction.4 But while this may be vital for some purposes it does not call attention to the process which Lewis was discussing. We can, of course, in a formal way, regard as parts of the capitalist sector those bits of the subsistence sector which come to accord with Lewis' definition. But the process of transformation of the "subsistence" sector is gradual and piecemeal. The mixture of regimes within it modifies the functioning even of its "capitalist" units. Whatever it is called, there is value in conjuring up as a starting point for analysis a residual sector, which, in all its variety and change, does not yet possess all the characteristics of a fully operating capitalist economy, and which provides some at least of the resources on which the growth of the capitalist sector depends.

          At any rate the Lewis model can probably be absolved from the strictures made against "dual economy" models that they present a false picture both of historical reality in the subsistence sector and of

12

the future prospects for development in a capitalist
sector. There is nothing in the nature of Lewis'
version of the subsistence sector that requires that
it be in a primeval state. The characteristics of
the sector required for the operation of the model
could have been generated by a prior history of
relationships with the metropoles. The initial
conditions of surplus labour and low incomes have been
generated by a variety of historical circumstances -
including monopoly of land by large landowners,
domination of rural markets by merchants, lack of
opportunities for investment, education and technical
advance - which themselves might well have been the
product of colonial and non-colonial relationships
with the capitalist countries. These are a very
relevant topic of investigation but they do not prevent the operation of the model.

        The mechanisms outlined in the model form,
in fact, a useful framework for the discussion of how
some of the phenomena of "the development of under-
development" arose. The interests of landowners and
mine-owners in preserving rural poverty; the use of
force and taxation by colonial governments to keep
incomes down, and to generate a labour force and a
food surplus,[5] the role of the terms of trade in
extracting a surplus from peasants; the way in which
low peasant incomes are linked with poor international terms of trade for tropical produce (a low wage on
plantations is one alternative for poor farmers and,
in some circumstances, peasant production of export
crops at low prices is another), are all illuminated
by the framework of the model, and Lewis has himself
written extensively on them.[6]

        Nor does the model necessarily require an
unimpeded and rapid progress of indigenous capitalism.
The capitalist sector could be in foreign ownership -
as Lewis says, most countries initially import their
capitalists. It is not required that all profits be
invested. The growth of indigenous capitalism may
well meet obstacles whose analysis requires an
investigation of the relationship between it and the
landowning class, the state, and the international
centres of capitalism. These obstacles may include an
inadequate level of internal or external demand for
capitalist sector products, though it is apparent that
capitalist development can proceed quite a long way

without being held up by the low incomes of poor farmers.

It may be that one focus should be on the drama being enacted in the Informal Sector where, on the one hand, the seeds of indigenous capitalism are sown and, on the other hand, destruction or frustration of indigenous activities, by competition from products stemming from international trade, ownership and technology, are experienced. Another focus needs to be on the contradictory but ever present economic activities of the state in the Third World countries. It is true that if no capitalist development is in prospect then the Lewis mechanism is irrelevant. But it would be a very extreme version of the under-development thesis which would assert that this is currently the case.

Nor is it necessary for observers to like what they see happening. Some of the literature generates confusion because we use normative concepts of "development". The word is reserved for processes which we consider desirable and if the reality is un-pleasant, generating unemployment, worsening the distribution of income, etc., then we tend to deny that development is taking place. Whether or not we need a separate term to describe the process of social and economic change which is actually taking place in the Third World - a combined process of the growth of capitalism, the enlargement of State activity, the impact of the metropoles, and the dis-solution of the pre-capitalist and pre-statist social order - clarity demands that we keep the study of this process separate from the discussion of what is desirable from a policy point of view.

POLICY MODELS

For policy purposes models cannot assume the whole gamut of historical change (though they would make fewer mistakes if they were more aware of it), but must specify certain variables whilst holding all else constant. It was by this test that some commentators found the Lewis model wanting, for instance in the discussion of the marginal product in agriculture. It could, however, be argued that the

Lewis model is a perfectly satisfactory framework for discussion of many policy issues. It does not necessarily induce the conclusion that industrialization without attention to agriculture is unproblematic, but can be used to draw out circumstances in which there will be difficulties both in commencing a process of industrialization and in sustaining it. It could be applied to non-industrial development, for instance to the rural development schemes discussed at about the same time as the Lewis model appeared, by Nurkse (1953) and by Vakil and Bramanand (1956),[7] or for that matter to the investment process going on in a Chinese commune. It must be noted, however, that many policy models assume state control of the direction of the economy. It would be of interest to discuss in a Lewis context the prospects for private capitalist development in the circumstances of rising peasant incomes. (In one reference to this Lewis agrees that, unless peasant incomes rise in every poor country simultaneously, capital would leave the countries whose peasants were benefitting).

THE MODEL AND HISTORICAL ANALYSIS

However the Lewis model was mainly intended to shed light on historical change. As such of course it faces problems. The model is specified in terms of a limited number of variables, whilst in reality there are many. We have to call upon history to explain the model as much as we call upon the model to explain history. We can do two things with a model in this situation. We can formulate it rigorously and reject it if we find it wanting against the test of fact. Or we can regard it as a useful framework within which to discuss reality, not taking the homogeneity of its sectors literally but looking behind this to the internal structure of each, designating new sectors where significant relationships are thereby revealed. It is clear that the contributors to this issue of *The Manchester School* are all thinking along the lines of the importance of the structural heterogeneity of the economy in determining its working. This applies to policy-based discussion as well as to historical analysis, as demonstrated for instance by the "basic needs"

approach taken in the paper by Griffin and James.**
This approach has itself stemmed from a rejection of
the homogeneity of the one sector-models which seek
simply to maximize GNP.

Lewis himself gave the lead in this direction by his descriptive reminders of the heterogeneity
of the sectors, by his refusal to formulate the model
precisely and mathematically, and by his emphasis on
the structural differences between the sectors.
Consequently his model is still a very illuminating
framework within which to discuss the process of
development. Possibly if those who sought to anni-
hilate it, and one another,in the course of the
evolution of development economics had instead built
on it the discipline would not now, twenty-five years
on, be so characterized by the mutual incomprehension
by each school of thought of the work of the other.

**Editors' note: The reference here is Griffin K. and
James J. (1979): "Problems of Transition to
Egalitarian Development" The Manchester School
Vol. 48, No. 3 pp. 248-269.

* Helpful comments by Michael Artis, Martin Godfrey and Ian Steedman are gratefully acknowledged.

1. The argument of the original, 1954 article was further developed in Lewis (1958).

2. A list of many, though not all, of the earlier critical writings, is contained in Lewis (1972). Amongst those not listed, but of interest as a general evaluation, is Bauer (1956). Attacks on "dual economy" models from the "development of underdevelopment" standpoint have been a more recent concern. Comprehensive references to this literature (not by any means all focussing on "dual economy" models) are given in Palma (1978). A very relevant article not, however, included in Arrighi (1970). The Lewis model still, of course, receives evaluative treatment in textbooks on development. Two recent examples are Meier (1974) and Todaro (1977). Criticism of Lewis in the latter reflects the current concern in the literature with urban unemployment, migration, and the size of the gap between urban wages and farmers' incomes.
    The mode of presentation of his model by Lewis has often meant that critics, in search of a more precise target, have linked it with other, more rigorously formulated, models and the differences between them have not always been noted. Thus Todaro and others refer to the "Lewis-Fei-Ranis" model in discussing the industry-agriculture, urban-rural distinctions. Griffin (1969) lists Lewis with the neo-classical, Jorgenson, model in discussing dual-economy models in general. Arrighi attacks more specifically the agricultural underemployment assumptions of Barber (1970).
    It is also fair to say that Lewis's answer to his critics (Lewis, 1972) contained changes of emphasis and additional points, some of which could be said to be concessions to the critics.

3. Lewis (1972).

4. Lewis' original discussion was based on a peasant farmer regime. He did make one reference to landlords and rent (Lewis, 1954). Ranis and Fei couch their model in terms of landlord-employers and utilize this mechanism to prevent the incomes of the rural labour force from rising. Later, Lewis brought in agricultural workers as well as independent farmers. He also, in his discussion of inter-sectoral trade, went along with the Ranis-Fei division of sectors into agriculture and industry (Lewis, 1972, pp. 88-92). In the present issue of this journal Lewis has moved to yet another terminology, referring now to the two sectors as the "modern" and the "traditional".

5. Arrighi's discussion provides an example of how Lewis' two variants (the one involving trade between the sectors; the other simply involving labour transfer) may not just be alternatives, applying in different circumstances, but may be different phases of the growth of the capitalist sector, with capitalist agriculture rendering peasant sales unprofitable and enforcing greater reliance on the sale of labour by peasant families.

6. E.G., Lewis (1978).

7. Lewis refers to these schemes in his "Further Notes" (Lewis, 1958, pp. 4-7).

REFERENCES

Arrighi, G. (1970), "Labour Supplies in Historical Perspective. A Study of the Proletarianization of the African Peasantry in Rhodesia", *Journal of Development Studies*, Vol. Vl, No. 3, pp. 197-234. (Reprinted in G. Arrighi and J.S. Saul, *Essays on the Political Economy of Africa*, New York, Monthly Review Press, 1973, pp. 180-234).

Barber, W.L. (1961). *The Economy of British Central Africa*, London, Oxford University Press.

Bauer, P.T. (1956), "Lewis Theory of Economic Growth", *American Economic Review*, Vol. XLVl, No. 4, pp. 632-641. (Reprinted in P.T. Bauer, *Dissent on Development*, London, Weidenfeld and Nicholson, 1971, pp. 435-477).

Fei, J.C.H. and Ranis, G. (1964). *The Development of the Labour Surplus Economy. Theory and Policy*, Homewood, Illinois, Richard Irwin.

Griffin, K. (1969). *Underdevelopment in Spanish America*, London, Allen and Unwin. (Extracts reprinted in C.K. Wilber (ed.), *The Political Economy of Development and Underdevelopment*, New York Random House, 1973, pp. 15-25 and pp. 68-81).

Lewis, W.A. (1954), "Economic Development with Unlimited Supplies of Labour", *The Manchester School*, Vol. XXll, No. 2, pp. 139-191. (Reprinted in N. Agarwala and S.P. Singh (eds.), The Economics of Underdevelopment, London, Oxford University Press, 1958, pp. 400-449.

Lewis, W.A. (1958), "Unlimited Labour : Further Notes", *The Manchester School*, Vol. XXVl, No. l, pp. 1-32.

Lewis, W.A. (1972), "Reflections on Unlimited Labour" in Luis Eugenio Di Marco (ed.), *International Economics and Development. Essays in Honour of Raoul Prebisch*, New York Academic Press, pp. 75-96.

Lewis, W.A. (1978). *The Evolution of the International Economic Order*, Princeton, N.J., Princeton University Press.

Meier, G.M. (1976). *Leading Issues in Economic Development* (3rd Edition), New York, Oxford University Press, pp. 157-163.

Nurkse, R. (1953). *Problems of Capital Formation in Underdeveloped Countries,* Oxford, Blackwell.

Palma, G. (1978). "Dependency, A Formal Theory of Underdevelopment or a Methodology for the Analysis of Concrete Situations of Underdevelopment", *World Development*, Vol. Vl, No. 7/8, pp. 881-924.

Ranis, G. & Fei, J.C. 11 (1961) "A Theory of Economic Development" *American Economic Review*, Vol. Ll, No. 4, pp. 533-565.

Todaro, M.P. (1977). *Economics for a Changing World*, London, Longman, pp. 215-217.

Vakil, C.N. and Bramanand, P.R. (1956). *Planning for an Expanding Economy*, Bombay, Vora & Co.

INDUSTRIALIZATION AND DEVELOPMENT:
REFLECTIONS BASED ON THE LATIN AMERICAN EXPERIENCES

by
Werner Baer

INTRODUCTION

Industrialization was chosen as the principal strategy for economic development by the policy-makers of Latin America's major countries in the two decades following the second World War. The motivation and justification for this option can be traced to the influence of three basic perceptions by the people in charge of economic planning. First, there was the historical association of economic and political power of Western European, the United States and the Soviet Union with the growth of industry.[1] Second, there was the colonial or neo-colonial type of dependency associated with the 19th and 20th century world division of labor, in which Third World economies specialized in the export of primary products. This specialization placed them at the mercy of business cycles generated in industrial countries, against which they could not adopt autonomous anti-cyclical policies.[2]

Finally, "center-periphery" theories, of which the Prebisch-ECLA variety became the most widely known,[3] convinced most Latin American (and other Third World) planners that maintaining their economy's traditional specialization would either lead to a transfer of resources to industrial countries through declining terms of trade and/or to a steady decline in their share of world trade, as industrial goods seemed to be the most dynamic export commodities.

In this essay I shall examine the past impact of the industrialization in Latin America--that is, its positive and negative aspects--the problems facing the industrial sector of the region in the 1980's, and industry's future role in the region's domestic and international growth.

EARLY INDUSTRIAL GROWTH

Until the 20th century Latin America fitted into the world division of labor as a supplier of primary products and few attempts were made to promote industry. There was little political desire to change the structure of the economies because favorable external markets for the region's primary exports benefitted the elites of those days.[4] In the 19th and early 20th century, moreover, Latin American countries did not have the entrepreneurial classes, the skilled labor force, economic or social infrastructure, market size and administrative capacity to cope with industrialization. Finally, in a number of countries European powers had enough leverage to force governments to maintain free trade policies, which effectively blocked any possibility for the development of industries, as domestically produced manufactures could not compete against lower cost and better quality imports.

Latin America did not, however, remain completely devoid of manufacturing activities prior to the 1930's. In the latter part of the 19th century workshops and small factories appeared in the textile, clothing and food products sectors in Argentina, Brazil, Mexico and a few other larger countries; machine tools and spare parts workshops were started to service railroads, sugar refining mills, and other economic activities. The early industrialists were often importers who turned to producing goods they formerly bought abroad. They were able to do this by investing their accumulated profits, and their main motivation was the growing size of the market. On the eve of World War 1 these light industries had grown to such an extent that most local textile and food products consumption in the larger countries was already furnished locally.[5] Interruption of supplies during World War 1 spurred domestic manufacturing and installed capacity was used intensively. In the 1920's, however, industrial production stagnated due to U.S. and European competition and the refusal of Latin American policy-makers to protect domestic industries. It was believed that World War 1 had been an aberration from the natural order of things, and governments were thus reluctant to impede the movement back to the apparent "normalcy" of the 19th century world division of labor.

Until the great depression of the 1930's no Latin American country had undergone a process of industrialization. Although some industries made their appearance in certain regions, export agriculture remained the leading and dominant sector of the economy. One can hardly speak of this process as "industrialization," since industry did not become the economy's leading sector, causing pronounced structural changes.

For some countries, like Argentina and Brazil, the great depression marked the beginning of an industrialization process. Industry became the leading sector of the economy and substantially increased its share of the GNP. Industrialization at the time was, however, more the result of a defensive policy--i.e., of attempts to deal with the impact of the world depression on the balance of payments-- rather than of deliberately choosing industrialization as a method for promoting economic development.[6]

However, as Sir Arthur Lewis observed, the impact of the great depression had lasting effects. It "...gave a direct fillup to industrialization for import substitution, especially in Latin America. Even more important, it broke the back of the political resistance to industrialization--whether it had been the resistance of imperial powers or the resistance of domestic vested interest in primary production."[7]

POST WORLD WAR 11 IMPORT SUBSTITUTING
INDUSTRIALIZATION PERIOD

It was only after World War 11 that industrialization was adopted as the strategy for economic development. The type of industrialization pursued became known as Import Substituting Industrialization (ISI). It consisted of establishing domestic production facilities to manufacture goods which were formerly imported. Most of the large Latin American countries explicitly or implicitly accepted the CEPAL (Economic Commission for Latin America)

analysis of the futility of gearing their economies
to the traditional world division of labor. Continued reliance on the export of food and primary products
was thought to be inimical to economic development
because of the market instability of such exports and
the slow growth of world demand for them, which, it
was agreed, would turn the terms of trade against
them. ISI was viewed as introducing a dynamic
element into the Latin American economies which
would increase their rates of growth. The latter was
deemed essential to deal with the population explosion of the region and to meet the demands of the
increasingly urban population for the ways of life of
the masses in more advanced industrial countries. It
was also thought that ISI would bring greater economic
independence, with self-sufficiency in manufactured
goods placing Latin American economies less at the
mercy of the world economy and the economic fluctuations originating in the industrial centers of the
world.

The principal policy instruments used to
promote and intensify ISI consisted of: protective
tariffs and/or exchange controls to restrict the
imports of consumer goods; special incentives for
domestic and foreign firms importing capital goods
for new industries; preferential import exchange
rates for industrial raw materials, fuels and intermediate goods; government construction of infrastructure especially designed to complement industries;
and the direct participation of government in certain
industries (especially heavy industries like steel)
where it was assumed that neither domestic nor
foreign private capital was willing to invest.8

The promotion of ISI industries was
indiscriminate. No attempts were made to concentrate
on industrial sectors which might have had a potential
comparative advantage. Some countries followed a
sequence which began with the promotion of consumer
goods and building materials products, which used a
relatively simple technology; this was followed by
consumer goods using a more sophisticated and capital
intensive technology; and, finally, by heavy and
capital goods industries. This road was followed by
such countries as Argentina, Chile, and Colombia.
Other countries, like Brazil, followed policies which

24

stressed a maximum amount of vertical integration, that is, they simultaneously promoted final consumer goods, intermediate goods and capital goods industries.

An important feature of Latin American ISI has been the participation of foreign capital. Although its proportion of investment was often below 10 percent, it was instrumental in setting up key manufacturing industries by transferring know-how and organizational capabilities. This was also the case with infrastructure and heavy industry investments by government-owned enterprises, which depended on foreign financing and technical aid.

The ISI policies were responsible for high real rates of economic growth in many of the region's major countries in the 1950's, among them Brazil, Mexico, and Colombia. Even where overall growth rates were not very high (e.g., Argentina), industry was usually the leading sector. By the early 1960's it had surpassed agriculture's share of GNP in all the major countries.

SHORTCOMINGS OF ISI BY THE EARLY SIXTIES

Some economists have viewed ISI as an inefficient way of using resources to achieve growth. The more conservative among them believe that since world production can best be maximized by having each country (or area of the world) specialize in sectors where it has its greatest comparative advantage, Latin America should have continued to concentrate on the production of primary products. This would have maximized world output and made possible a higher level of income in all parts of the world.

Because of the declining share of food and primary products in world trade, more moderate critics recognized the need for some ISI. Their main objection is to the indiscriminate way in which it was carried out, with the across-the-board promotion of industries without regard even to potential comparative advantage. The Latin American ISI strategies are seen as drives toward national self-sufficiency in total disregard of the advantages of a possible international division of labor along newer lines. This emphasis on autarky was considered as prejudicial to rapid economic growth for a number of reasons.

Given the small markets, limited capital, and a dearth of skilled manpower, autarkic growth leads to the development of inefficient and high-cost industries. This is especially the case in sectors having high fixed costs. They require large-scale output to bring costs down to levels prevailing in advanced industrial countries. Outstanding examples are the steel and automobile industries which have been established in many Latin American countries. In the case of automobiles the situation was worsened because many countries permitted the establishment of a large number of firms, thus completely eliminating the possibility of economies of large scale production. Even in the largest market, Brazil, only in recent years have a few of the major manufacturers achieved the economies of scale regarded as normal in the older industrial countries. The reason for such large numbers of firms was the impression of policy-makers that this would bring on the benefits of competition. If the latter existed at all, it was overcome by the lack of scale economies. In the latter sixties and the seventies a number of smaller countries substantially reduced the quantity of automobile firms operating within their borders.

Inefficiency in the industrial sectors has also been the result of overprotection. In many countries the rate of "effective protection" has been much greater than "nominal" protection. The latter measure only the percentage by which prices of protected goods exceed their world prices. "Effective" tariffs indicate the percentage by which value added "...at a stage of fabrication in domestic industry can exceed what this would be in the absence of protection; in other words, it shows by what percentage the sum of wages, profits, and depreciation allowances, payable by domestic firms can, thanks to protection, exceed what this sum would be if the same firms were fully exposed to foreign competition."[9] Thus, if a product uses a considerable amount of imported inputs on which there is no tariff or on which the tariff rate is lower than the tariff on the finished product, protection is higher than is indicated by the nominal tariff, since the margin available for domestic value added is larger than the difference indicated by the tariff. In a number of Latin American countries the effective tariff on consumer goods was much higher than for intermediate or capital goods. (At one time in the 1960's effective protection for manufactured products in Brazil was about 250 percent as compared with nominal protection of about 100 percent.) Such high levels of effective protection eliminate incentives to increase production efficiency and make it difficult to bring the cost of production to international levels.

It has been argued that the stress on autarky in the region's industrialization (i.e., the maximizing of internal vertical integration of industry, promoting not only final goods production, but also intermediate and capital goods), impedes growth because resources are not used in sectors where they will produce the highest possible output.

The promotion of industry has been prejudicial to the agricultural sector in a number of countries. The allocation of investment resources to new industries has often meant that fewer resources were available to increase agricultural productivity. Overvalued exchange rates, which favored industries by providing cheap imported inputs, hurt agriculture by making its goods less competitive in the international market and/or by making it less profitable to produce for the agricultural export sector. The combination of higher industrial prices caused by protection and the price control of agricultural goods, moreover, turned the internal terms of trade against agriculture. All these factors hurt agricultural production and exports. (Argentina is probably the outstanding example of ISI taking place at the expense of agriculture.)

NEGLECT OF EXPORTS

Until the 1960's Latin America's policy-makers concentrated exclusively on ISI. They neglected the export of traditional goods and made no effort to diversify the commodity structure of exports in accordance with the changing internal economic structure which ISI had brought about. It

27

gradually became obvious, however, that ISI had not made Latin American countries self-sufficient. It had only changed the nature of their trade linkages with the outside world. Whereas previously imports were principally made up of final consumption goods, they now increasingly consisted of raw materials and capital goods. The latter represented imported inputs into the newly established industrial sector which could not be obtained domestically.

It was thus ironic that the net result of ISI placed Latin American countries in a new and more dangerous dependency relationship with the advanced industrial centers than before. In former times a decline in export receipts acted as a stimulus to ISI. Under the new circumstances, a decline in export receipts not counterbalanced by capital inflows can result in forced import curtailments which, in turn, can cause an industrial recession. This has been experienced by a number of Latin American countries. Most of the major countries of the region gradually perceived that to adjust to this situation, they would have to make efforts to diversify exports.

POST-ISI ADJUSTMENTS

During the 1960's and 1970's attempts were made to adjust to some of the shortcomings of ISI. The export of non-traditional, especially manufactured, exports was promoted by the use of both fiscal incentives and subsidized credits. By the late 1970's these efforts proved to have been fairly successful. The share of manufactured goods in the value of Latin America's total exports increased from 13 percent in 1970 to about 25 percent by the late 1970's. Especially notable was the share of manufactures in Brazil and Mexico's exports, which in the late 1970's amounted to about 33 percent.

The smaller countries of Latin America which had industrialized faced many problems because of their small internal market size, which prevented them from benefitting from economies of scale and thus to eventually produce at competitive prices. These countries were the most fervent advocates of regional economic integration, which was seen as a way out of their narrow market. When progress of LAFTA became stalled, the smaller countries of South America formed the Andean Group. One of its basic goals was to rationalize the existing industrial base of member countries to provide for future integrated growth. These countries, for instance, substantially reduced the number of automobile firms in their respective countries, and those firms permitted to stay on had to fit into an agreed-upon division of labor for the production of various types of vehicles and their parts. Central American economic integration, which began even prior to the Andean Group, was promoted in order to get the industrialization process started, since the very small size of Central American countries precluded even the beginnings of many manufacturing industries.

THE CURRENT ROLE OF INDUSTRY

In the contemporary major Latin American economies industry plays a key role. Manufacturing accounts for over 35 percent of the domestic product in Argentina, about 30 percent in Brazil and Mexico, 25 percent in Peru and about 20 percent in Colombia. Including construction and public utilities would substantially increase this share; for all of Latin America it would rise from 27 to 39 percent in the late seventies. Much of the region's manufacturing was concentrated in three countries--Argentina, Brazil and Mexico--which accounted for 78 percent of its value added (while they contained only 65 percent of Latin America's population).

The industrial achievements of Latin America are impressive in absolute terms--i.e., amount of transport equipment produced; tons of steel; output of consumer durables, of capital goods, or petrochemical products. Over the last decade there has also been a noticeable diversification of the industrial structure away from the traditional sectors (especially textiles and food products). In the late seventies machinery and equipment accounted for 30 percent of industrial value added in Brazil, 24 percent in Argentina and 20 percent in Mexico; while chemicals amounted to 13 percent of industrial value added in Argentina, 12 percent in Brazil and 14 percent in Mexico. As already mentioned, there has been an impressive growth of manufactured exports in the 1970's, which includes even some exports of capital goods and industrial projects, especially from Argentina and Brazil. In absolute terms, there also exists a large and by now well-trained skilled industrial labor force, and a substantial amount of engineering and managerial capabilities.

The nature of Latin America's industrialization has, however, brought problems and/or aggravated already existing ones, which defy short-run solutions. Let us examine some of them.

1. _Employment_. The employment impact of industrial growth in most countries of Latin America has been disappointing. The rate of growth of industrial output (especially in the manufacturing sector) has been substantially higher than the rate of growth of industrial employment. By 1978, while industry's share of the GNP in Argentina was 45 percent, it only employed 29 percent of the labor force; for Brazil the difference in the ratio was 37 and 22 percent; for Mexico 37 and 26 percent; in the U.S. the ratios in the late seventies were 34 and 33 percent, while in West Germany they were 48 and 48 percent. This low labor absorption capacity of the industrial sector has to be viewed in the context of a high rural-urban migration in most countries of the region. Thus, a large proportion of the urban labor force has been forced to find employment in the low productivity urban sectors, especially in services. Industrial-urban growth, of course, calls for the expansion of many complementary service jobs. But even the latter have not expanded at a satisfactory rate, i.e., relative to the labor supply.[10]

The principal reason for the low job-creating capacity of industry is its capital-intensive technology. There was little adaptation of imported technology to local factor supply conditions. The reason for this rigidity has never been satisfactorily established. Some economists have claimed that developing countries have artificially distorted factor prices in their desire to stimulate ISI. In other words, they have made the price of capital artificially low relative to that of labour, thus

30

stimulating the introduction of capital-intensive technology. This argument, however, has never been satisfactorily proven. In fact, in the early ISI spurt, much of the imported equipment was second-hand and one could thus argue that at the time a choice was made favoring relatively more labor-intensive technology. Yet even with the latter, industry's labor absorption was low.

With the advent of non-traditional export promotion in the 1960's and 1970's, both domestic and multinational firms in Latin America switched to new equipment in their investment programs in order to compete more effectively in the international market. The cost of diversifying exports was thus to make the industrial sector even less labor absorptive than before.

    2. <u>Income Distribution</u>. In Latin America the distribution of income has traditionally been very concentrated and industrialization has tended to accentuate this characteristic. In fact, in the major industrial countries periods of high industrial growth rates have brought about substantial increases in the relative inequality of the income distribution. This may have been caused, in part, by the capital-intensive nature of newly-built industries. A high capital/labor ratio means that a large proportion of the increment in the national income contributed by the industrial sector goes to non-wage earning groups. Within the wage earning groups, moreover, a high capital intensity may favor certain types of skilled labor at the expense of poorer workers. Since the industrial sector is the most dynamic in the economy and since its capital/labor ratio is higher than the national average, growth (<u>ceteris paribus</u>) will inevitably favor the non-wage sector (even if average wages in the dynamic industrial sector are higher than the national average).

The traditional justification for industrialization policies which resulted in these trends in the distribution of income is that concentration increases the capacity of a society to save (i.e., the upper income groups have a higher propensity to save than the lower ones), making it possible to invest in new productive capacity. With time the total productive capacity will be large enough to support both a continuing high rate of growth and a more equitable distribution of income. There is thus, at first, a negative relation between growth and equity, but beyond a certain point this conflict may disappear as growth makes all groups better off.

The experiences of the large countries of Latin America have thrown some doubts on this argument, even if we ignore the political power to resist change that may be generated by increasing inequality. The type of industrialization which takes place under conditions of increasingly concentrated income will not necessarily be adequate for a possible future situation of greater equality. Latin America's actual production profile reflects the demand profile which, in turn, is influenced by the distribution of income. How flexible is the productive apparatus built up to accommodate a specific structure of demand? Could it be used under new socioeconomic conditions which would result in a changed demand profile? Obviously the basic economic infrastructure and industries in the capital goods and steel sectors would have more flexibility than other industries which are further downstream (i.e., closer to the consumer). Finally, one should also take into account the firms which have a vested interest in the existing productive structure--how effectively would they resist reforms which would threaten their markets?

3. <u>Regional Concentration</u>. Regional disparities in the growth of economic activities and the distribution of the national product have been a common feature in large Latin American countries. The process of industrialization has accentuated this concentration and made redistribution more difficult.

There is a logic to this trend. Since industrialization in a poor country begins with a small market with few opportunities for economies of scale, especially if export opportunities are regarded as limited, any attempt at regional deconcentration in the early stages will tend to increase the difficulties in making the new sector efficient. One should also consider the various external economies associated with geographical concentration which also contribute to decreasing the cost of industrial production.

There are thus obvious conflicts between regional balance and rapid and efficient industrial growth. To date the latter has usually been given priority.11

4. <u>Multinationals</u>. Since rapid ISI was possible only with a substantial influx of foreign direct investments, it is not surprising that in many of the most dynamic sectors multinationals play a key role. Some countries allow only subsidiaries of multinationals to function with local participation (e.g., Mexico), while others allow them to be totally owned by the parent company. Regardless of the formal rules of operation, however, there can be little doubt of the important role multinationals play in the dynamic industrial sectors of Latin America.

Although multinationals were a fundamental factor in enabling Latin American countries to industrialize rapidly--in providing capital, technology, organizational skills, and, at a later stage, in providing marketing outlets for the export of manufactured goods--their presence has raised a number of issues which have or will soon affect not only relations between multinationals and the host governments, but also relations between the government of the host country and the government of the parent-firm country. The major problems are the following:

a) <u>Profit Remittances</u>. Besides the issue of what would be a reasonable maximum profit remittance per year which the host government could impose, there is also the question of control. The phenomenon of "transfer pricing" makes possible hidden transfers of profits. The technique is used to understate profits in the host country not only to circumvent profit remittance controls, but also to decrease tax payments. Disputes about such practices are bound to rise in the future since it is difficult for any control agency to make unambiguous rules for pricing imports from the parent companies or for pricing technical assistance from parent to subsidiary.

b) <u>Technology</u>. Multinationals have been accused of not adapting the technology they implant to Latin American conditions, that is, making it more labor intensive. As was already discussed above, it is not clear whether such adaptation is either feasible or desirable.

Emphasis on old or artisan-type technology, however, may not satisfy the desire of policy-makers to strengthen their country's economic and political position vis-a-vis the industrial centers of the world. Many feel that only modern technology and the capacity for generating new technology within their countries will improve their relative position.

Although multinationals have responded by introducing fairly up-to-date technology, they have been reluctant to engage in genuine Research and Development activities in the host countries. Most R & D of multinationals takes place in the parent company's country. A major reason for this is that technology is the strongest card a multinational has in its international bargaining position, and this advantage is thus to be guarded as much as possible.

For the host country, it is important to acquire the capacity to produce technology to increase its relative bargaining position and to reduce the cost of importing technology. Thus the development of local R & D capacity will be an increasing bone of contention between major Latin American countries and multinationals in the next decades, as the ambition of these countries grows from merely building new industries to acquiring a share in the world's technology-producing capacity.

5. The Role of State Enterprises. A notable feature of Latin America's industrialization has been the role of state enterprises and state financial institutions.[12] In most countries a large proportion of the steel industry is owned by state enterprises; most public utilities are run by state companies; the state owns mining and derivative firms; in a number of countries it has a monopoly of oil exploration and state petroleum companies have a large stake in refining and petrochemical industries. The state is also the owner of development banks and a large proportion of commercial banks.

The direct state participation in economic activity is due in large measure to the industrialization ambitions of these countries. This called for

34

the development of a number of basic industrial sectors with large capital requirements and long gestation periods. As there were few local private groups
with the financial and technical capabilities to
enter these activities and as multinationals were
reluctant to commit huge sums to projects which would
only begin to pay off in the distant future (if at
all), governments were forced to organize state enterprises to do the job. In certain cases, of course,
governments entered for nationalistic reasons (e.g.,
petroleum and mining), since they deemed it against
the national interest to have such sectors in foreign
hands.

In a similar fashion, the large presence of
the state in development (or investment) and
commercial banking is linked to the industrialization
process. Rapid ISI required an adequate financial
system to provide funding for both the private and
the state sectors. As capital markets were still
underdeveloped, the founding of state financial
institutions became a necessity.

In the region's countries the domestic
private, the multinational and the state sectors have,
in most cases, worked harmoniously together, i.e.,
complementing rather than competing against each
other. It is doubtful that the state will (or can)
reduce its share of economic activities in the short
or even medium-run, since there are few sources of
funds for the private sector to buy out large state
undertakings and since it would be politically un-
feasible to sell these to multinationals.

Our present state of knowledge on how state
enterprises operate is still rudimentary. It is un-
clear where decision-making powers lie concerning
pricing, investments, imports of equipment, or
domestic vs. foreign procurement, for example. The
few studies which exist make it clear that these huge
enterprises are not necessarily under the control of
the central government. Often their own economic
power makes itself felt on the decisions of government
ministries, rather than vice versa.

A recent trend, which merits further
examination, is the appearance of joint ventures
between Latin American state enterprises and

multinationals. These have been especially prevalent
in mining, steel mills, aluminum plants, petrochemi-
cals, and some other areas. Usually the state firm
has 51 percent control of such ventures. There are
obvious advantages to both sides. The state firm has
access to technology and equity finance, while the
multinationals sells equipment, technology, shares in
the earnings, and has a politically safe investment.

COMPLEMENTARY VS. COMPETITIVENESS
IN ECONOMIC RELATIONS

          The recent emphasis on trade diversifica-
tion, in which exports of manufactures have played a
prominent role, has raised questions about the share
of world markets for manufactured goods which Latin
American countries will be allowed to have.

          The success of Mexico, Brazil, Argentina
and other countries in selling manufactured goods in
the U.S. and Europe brought about a reaction in the
late seventies in the form of demands to eliminate
various types of export incentives. Some countries
(e.g., Brazil) have complied with these demands and,
in compensation, have drastically devalued their
currencies.

          Although it is generally recognized that
export diversification is important to increase the
foreign exchange earnings capability of Latin
American countries (which has become even more
important for petroleum importing countries), most
advanced industrial nations have not been very
receptive to the idea of providing a permanent market
for Latin American manufactured goods. One of the
major issues in the next decade will be the degree of
accommodation which the industrial centers of the
world will offer in the matter--i.e., to what extent
they will agree to a new world division of labor in
the production of manufactured goods.

          A further issue in industrial trade rela-
tions concerns the growing vertical division of labor
between Latin America and advanced industrial countries. A growing proportion of trade consists of
semi-finished products, many of which are goods sent

from subsidiaries of multinationals to parent firms, or to other subsidiaries. For example, U.S. auto manufacturers make engines in some of their Latin American subsidiaries, which are then shipped to the U.S. for final assemblage. Although such a new inter-relationship may have benefits from an efficiency point of view, it can also produce situations of con-flict.

This trend results in some sacrifice in decision-making autonomy within Latin America as it becomes a more integrated piece of an international system of production. The level of production of the subsidiaries of multinationals, especially those vertically integrated on an international level, thus depends on decisions of multinationals concerning their world production objectives, such as the inter-national division of their activities.

International bargaining for shares in the international production scheme of multinationals is still in its infancy. On the Latin American side, the multinationals increasingly are feeling the pressure of governments interested in pushing their export diversification programs. They are feeling the political pressure of the governments but are also attracted by tax incentive schemes to increase exports. In the U.S., on the other hand, there has been a mounting pressure by labor unions and other interest groups to limit the expansion of overseas production facilities of U.S.-based multinationals, on the grounds that such operations in effect "export" American jobs.

It is possible that the huge foreign debt of the major countries of Latin America may paradoxically have given their governments some bargaining strength. The large stake of both multinationals and the larger banks in the U.S. and other developed country finan-cial centers in the economic growth and balance of payments strength of the borrowers in an obvious con-sequence of their past financial commitments. It is probably no exaggeration to state that the continuing ability of the larger countries (notably Brazil and Mexico) to service their external debt is essential to the solvency of many of the principal members of the international financial community. For this reason, their past borrowing and receptivity to foreign direct investments has given the major Latin American nations a group of allies in their effort to obtain favorable trade policies from the developed world, especially to facilitate the further growth of their manufactured exports.

FOOTNOTES

1.　Alexander Gerschenkron, <u>Continuity in History and Other Essays</u>, (Cambridge, Mas.: Harvard University Press, 1968). On page 88, Gerschenkron states that "...A government may do a great deal to promote the cause of industrialization. It may do so because in its estimation the creation of an industrial apparatus and the concomitant increase in economic potential of the state will increase the power of the latter. In this sense, the motivation of the industrial policy of the government is clearly political."

2.　A good recent summary of the dependency literature with respect to industrialization can be found in E.V.K. Fitzgerald, <u>The Political Economy of Peru 1956-78</u> (Cambridge University Press, 1979), chapter 2, "The theoretical issues."

3.　Joseph L. Love, "Raul Prebisch and the Origins of the Doctrine of Unequal Exchange," <u>Latin American Research Review</u>, Volume XV, Number 3, 1980, pp. 45-72; <u>International Economics and Development: Essays in Honor of Raul Prebisch</u>, edited by L.E. DiMarco (New York: Academic Press, 1972), see especially articles by DiMarco, Dadone and DiMarco, Pinto and Knakal.

4.　Sir Arthur Lewis has stated that "Imperial power was of course an obstacle in the colonial countries, but is not a necessary explanation since the same happened in the independent countries. The fact is that the very success of the country in exporting created a vested interest in those who lived by primary production--small farmers no less than big capitalists--and who opposed measures for industrialization, whether because such measures might deflect resources from agriculture and raise factor prices, or because they might result in raising the prices of manufactured goods. The outcome therefore depended on the relative political strengths of the industrial and the agricultural interests." In W. Arthur Lewis, <u>The Evolution of the International Economic Order</u> (Princeton University Press, 1978), p. 24.

5. Werner Baer, The Brazilian Economy: Its Growth and Development (Columbus, Ohio: Grid Publishing, Inc., 1979) pp. 31-7; Carlos F. Diaz Alejandro, Essays on the Economic History of the Argentine Republic (New Haven, Conn.: Yale University Press, 1970), pp. 209-218.

6. Baer, op. cit., pp. 41-2; Diaz Alejandro, op. cit., pp. 218-69.

7. Lewis, op. cit., p. 31.

8. Ian Little, Tibor Scitovsky and Maurice Scott, Industry and Trade in Some Developing Countries, A Comparative Study (Oxford University Press, 1970), chapters 2, 5, and 6; Werner Baer, "Import Substitution Industrialization in Latin America: Experiences and Interpretation," Latin American Research Review, Vol. Vll, No. 1, Spring 1972, pp. 95-122.

9. Little, et. al., op.cit., p. 39.

10. Werner Baer and Larry Samuelson, "Toward a Service Oriented Growth Strategy," World Development (forthcoming in 1981).

11. Lewis has presented the problem in the most succinct matter, when he stated that "...industry is itself gregarious; most industrialists prefer to establish themselves in existing industrial centers, which already have not only the requisite physical infrastructure but also the network of institutions that binds industrial establishments together. One can work hard at establishing rural industries, but except in police states, success is bound to be limited." In Lewis, op.cit., p. 43.

12. Baer, The Brazilian Economy, chapter 7, "Brazil's Extended Public Sector."

INTERNATIONAL TRANSFER OF
TECHNOLOGY, INDUSTRIAL DEVELOPMENT AND
DEVELOPING COUNTRIES: SOME OBSERVATIONS

by
Frank Long

INTRODUCTION

Technology transfer is of central concern
to contemporary development policy. In terms of
restructuring the international economy, for instance,
it is a key ingredient in proposals for a New
International Economic Order; further, a cursory
observation of the development policy objectives of
many developing countries is enough to indicate a
widespread concern. This chapter proposes a brief
review of aspects of technology transfer within the
context of recent industrial experience of developing
countries.

PRELIMINARY REMARKS

Technology may be defined as know-how,
necessary for the productive functioning of an
enterprise. In other words, knowledge about production methods, processes, techniques, etc. and application of this knowledge to economic activity. The
history of measuring the importance of technology to
economic growth is of fairly recent origin. In the
U.S.A., Solow found that it accounted for over 80% of
the growth in that economy. (Solow 1957). A study
by Denison also reached similar conclusions -
(Denison 1974). Statistical evidence from the U.S.S.R.
has likewise shown that technology accounted for over
75% of real growth in that economy within recent times.
(UNESCO 1979). If the statistical importance of
technology to growth is accepted, prima facie, technology can be regarded as being specially relevant to
developing countries. Because of the challenges of
development and growth, for example, it can be argued
that accelerated increases in goods and services are
a necessary (though not sufficient) condition for
alleviating conditions of open poverty and other

symptons of under-development.

TECHNOLOGY TRANSFER

          The relevance of "technology transfer" to
developing countries stems largely from the fact that
such countries often lack an indigenous capacity to
generate the technology they need for economic activity. For example, available data for 1973 show the
following: Developed countries accounted for 87.4%
of R & D scientists and engineers and developing
countries 12.6% (UNIDO 1979). In terms of global
expenditures in technological innovation, developed
countries at the same time accounted for 97% of these;
developing countries 3% (UNIDO 1979). In terms of
global exports of technology intensive goods, developing countries in 1976 accounted for only 4% of
these and developed countries 96%. At the same time,
developing countries imported some 90% of basic
capital goods from developed economies. (UNIDO 1979).
Thus, a technology resource gap problem is clearly
evident in developing countries. Given the need to
accelerate development then, foreign technology is
often called upon to play an important part in the
development efforts of most Third World economies.
Most of this technology emanates from western industrialized countries.

          The literature identifies the following, as
some of the main vehicles for transferring technology
to developing countries:

          (1)   Foreign direct investment including
                 joint ventures.

          (2)   Licensing arrangements including
                 patents and trademarks.

          (3)   Imports of goods and services
                 (embodied technology). These
                 incidentally constitute the
                 major portion of direct costs for
                 technology transfer. In 1968, for
                 example, out of $25.7 billion (U.S.)
                 expended by developing countries
                 for foreign technology, imports of
                 machinery and equipment constituted

42

$18 billion (U.S.) or 72%
(UNCTAD 1975).

(4)   Technical assistance such as
        those affecting bilateral and
        multilateral arrangements.

INDUSTRIALIZATION AND DEVELOPMENT

        Before examining aspects of technology
transfer in industrialization, it is necessary to look
first at some broad issues concerning industrialization and development.

        Some of the potential benefits which are
sometimes attributable to industrialization are:

(1)   Increased processing of primary
        products i.e., agro-industrial
        activity, mining and the like,
        thereby augmenting local value
        added.

(2)   Stimulation of linkage effects
        in the macro-economic production
        process thereby adding greater
        structural depth and inter-
        connectedness to economic activity
        because of (1).

(3)   Increased economic growth, as a
        result of addition to real output
        of goods and services.

(4)   Generation of employment opportunities.

(5)   Increased export earnings capacity
        when industrial production is
        geared towards satisfying overseas
        demand.

(6)   Reduced dependency on account of
        the production of goods formerly
        imported. That is, benefits allied
        to import substitution.

(7) As a result of (1), (2) and
     (5), the reduction of econo-
     mic vulnerability by reducing
     undue dependency on exports
     of primary products which face
     a volatile world market.

On account of some of the foregoing points,
industrialization is generally regarded as central to
economic transfromation of developing countries.
Further, as a recent study argues "industrial growth
can expand occupational choice of the population of a
country, promote greater equality in social as well
as economic terms, promote national pride, national
self-reliance and national independence for countries
which were, until recently, colonies of Northern
powers." (UNIDO 1979)

'TWO SECTOR MODELS' INDUSTRIALIZATION
AND TECHNOLOGY

The theoretical foundations of the optimism,
concerning the role of industrialization in development, can be traced to the dual sector models of
economic development, which were popularised to an
important extent by Arthur Lewis. (Lewis 1954). In
simple terms, within the dual sector framework, an
economy is said to be made up largely of two sectors -
a subsistence sector and a modern sector. The subsistence sector is akin to agriculture in the main.
It is characterised by the following: Surplus labor
and therefore high rates of disguised unemployment,
low levels of productivity, primitive technology,
low rates of capital accumulation and a high incidence
of poverty. There is also little marketable surplus
generated by this sector, the rates of auto consumption being quite high. Conversely, the modern sector
is made up importantly of manufacturing activity. It
is noted for modern technology, relatively high ruling
wage rates, levels of productivity are comparatively
high, there is a reinvestment of economic surplus for
progressive expansion of capital to provide the
foundations for the economic dynamism of this sector.
Thus argues Lewis:

        "The key to the process is the use
        which is made of the capitalist

44

> surplus. In so far as this is
> reinvested in creating new capital,
> the capitalist sector expands, tak-
> ing more people into capitalist
> employment out of the subsistence
> sector."

(Lewis 1954). Economic development is therefore seen as a gradual withdrawal of surplus labour from a relatively inefficient agricultural sector to the modern sector.

Although technology transfer does not constitute key feature of the Lewis model, the initial model does explicitly recognize the general importance of technology to development. A few illustrations suffice. "Inside the capitalist sector knowledge and capital work in the same direction to raise the surplus and to increase employment." (Lewis 1954). Further, "...the application of new technical knowledge usually requires new investment." (Lewis 1954). Moreover, "capital and technical knowledge also work together in the sense that in economies where techniques are stagnant savings are not so readily applied to increasing productive capital." (Lewis 1954). Given the importance of savings and the regeneration of surplus to economic activity to this model, it is clear that technological change constitutes a central consideration to the analysis of the modern sector in particular, and economic development in general.

Theoretically, if the model is viewed in terms of a closed economy, the subject of technology transfer must be ruled out. Conversely, a discussion of technology transfer can be readily accommodated if open economy assumptions apply. Once the importance of modern technology to industrial activity is accepted, as well as the importance of imported technology in meeting the technological requirements for industrialization, the connection between a Lewis type framework and technology transfer can be readily appreciated.*

*We are by no means ignoring the fact that modern technology also applies to primary agriculture. Evidence from developed economies i.e. U.S.A., Canada, Denmark and Holland illustrates the point that rapid technical change is a characteristic of 20th century agriculture.

Before we focus on aspects of technology transfer in relation to the contemporary industrialization of developing countries some comments on industrialization development policy are necessary.

INDUSTRIAL DEVELOPMENT POLICY - SOME REMARKS

The early post-war period saw concerted attempts by many developing countries to charter new horizons for development based on industrialization. This was partly influenced by the dualist model, just looked at (and subsequent versions of it) which has an intuitive appeal to development analysis because of its simplicity, secondly because of its apparent realism, thirdly because it seemed to provide a ready panacea for under-development. Industrialization and modern technology associated therewith were seen by economists and policy makers as the necessary ingredients to rid poor countries of Hla Myint's 'low level equilibrium trap.'

To the economic historian, casual empirical observation seemed to strike home the point. This was the path followed by metropolitan countries which were not only industrialized countries, but simultaneously constituted in Rostow's language, the quintessential stage of 'self sustained development.' (Rostow 1959). Agricultural specialization, because of low price and income elasticity of demand, and consequently its overall sluggish nature, seemed to offer to many developing countries limited scope for rapid economic development.

Further, reasoned some economists, savings (because of its importance to investment) constituted the key transformational link between agriculture and industry (Nurkse 1953). Poor countries, it was argued, saved little and because of this, could not generate adequate investment capital for stimulating economic activity in the modern sector. Low levels of savings resulted from low levels of income and Engel's Law (which postulated that at low levels of income, the marginal propensity to save was low, meaning little room was left for savings). Low levels of real income, in turn, were induced by low levels of productivity. In this "vicious circle world" (which became

46

associated with Nurkse) massive injections of capital were considered necessary to bring about industrial development in poor countries. Given the internal savings constraint already referred to, such capital it was further reasoned, had to come from overseas; that is to say, from capital surplus developed econo- mies. The grand era of industrialization via foreign capital was thus born during the 1950's. For example, in 1940 overseas investment in manufacturing activity in developing countries was virtually non existent. By 1967, however, estimates showed that nearly US$10 billion or 29% of local foreign direct investment in developing countries was in the manufacturing sector (OECD 1972).

THE INDUSTRIALIZATION EXPERIENCE,
DEVELOPING COUNTRIES AND TECHNOLOGY
TRANSFER ISSUES: SOME ISSUES

Ultimately, industrial policy measures are based on some form of theory, for it is theory that gives some stature as to what such measures are like- ly to accomplish in real terms, under particular assumptions. But policy prescriptions aximotically, may be based on good theory or bad theory. In the latter case, new prescriptions are called for.

One of the major shortcomings borne out by the industrialization experience in developing countries relates to the question of technology transfer. An elaboration is now necessary. Such industrialization attempts, can be broken down into two groups, import substitution and export promotion. Import substitu- tion industrialization, was primarily geared to satis- fying the needs of the home market; in particular, light manufacturing goods such as textiles, beverages, food, etc. and the like. In the literature this is largely referred to as the easy phase of import sub- stitution, given the protective nature of the domes- tic market. For one, with adequate protection, domestic demand in most developing countries is such that a ready market exists for a range of light consumer goods normally imported. However, in many instances, especially initially, this is associated with relatively high cost products, given limited "learning by doing" which takes place. Sooner or

later, as evidence seems to confirm, the domestic
market becomes a limiting factor for import substitution industrialization and exports have to be resorted to in order to push the process of industrialization further (Bruton 1970). Producing for a heavily
protected domestic market and a keenly competitive
foreign one, however pose different problems. And
often, as evidence seems to show, the jump from the
domestic to the international market, especially for
indigénous third world firms using inefficient production techniques, is not that automatic if they are
able to be competitive at international prices. Also,
if it is optimistically assumed that production cost
curves are low enough for firms to compete internationally, various tariffs and non-tariff barriers to
trade tend to be a limiting factor to industrialization. Further, the import substitution experience in
the capital goods or technology intensive sector in
developing countries has been less spectacular than
in the light manufacturing sector, already referred
to. An analysis of the causes of this is outside
the scope of this paper but three factors seem to be
important - very limited market for producers goods,
high cost of production, limited know how relating to
the capital goods sector. The strategy of import
substitution was prominent in Latin America in the
1950's and 1960's, and is also presently common to the
Caribbean and African experiences.

Be that as it may, formal attempts at
regional integration by many developing countries in
Asia, Latin America, the Caribbean and Africa seemed
to provide larger regional markets by which transnationals, through subsidiaries or through licensing
arrangements, anxious to jump tariff walls, and to
seize on prospects for a wider market, were able to
benefit from import substitution possibilities at the
regional level.

Meanwhile, in the Caribbean, for example,
export led industrialization gained much currency
given the small nature of the domestic market, the
limited resource base to be found in some countries,
and the attempts to reduce undue reliance on plantation agriculture. Barbados, Jamaica, Trinidad, Puerto
Rico, and recently Haiti, are examples of such
economies, which, with varying degrees of emphasis,

resorted to this strategy. Taiwan, Hong Kong,
Signapore, and South Korea, are examples of other
developing countries, which have been making considerable headway with this type of industrialization
strategy, characterised by elaborate export processing zones. These countries' hopes for industrializa-
were in their ability to exploit relatively abundant
supplies of cheap labor or natural resources, within
the existing sphere of international division of
labor. Two broad features are detectable in the
literature - traditional types using largely unskilled
labor, and modern high technology types such as
electronics, computer, engineering and precision
insturments and the like, where the use of skilled
labor inputs are of growing importance (Helleiner
1973). For example, the experience of a number of
export processing zones in Asia lends evidential
support to the latter.

The approaches to industrialization - import
substitution and export led - although conceptually
dissimilar, had two main features in common. The
establishment of lavish incentives scheme to attract
foreign investment, largely transnational corporations,
and the widespread acceptance of imported technology
as part of the industrialization strategy. In cases
where import substitution did not rely on foreign
investment, but stressed the active participation of
the indigenous capitalist sector, many developing
countries still had to depend significantly on foreign
technology to lubricate the industrialization process.
In many instances too, most basic inputs - raw
materials, intermediate products, machinery and
equipment - were supplied from abroad. In the case of
transnationals, this was done through their vertically
integrated world production network. Thus 'growth'
impulses were often externally induced.

To be sure, between 1960 - 1977 developing
countries share in the world value added of manufactures rose from 6.9% to 9%. (See Table 1). Between
1960 - 1965, the annual growth rate of world manufacturing value added for developing countries was 6.7%;
between 1970 - 1975 it was 8.7%, 1976 it was 8.5% and
1977 it represented 10.4%.

TABLE 1

WORLD VALUE ADDED TO MANUFACTURES

	1960	1965	1970	1975	1977
Share of developing countries in world manufacturing value added	6.9	6.9	7.3	8.6	9.0

SOURCE: UNIDO Industry 2000, New Perspectives (New York: UN 1979).

As Table 11 shows, the corresponding averages for developed market economy countries, at the same time were 6.7%, 3.2%, 9% and 4.1%.

TABLE 11

GROWTH RATES OF WORLD MANUFACTURING VALUE ADDED ANNUAL PERCENTAGE CHANGES

Year	Developing Countries	Developed Market Economies
1960 - 65	6.7	6.7
1970 - 75	8.7	3.2
1976	8.5	9.0
1977	10.4	4.1

SOURCE: UNIDO Industry 2000, New Perspectives (New York: UN 1979) p. 89.

Thus, judging from the data (i.e. Table 1) developing countries as a group, have been able to progressively increase their involvement in the world division of labor as it affects manufacturing activity. For some countries, such as Mexico, Brazil, South Korea, Taiwan, Signapore, Hong Kong, Pakistan - sometimes referred to as rapidly industrializing countries, growth in world manufacturing value added has been more significant than the weighted average of developing countries as a whole, cited in Table 11. For example, between 1962 - 1969 the manufacturing growth rates of the respective countries cited were Mexico (19.8%), Brazil (16.2%), South Korea (77.1%), Taiwan (36.5%), Pakistan (23.7%), Hong Kong (20.1%), (Helleiner 1973). For other countries, such as land locked economies in Africa, this involvement has tended to be below the average, cited in Table 11.

It is difficult to generalize about the impact of the industrialization experience in developing countries, given the unevenness of the rates of industrialization, varying emphases of industrialization, different resource configurations facing such countries as well as varying social policies associated with industrialization strategies. However, when allowance is made for the preceding point, the benefits of industrialization have somehow failed to live up to theoretical expectations in a significant number of instances. For example, as is argued "In undertaking such imitative industrialization, developing countries too often overlooked the real social costs which have been inflicted by the industrial development process..." (UNIDO 1979). Or "...There is no doubt that the numbers of the poor have increased, inspite of the rapid economic growth in most developing countries" (ILO 1976).

As a result of considerable research which has taken place over the impact of technology transfer in recent attempts at industrialization by developing countries, an attempt is now made to itemize some of the main problems identified in the literature -

(1)   Increased economic dependency
      on foreign technology suppliers
      which is said to militate against
      the self reliant development.

(2)   Associated with (1), forms of
      economic control by technology
      suppliers. For example, tying
      technology inputs and the use
      of restrictive business prac-
      tices. Often "tie in clauses"
      prohibit the use of alterna-
      tive technology as part of the
      technology package. This has
      limited prospects for the use
      and development of indigenous
      technology in developing
      countries. Further, it pre-
      vents developing countries from
      resorting to cheaper technology
      substitutes or complements, when
      these are available in the
      international market.

(3)   Because of (2) the linkage
      potential in developing countries
      has been kept to a minimum. This
      has raised doubts about the
      effectiveness of imported technolo-
      gy in terms of structural trans-
      formation. Also, it is sometimes
      held that imported technology is
      not properly absorbed and
      assimilated in developing countries.

(4)   Relatively high price in such
      countries tend to be associated
      with imported technology (royalties,
      management contracts, licence fees,
      know how agreements), largely
      because of the oligopolistic nature
      of the world technology market on
      one hand, and weak bargaining
      position of technology buyers from
      developing countries, on the other.
      This has added to a balance of
      payments difficulties of develop-
      ing countries.

(5)   Imported technology tends to be
      capital intensive and has failed
      to make impact on problems of
      unemployment in developing countries.

The capital intensive bias of such technology is a function of the 'factor configuration' facing developed countries themselves as suppliers of technology. As a result, the technology they export hardly satisfies the 'surplus' labor supply situation in developing countries, which more often than not, demands the use of labor intensive techniques. Hence the relevancy of the concept of appropriate or intermediate technology in the development objectives of many developing countries.

(6) Because of the nature of the distortions which tend to occur in the factor market, imported technology has tended to aggravate income distribution problems and therefore economic inequality in developing countries. For example, the use of a capital intensive technique means that the share of income going to the owners of capital, is greater than that going to labor.

(7) It has failed, in a number of instances, to make an impact on the development of key industrial skills in developing countries. For example, engineering, management, product development, etc. In the main, it is sometimes held that 'vital' technological know how associated with industrialization has been retained by transnationals.

(8) Further, limited technological research on industrial activity takes place in developed

countries in global activities
by such corporations.

(9)   Technology embodied in consumption has tended to favor income
needs of relatively well to do
social classes, to the neglect
of 'basic needs' of the rest of
the population. From this point
of view, it can be argued that
consumption technology, in many
instances, has been found to be
inappropriate to the welfare
needs of developing countries.

(10)   Transfer pricing strategies
between parents and subsidiaries
of transnationals has tended to
result in tax evasion, for
maximization of global profits
of such firms. For example, by
under and over invoicing of input supplied to or from overseas
networks. This has tended to
deprive some countries of vital
sources of public revenue for
development. Limited empirical
work, however, has been done to
quantify the loss of tax revenue
from this type of corporate
behaviour.

If the above holds, it would seem to follow
that technology transfer can be regarded as a central
explanation for the limited impact of industrialization in many developing countries. Further, it would
also seem to be an important constraint to generally
acceptable goals of development policy e.g. reduction
of income inequality, basic needs, reduction of unemployment, reduction of economic dependency, etc.
in a wide cross section of countries. On the other
hand, it can be argued that imported technology is a
main factor for accelerated growth performance in many
rapidly industrializing developing countries. However,
the point being raised here concerns the net social
costs of growth and limited welfare gains arising
therefrom. Bearing this in mind, an optimal development policy would be one aimed at keeping such social

costs to a minimum in the acquisition of industrial technology.

Presently, an International Code of Conduct on Technology Transfer is being elaborated to minimise some of the problems facing developing countries as a result of technology transfer. But this can merely constitute a partial solution to the manifold problem discussed above, since internal policies in such countries also help to condition a development process. In many instances, these policies have tended to reflect the preferences of privileged social classes in their positions of power as decision makers.

SUMMARY AND CONCLUSION

This paper has tried to look at the question of technology transfer with reference to a dual sector framework.

Inspite of the fact the Lewis model does not explicitly deal with the subject of technology transfer, the argument advanced here is that an open economy version of the model has important implications for the question of technology transfer. For example, the role of imported technology in creating dynamic impulses in the modern sector for industrial and economic development. Further, the model has played an important role in shaping development policy objectives of a number of developing countries; in particular the emphasis of the modern sector in development plans.

The evidence, however, suggests that the industrialization experience of many developing countries based on modern (imported) technology, appears to have fallen much short of theoretical expectations. Growth has taken place in a large number of instances, but development remains questionable, partly but importantly, as a result of technological distortions. Other factors militating against development such as unequal access to economic resources, institutional factors, and political considerations for example, were not analysed in the Study.

The Lima Declaration has set a target of increasing the share of developing countries to world industrial output by 25% in the year 2000. From the evidence before us, it can be held that this target is unlikely to make any meaningful impact on Third World development, unless a radical redressing of technological induced distortions, just looked at, takes place.

FOOTNOTES

1. R. Solow,"Technical Change and the Aggregate Production Function", Review of Economics and Statistics, Vol. 39, 1957.

2. E. Denison, Accounting for U.S. Economic Growth 1929 - 1969 (Washington: Brookings Institute 1974).

3. See U.S.S.R. Report in National Science and Technology Policies in Europe and North America (Paris: UNESCO 1979) p. 385.

4. UNIDO Industry 2000, New Perspectives (New York, UN 1979) pp. 72, 81.

5. UNCTAD TD/8/AC/11/10/Rev. 2, March 1975, p. 28.

6. See Arthur Lewis "Economic Development with Unlimited Supplies of Labour", The Manchester School, May 1954, p. 139-191. See also, C. Fei and G. Ranis, Development of the Labour Surplus Economy (Homewood 1964) for further extensions.

7. See W. Rostow, The Stages of Economic Growth 2nd (ed.) (London: Cambridge University Press 1971).

8. See R. Nurkse, Problems of Capital Formation in Underdeveloped Countries (Oxford: Blackwell 1953).

9. See H. Bruton "The import substitution strategy of economic development: A survey", Pakistan Development Review, Summer 1970.

10. G.K. Helleiner "Manufactured Exports of Less Developed Countries and Multinational Firms", Economic Journal, March 1973.

11. ILO, Employment, Growth and Basic Needs (Geneva: ILO 1976), p. 23.

12. OECD Stock of Private Direct Investment by DAC Countries in Developing Countries (Paris: OECD 1972).

ECONOMIC ANALYSIS, POLICY ANALYSIS, AND AGRICULTURAL DEVELOPMENT

by
Bruce F. Johnston

The thesis of this paper is that progress in advancing understanding and effective action in attaining the goals of development requires a combination of economic analysis and policy analysis. In particular, I argue that the failure of so many of the contemporary developing countries to reduce the poverty which continues to be so serious and widespread among their rural populations can be attributed in no small measure to a common failure to supplement formal economic analysis with a policy analysis perspective. At the very least, it can be asserted that research and analysis on development problems has failed to provide useful policy guidance to decision-makers to the extent that is possible and desirable.

INTRODUCTION

It is only in recent years that efforts to make research and analysis more responsive to the actual needs of decision-makers has led to an explicit focus on policy analysis. To a striking degree, however, W. Arthur Lewis's contributions to the development literature have combined economic analysis with a policy perspective. This is perhaps particularly true of his 1955 treatise on The Theory of Economic Growth, a splendid book with an unfortunate title as he recognized at the time. It is also true of his classic articles on "Economic Development with Unlimited Supplies of Labour" (Lewis, 1954, 1958). Those articles come closer to being examples of conventional economic analysis. However, in directing attention at certain highly significant structural and behavioral characteristics of developing countries and the constraints and opportunities highlighted by those characteristics, the two-sector model outlined in his 1954 article provided a valuable point of departure for a policy analysis perspective on problems of agricultural and rural development. It was the analytical framework underlying much of his 1955 treatise, and many other contributors to the development literature have also built on that framework.

Nevertheless, the principal response of our discipline to Lewis's seminal articles was to recast them and debate their implications at great length within the limited perspective of formal economic analysis and more elaborate model-building exercises. Thus Fei and Ranis (1964) formally incorporated a state of "redundant" agricultural labor characterized by zero marginal productivity as an important feature of their approach to modeling "the development of the labor surplus economy." The well-known critique by Jorgenson (1969) of the "classical" model of development is directed at the Ranis-Fei version which is more fully elaborated than the essentially heuristic model presented by Lewis. Indeed, Jorgenson apparently does not regard Lewis's formulation as a "dual-economy model" because he believes that Lewis's only purpose in introducing a backward sector was to provide a physical location for the "industrial reserve army". Presumably he disregarded Lewis's emphasis on the role of the backward sector in providing the food supplies of the modern sector because this is handled as a verbal supplement to the more formal part of Lewis's analysis of the dual economy.

As contributions to economic analysis, the work of Ranis and Fei and Jorgenson's critique and his formulation of a neoclassical version of a dual-economy model, which rejects the possibility of redundant agricultural labor, are impressive and of considerable interest. A. K. Sen's (1966) analysis of the possibility of dualism in a peasant economy "with or without surplus labor" is perhaps particularly outstanding as an exercise in formal economic analysis. I believe, however, that with the benefit of hindsight it can be said that the large investment of analytical resources in the theoretical and empirical controversy about the existence or nonexistence of labor of zero productivity contributed very little to advancing understanding of the important issues to be confronted in the design of effective strategies for agricultural development.

Lewis took a much more flexible view of the concept of "surplus labor" and explicitly introduced the assumption that the effects on agricultural output of the transfer of farm workers to nonfarm employment might have to be offset by adjustments in agriculture, including willingness on the part of the remaining members of farm households to work harder. Johnston and Mellor (1961) argued that this implication of Lewis's model, with its emphasis on agricultural labor as a relatively abundant resource with low social opportunity cost because of limited demand for labor in the modern sector, is reinforced by the considerable scope that exists for expanding farm output by technological innovations which make only modest demands on a country's scarce resources of capital. Lewis (1955, pp. 187-88, 230-31) had also emphasized the scope for expanding farm output by fostering technical change and noted that Japan's experience had demonstrated the significance of that potential for increasing the productivity of the agricultural work force.

One other aspect of the debate of the 1960s over dual economy models merits attention. For both Lewis and Jorgenson an essential feature of sustained economic growth is the structural transformation of an economy that takes place with the emergence of an expanding industrial sector. A striking feature of Jorgenson's neoclassical version of a dualistic model is his assumption that the existence of a positive and growing agricultural surplus is a necessary and sufficient condition for economic growth, including the emergence of a growing industrial sector. And in turn, the necessary and sufficient condition for creating a growing agricultural surplus is a rate of technical progress in agriculture which exceeds the exogenously determined rate of population growth mulitplied by the elasticity of output with respect to land. In contrast, in Lewis's version, the transfer of manpower is limited by the demand for labor, which in turn is limited by the rate of capital accumulation.

Clearly, there is an important element of

truth in both views. The emergence of a growing nonagricultural sector necessarily depends upon the availability of food to meet the requirements of the increasingly large fraction of the population employed in the modern sector. It is equally true, however, that sustained economic growth and the process of structural transformation depend upon the expansion of employment opportunities in the non-agricultural sectors. And a necessary, though not a sufficient condition for the emergence of an agricultural surplus is a growing nonagricultural sector dependent upon purchased food.[1] That is, the growth of effective demand must provide "scope" for an increase in agricultural productivity to occur. Therefore in a particular country at a particular time the limiting factor in the process of structural transformation and economic growth may be either be either an inadequate rate of increase in food supplies for a growing nonfarm population or an inadequate growth of demand for labor outside agriculture because the rate of expansion of output and employment in the nonfarm sectors is too slow. We need to recognize and sharpen our understanding of the reciprocal relationships involved. Hence, it is essential to give serious and explicit attention to the sectoral interdependence between agriculture and the rest of the economy--and of the implications of the changing nature of those interrelationships (Johnston and Kilby, 1975). To be sure, development policies have some times been based on an "industrialization first" strategy which ignores or positively discriminates against agriculture on the naive assumption that agricultural output can be sustained following the removal of a substantial fraction of the agricultural work force without appropriate measures to increase farm productivity. But the opposite extreme of advocating a "food first" strategy which ignores the importance of concurrent expansion of the agricultural and nonagricultural sectors of a developing economy is equally untenable.

To conclude these introductory remarks it is useful to quote a statement by A. K. Sen made as a member of a group attempting to evolve "guidelines for rural development." Although best known as a theorist and welfare economist, in this context Sen argued:

> For developing countries the shift in
> focus to technological and institutional
> details is long overdue. . . . The most
> serious problems lie, not in the grand
> design, but in what has the superficial
> appearance of 'details' (Sen, 1975, as
> quoted in Hunter, 1978a, p. 37).

The point that I want to emphasize is that
good policy analysis, unlike economic analysis, must
take a broad view of a great variety of interrelated
factors that are relevant to the design of development strategies. The technological and institutional
"details" emphasized by Sen are important examples.
A notable feature of Lewis's 1955 treatise is his
attempt to examine a great many noneconomic as well
as economic factors in his analysis of the complex
process of economic development. For example, in
stressing the importance of "the will to economize,"
Lewis emphasizes the importance of attitudes, the
influence of experience in shaping attitudes and
performance, and the important effects of organizations and other institutions on economic growth.
In his Preface he remarks: "So many factors are
relevant in studying economic growth that it is
easy to be lost unless one has a general perspective
of the subject." There are, however, numerous
pitfalls in attempting to adopt a broad perspective.
In the following section I briefly sketch some
features of a policy analysis perspective which, I
believe, are particularly relevant to attempt to
provide policy guidance with respect to the complex
and ill-structured problems of development. In
section lll, I comment briefly on some of the factors
that have received insufficient or inappropriate
attention in research and analysis on development
problems with particularly serious consequences for
rural development.

SOME PROPOSITIONS FROM POLICY ANALYSIS[2]

What do I mean by policy analysis?
W. Granger Morgan, one of the ablest practitioners of
the art and craft of policy analysis has defined
"good policy analysis" as a systematic effort "to
evaluate, or to order, and structure incomplete

knowledge so as to allow decisions to be made with as complete an understanding as possible of the current state of knowledge, its limitations, and its implications" (Morgan, 1978, p. 971). When applied to a problem as complex and ill-structured as development, a host of variables and changing inter-relationships among those variables must be considered. Consequently, complete knowledge and understanding are impossible. Furthermore, judgements and decisions by policymakers will inevitably be influenced by opinions, subjective preferences, values, and vested interests. Therefore, according to Morgan, good policy analysis should order and structure that incomplete and imperfect knowledge "in ways that are open and explicit;" and it should avoid drawing "hard conclusions unless they are warranted by unambiguous data or well-founded theoretical insight."

In the context of economic development, policy analysis must focus on people and on their interactions with each other and with the enviornment. These interactions are mediated through a variety of organizations and their policies and programs. In order to fulfill their functions, organizations rely on various social techniques of calculation and control: markets and price systems, political organizations, bureaucracies, private firms and co-operatives, family and community groups, and many others.[3] Policies and policymaking processes in this broad sense can be viewed as social action programs through which people seek to devise and im-plement solutions to their problems. The range of policymaking processes which may be relevant includes planning, government interventions, institutional reforms, perhaps revolution.

Planners, economists, and other social scientists typically emphasize a "thinking-through" approach to problems and to the formulation of plans which tend to be regarded as "blueprints" which, it is hoped, will be adopted and implemented. But the emphasis is usually on the questions of "what to do." The "how to do it" questions receive short shrift.

Of the various propositions that are suggested by a policy analysis perspective, four appear to be especially relevant to the design and redesign of development strategies. These proposi- tions are summarized in the paragraphs that follow under the following rubrics: (1) power and per- suasion, (2) feasibility and desirability, (3) in- efficiency and the lack of consensus, and (4) cogitation and interaction. The general proposition underlying this section is that if we as economists (or whatever) want to be effective and constructive in influencing development policy and outcomes, we need to go beyond our disciplinary specialty and learn to function as "policy analysts."

POWER AND PERSUASION

A policy analysis perspective on power and persuasion simply emphasizes that politicians and policymakers have power, policy analysts do not. Hence, in order to be effective as policy analysts we have to learn how "to speak truth to power" clearly and persuasively enough so that development goals are achieved to the maximum degree that is feasible.[4]   Needless to say, the "truth" that we will be able to speak will almost always be partial and incomplete.

This relationship between power and per- suasion points up a kind of naivete that is a frequent source of ineffectiveness. It is often remarked, especially with respect to development programs aimed at helping the poor, that the failures, which are all too common, are "essentially" political failures. That is obviously true. Politics, power, and conflicting interests are inconspicuous features of development programs which are bound to influence "who gets what, when, and how." But to bewail the unequal distribution of power is no more conducive to resolving the "essentially political" problems of development than bewailing the unequal distribution of rainfall is to resolving "essentially agricultural" problems. In playing our role as policy analysts, we must learn to understand the constraints which inevitably shape feasible programs, constraints which are related to the world of power as much as to those imposed by nature and by the scarcity of economic, budget, and manpower resources.

FEASIBILITY AND DESIRABILITY

This second proposition concerns the unfortunate but common tendency to equate the feasible with the desirable. And the equation is applied in both directions. Many people assume that goals are highly desirable must be feasible as well. But in the world of economic and political constraints, resources are never adequate for all the important tasks at hand. In brief, we can't always get what we want.

On the other hand, some pragamtic politicians and advisors have a strong predilection to stick with demostrably feasible activities, i.e., with things that have worked in the past. Obviously this is better than sticking with things that won't work. But especially in low-income developing countries where resource constraints are severe, the opportunity cost of undertaking activities that are feasible but of low priority may be very high indeed. In brief, some activities may be too feasible. Therefore, we shouldn't always want what we can get.

An important conclusion is suggested by this analysis of feasibility and desirability. The conventional view of planning emphasizes a procedure in which objectives are first established and then the means required to attain those objectives are determined. Although there is an attractive logic about that approach, it is misleading, especially in dealing with ill-structured problems and in situations characterized by a severe scarcity of resources. Instead of that conventional approach, good policy analysis emphasizes the need for mutual adjustment of ends and means: the definition of objectives must be shaped by the abailability of resources--and vice versa to the extent that available resources can be enlarged or depolyed more effectively. A further important implication of this emphasis on the need for mutually adjusting ends and means is that particular attention should be given to the possibility of identifying means--sets of policies and programs which constitute a strategy-- which will be effective in furthering multiple objectives. I will have more to say about that in the next section when I discuss agricultural strategies and a few other components of a strategy for rural development. I also argue shortly that the mutual adjustment of ends and means requires a continuing, iterative process of policy design and redesign as initial judgments about feasibility and desirability are modified in the light of experience.

INEFFECTIVENESS AND THE LACK OF CONSENSUS

This third proposition derives its importance from the limited progress that has been made in achieving cumulative progress in better understanding of development problems and of the means for coping with them. Effective action often has been impaired by inadequate understanding and also by the lack of the degree of consensus required for effective action, particularly the sustained action that is often necessary in order to achieve more effective performance by new organizations and in the implementation of new programs.

Instead of leading to cumulative progress, research and analysis in the development field has tended to jump from controversy to controversy and to flit from fad to fad. The controversy has typically been aimed at demolishing an opponent's theory and establishing the unique superiority of some alternative version of the "truth". Such an emphasis on claims and counterclaims is singularly inefficient in identifying the really important issues on which there is inadequate understanding or faulty or insufficient evidence and thereby gradually broadening the areas of consensus. Perhaps the greatest disservice to policymakers in developing countries has been the proliferation of "options" which are often treated almost as panaceas as each "new direction" moves to center stage in the development debate. Thus those responsible for policy formulation have been pushed first one way and then another: an early emphasis on investment and growth as the answer, the burst of enthusiasm for investment in human resources and for manpower planning, then the focus on expanding employment as the all-important need, and more recently the advocacy of a "basic needs strategy" as the latest "new direction".

An obvious consequence of the inconclusive skirmishings and changing fashions that have characterized the development debate is that efforts to "speak truth to power" are unlikely to carry much weight. To be sure, in a field as complex as development, controversy is both inevitable and useful. However, the sort of criticism and emphasis on what is new and different that are appropriate in an academic context can easily be overdone and become counterproductive when carried over to policy analysis. In the absence of a workable consensus on what needs doing and how it is to be done, it is difficult to overcome the inertia of a government bureaucracy and undertake new initiatives. At the same time, in the absence of patient and persistent efforts to advance understanding and to build consensus for well-considered programs, there will be a tendency for governments to undertake hasty and sporadic action to respond quickly (and ineffectively) to the latest crisis. Hence, I believe we need to start paying more attention to reaching consensus and building the support required to carry good proposals through to effective implementation. These will probably not be the "optimal" proposals; and we are almost certainly incapable of knowing whether they are optimal or not.

COGITATION AND INTERACTION

The last of these propositions suggested by a policy analysis perspective has been influenced strongly by the work of Lindblom (1977) and Wildavsky (1979). Wildavsky has introduced the terms "intellectual cogitation" and "social interaction" to describe two alternative approaches to social problem-solving. (See also Lindblom 1977, chapters 19, 23.). The approach of intellectual cogitation assumes that we are equal to the task of "thinking through" solutions to our problems. The social interaction approach takes a more skeptical view of our capacity for calculation and analysis and relies on "acting out" solutions through social processes of voting, markets, bargaining and other interactive techniques.

It is useful to emphasize the extreme forms

of the alternative approaches. In fact, each has its strengths and weaknesses. A statement by Prime Minister Nehru of India illustrates the supremely ambitious, synoptic view of intellectual cogitation:

> (Planning) and development have become a sort of mathematical problem which may be worked out scientifically. . . . (Planning) for industrial development is generally accepted as a matter of mathematical formula. . . . (Men) of science, planners, experts, who approach our problems from purely a scientific point of view (rather than an Ideological one). . . agree, broadly, that given certain pre-conditions of development, industrialization and all that, certain exact conclusions follow almost as a matter of course (quoted by Karanjia, 1960, pp. 49 ff.).

However seductive such a vision of comprehensive planning might be, it is clearly an example of the arguable desirable but wholly infeasible goals that are so common in the development debate. Such synoptic approaches to thinking through development policies are infeasible because they exceed man's cognitive capacities and they presume the existence of agreed upon criteria of goodness or value on which alternative solutions can be judged (Lindblom, 1977, p. 322).

The interactive acting-out approach to social problem-solving is less ambitious and demands less of analytical talent and political harmony. It emphasizes the limitations of human thinking and the scarcity of human attention. As Herbert Simon (1977, p. 47) has argued, "The dream of thinking everything out before we act, of making certain we have all the facts and know all the consequences, is a sick Hamlet's dream". Simon recognizes that "it is costly, and frequently less reliable, to try through research and analysis to anticipate experience".

Although a strategy of incremental improvement or "muddling through" has advantages as compared to an unrealistic, excessively ambitious synoptic approach to comprehensive planning, it has its own limitations. I have emphasized already that the feasible is not always desirable: and a predilection for "getting on with it" may have a high opportunity cost and entail undesirable long-term consequences. For example, policies which promote a "bimodal" agricultural strategy based on the "crash modernization" of a subsector of atypically large and capital-intensive farm enterprises in a developing country tends to foreclose the option of pursuing a successful "unimodal" strategy involving the progressive modernization of a large and increasing fraction of a country's small-scale farm units. Furthermore, interaction learns only randomly from its own experience, and it is incapable of learning from the experience of others.

Policy analysis seeks an integration of cogitation or thinking-through approaches and interactive, acting-out approaches which recognize explicitly the strengths and limitations of each. Clearly, there is a need for systematic reflection on the key problems and issues, the major constraints, and the feasible opportunities for advancing development in a particular country or subset of developing countries. This reflection and the priorities suggested by analysis of problems, constraints, and opportunities provide valuable guidance for the design of a variety of program interventions. But our expectations with respect to those interventions should be modest. Shortcomings and mistakes are inevitable. To adapt a phrase from D. N. Michael (1973), "learning to plan" is important; but "planning to learn" is equally important. In brief, the challenge is to make good though imperfect choices--and then to learn from our inevitable mistakes in a continuing, interactive process of policy design, implementation, and redesign.

COMPREHENSIVE ECONOMIC PLANNING: THE
LIMITATIONS OF A "THINKING-THROUGH" APPROACH

What is the relationship between this

modest view of the role of intellectual cogitation and the tradition of comprehensive economic planning as pioneered by Tinbergen? The question is obviously important because of the extent to which enthusiasm for planning has influenced research and analysis focused on the problems of developing countries. Tinbergen's classic treatise, Economic Policy: Principles and Design (1956), was focused on the relatively well-structured problems of economic policy in the Netherlands and derived from his experience in the Central Planning Bureau and his participation in discussions in the Dutch political arena. In later books, Tinbergen (1958, 1967) has applied some of those principles of economic planning and programming to "the design of development" in less developed countries; and a host of development planners and economists have followed in that tradition.

Lewis's treatise on economic planning is considerably more modest in its view of the role of intellectual cogitation than the mainstream of the planning literature. In his Preface, for example, Lewis suggests that "the secret of successful planning lies more in sensible politics and good public administration" than in the techniques of planning; and he notes that "comprehensive planning is more important to advanced economies than it is to underdeveloped economies" (Lewis, 1966, p. 242). Tinbergen also recognized that development policy is so complex that it embraces not only the whole of economic life but extra-economic phenomena as well. Thus he stresses that analysis must go beyond "quantitative policy" and embrace qualitative analysis as well (Tinbergen, 1956, p. 86). He includes among "the qualitative means" the "institutions chosen by a country as the organizational framwork within which its economic and social life take place" (Tinbergen, 1967, p. 41). And in language which anticipates the emphasis of policy analysis on the mutual adjustment of ends and means, he notes "inconsistency of a set of means and aims need not be ascribed to insufficiency of the means considered" because "it may also be attributed to overambitiousness in the aims set" (Tinbergen, 1956, p. 26).

Unfortunately, much of the planning

literature, formal economic analysis, and model-building has tended to ignore the limitations of intellectual cogitation and the need to supplement thinking-through approaches with interactive acting-out approaches to social problem-solving. Lindblom and Cohen (1979) have argued that this is a common characteristic of "professional social inquiry" (PSI). They suggest that practitioners of PSI have a tendency to greatly exaggerate the distincitiveness and importance of their approach. In their view, the "conclusiveness" and "authoritativeness" of the results of investigations by social scientists are distinctly limited. In fact, they even suggest that PSI "often positively obstructs social problem-solving" (Lindblom and Cohen, 1979, p. 86). The important point to be emphasized is that formal models, analyses of survey data, and statistical tests of hypotheses can only offer evidence in support of an argument. The complexity of problems such as development "denies the possibility of proof . . ." (Lidblom and Cohen, 1979, p. 81).

I am not arguing against the importance of empirical research and efforts to quantify the effects of past or projected activities. In seeking policy guidance for a process as complex as development, the analysis and interpretation of the steadily expanding body of historical experience is an especially significant source of insights and understanding of the critical variables and their interrelationships. And simulation models can play a valuable role in exploring the future implications of possible changes in population, of investment, of the effects of technical change on input-output relationships, and of many other important determinants of the growth of output and its distribution. I do argue in the following section, however, that the allocation of scarce analytical resources to formal analytical exercises such as the elaboration of systems models and a hypothesis-testing approach to the collection and analysis of survey data has been grossly disproportionate to the contribution of those exercises in furthering understanding and effective action to achieve development objectives. Moreover, this preoccupation with formal analytical techniques has had a high opportunity cost in diverting attention and scarce resources of trained manpower away from other approaches to research and analysis which could provide policy guidance of much greater value to decision-makers and administrators in developing countries.

RURAL DEVELOPMENT AS A LEARNING PROCESS

The shortcomings of an excessive emphasis on cogitation and a thinking-through approach appear to have had especially serious adverse effects on the design and effective implementation of strategies for rural development. In the first part of this section, I review in very summary fashion the evidence which suggests that there had been an increase in rural poverty in many developing countries during the past two decades. I then focus on shortcomings in three program areas which, I believe, bear much of the responsibility for this failure to reduce the extent of poverty in rural areas: (1) the failure to design effective strategies for fostering broadbased agricultural development; (2) limited success in slowing rapid growth of the total and rural population and labor force, especially in the low-income developing countries; and (3) the lack of progress in creating effective problem-solving organizations at the local level and in improving the performance of development bureaucracies. It is then argued that formal economic analysis and other types of "professional social inquiry" have made grossly inadequate contributions toward the resolution of these problems and that much greater attention should be given to some alternative approaches to research, analysis, and policy design and redesign.

The emphasis throughout is on the distinctive subset of developing countries which are "late-developing" in the sense that some 60 to 80 percent of their population and labor force is still dependent on agriculture and per capita GNP is still extremely low. This subset includes virtually all of the 38 "low-income developing countries" as classified by the World Bank and a number of the "middle-income" countries as well.[5]

THE INCREASE IN RURAL POVERTY

A major factor responsible for the increase in the extent of rural poverty is simply the increase in the size of rural populations. One result of the unprecedentedly rapid population growth that has characterized the contemporary developing countries is that their agricultural sectors have had to absorb a large fraction of the population increase. In spite of high rates of urban growth, the rate of urbanization--the increase in the percentage of the population in urban centers--has often been slow. Urbanization is, of course, highly correlated with the process of structural change whereby a pre-dominantly agrarian society with some 60 to 80 percent of its labor force dependent on agriculture is transformed into an industrial economy with the bulk of its labor force engaged in manufacturing and other nonfarm sectors.

More than two decades ago Dovring (1959) emphasized that structural change in the contemporary developing countries would be a relatively slow process because the rates of growth of population and labor force were so high and such a large fraction of the labor force was still dependent on agriculture. Highly protectionist import substitution strategies and related economic policies which encourage an inappropriately capital-intensive pattern of investment in the modern, industrial sector has also slowed the structural transformation process by limiting the rate of growth of nonfarm employment opportunities.[6] It is therefore not too surprising that for the 38 "low-income developing countries," the percentage of the labor force in agriculture declined only from 77 to 72 percent between 1960 and 1978 (World Bank, 1980, p. 146). According to the same source, the share of India's labor force dependent on agriculture remained unchanged at 74 percent.

In India, as in many other Asian countries, the growth of the rural population during the past two decades has been associated with a very slight increase in the cultivated area. The increase in India between 1953-54 and 1971-72 was from 305 to 311 million acres (Vyas, 1979). According to this analysis by Vyas, the average size of a farm holding in India declined form 6.3 acres in 1953-54 to 3.8 acres in 1971-72. Over that same period the number of marginal holdings of less than 1 acre more than doubled: and increase from 15.4 to 35.6 million households in that category was associated with a decline in their average size form .24 to .14 acre.

An increase in the size of some large holdings and a tendency for landowners to evict their tenants and go in for direct cultivation because of the profitability of the new high-yielding varieties and the availability of tractors at relatively cheap prices has accounted for some of the increase in the number of marginal holdings. However, the instances of increasing concentration of land in some large holdings have been more than offset by the subdivision of many other large holdings associated with a 66 percent increase in the total number of farm households between 1953-54 and 1971-72. The number of "big" landowners (15 to 50 acres) declined moderately from 4.3 to 4.1 million units and the number of "large" holdings (50 acres and above) was reduced form 604 to 350 thousand. And the share of the total land area owned by those two categories declined from 53 to 39 percent over the same period. The two intermediate groups of "small" and "medium" farmers (with 1 to 5 or 5 to 15 acres) were able to expand their land area almost as rapidly as the increase in the number of households in each category so that there was only a slight decrease in the average size of farm units. Thus the large increase in the number of landless and nearly landless households in India is to be attributed primarily to the growth in the total number of farm households which led to a particularly large increase in the number of marginal households.

The limitations on expanding the area under cultivation have been much less severe in the countries of Sub-Saharan Africa. Nonetheless, there clearly has been a substantial increase in the extent of rural poverty in many of the countries of tropical Africa.[7] At least, it seems reasonable to infer such an increase from the substantial growth of the rural population in those countries together with the fact that food production has failed to keep pace with the growth of population. It is estimated that per capita food production in the region in the late 1970s was some 10 percent below the level prevailing in both the early and late 1960s (FAO, 1979, p. 16). And a report prepared by an Inter Agency Working Group (1980, p. 1) as a working document for an "OAU Extraordinary Summit" states that "Over the last two decades, the food and agricultural situation in Africa has undergone a drastic deterioration". There are certainly many reasons for that deterioration. Knowledge and understanding of the principal causal factors is quite inadequate, and the attempts by Lele (1975), Anthony, Johnston, Jones, and Uchendu (1979), and others to offer interpretations of recent African experience have evoked considerable controversy. In a number of areas increasing population pressure has begun to be a problem, but I believe that the most general and fundamental problem is doubtless the difficulty that is being encountered in shifting from a resource-based to a science-based agriculture (Johnston, 1978).

The problems that lie ahead in absorbing a rapidly growing labor force into productive employment appear to be especially serious. The small size of their fledgling industrial sectors makes it especially difficult to expand nonfarm employment opportunities rapidly enough to absorb more than a small fraction of the annual additions to the labor force. In addition, the rates of natural increase in Sub-Saharan Africa are considerably higher than in most Asian countries and the prospects for slowing population growth are considerably less promising.

I suggested earlier that the shortcomings of efforts to achieve development objectives and a reduction of rural poverty during the past two decades have been influenced strongly by weaknesses in three program areas: the design of broad-based strategies for agricultural sevelopment, limited success in slowing the rapid growth of population, and the lack of progress in creating and strengthening local organizations and development bureaucracies. There have, of course, been many other important factors involved. I believe, however, that the weaknesses in these three program areas are especially significant and that in each instance undue preoccupation with formal analytical techniques and a thinking-through approach has diverted analytical resources and the attention of policy-makers away from a more promising approach to research, analysis, and policy design and redesign.

The discussion in this section of some neglected factors which have impaired rural development is extremely sketchy and impressionistic. Sen's emphasis on the need for attention to the "details" of development not only underscores the importance of detailed analysis but also of focusing on a variety of socioeconomic and agroclimatic factors; and the latter especially tend to be highly location specific. The discussion here is intended to illustrate some general problems of research methodology and analytical approach, not to substitute for the careful and painstaking analysis that is needed of problems, constraints, and opportunities in individual countries and in different farming regions within a country.

SOME GENERAL PROBLEMS RELATED TO THE EMPHASIS ON COGITATION AND FORMAL ANALYTICAL TECHNIQUES

Before turning to problems in the three program areas, it is useful to mention several general propositions about the excessive concentration of analytical resources on thinking-through approaches and formal techniques. Perhaps the most general problem is the common presumption that formal analytical techniques can provide definitive "answers" rather than relevant "evidence." This attitude has, I believe, had especially unfortunate consequences for the "learning process approach" that seems to be needed. Because of the complexity and uncertainty that characterize the important issues of rural development, it is essential to recognize that failures and shortcomings are inevitable. The realistic challenge is therefore not to avoid mistakes, which is impossible, but to learn from our mistakes.

One of the most serious weaknesses of large-scale, "black box" models such as the

ILO BACHUE model for the Philippines or the
Adelman-Robinson model for South Korea is that they
are not useful as a guide to learning. Too often,
even the model-builders have only limited understanding of the assumptions and relationships
which drive their models. Most of these models have
also been flawed by technical deficiencies and
questionable assumptions (Sanderson, 1978, 1980).
And because of their complexity, these almost
inevitable technical and conceptual errors are not
likely to be detected. Another common difficulty is
that a mantel of false complexity often cloaks
simplistic structural assumptions. Arthur and
McNicoll (1975, p. 257) have pointed out, for example,
that the "robust" conclusion of the TEMPO model that
slower population growth translates into more rapid
growth of per capita GNP is nothing more than the
necessary result of their use of a Cobb-Douglas
production function in the model.

        This is not to say that formal models do
not have a useful role to play. Experience does seem
to suggest, however, that that role in the overall
process of policy design, implementation, and
redesign is rather limited. Practical evaluations of
various modeling-based approaches to environmental
policy design conducted under the auspices of the
International Institute for Applied Systems Analysis
(IIASA) by C. S. Holling and his coworkers has also
emphasized the need for simplification at all stages
of the modeling and analytical effort. They argue
that such simplifications are essential "to
encapsulate understanding and help intuition play its
central role in the analysis" and also "to facilitate
communication" (Clark, Jones, and Holling, 1977, p.
38). We should not lose sight of the fact that
models or any other analytical technique intended to
assist in policy design are of little value unless
they contribute to constructive interaction between
those doing the analysis and decision-makers and
managers.

        Another feature which limits the usefulness
of systems models is the problem of "sub-optimiza-
tion". In summarizing Gunnar Myrdal's critique of
the well-know Coale-Hoover demographic model,
Perlman (1975, p. 256) notes that models of that

nature tend to be "inadequate in their specifications
. . . . Some of the key variables are omitted
because they are impossible to quantify. Some
variables may be so unstable that they cannot be
used".

A case in point is the emphasis which
Pyatt and Thorbecke (1976, p. 54) place on the need
for detailed case studies to determine the form of
the production functions to be used in estimating a
"social accounting matrix" to trace through the
effects of production activities on labor markets
and markets for other factors and ultimately on the
determination of income levels and income distribution among household groups. The proper
specification of production functions in such a
model is clearly important. But in their discussion
of "planning techniques for a better future," Pyatt
and Thorbecke virtually ignore much more important
questions, including the critical question of how
to shift agricultural production functions through
research, extension programs, investments in
infrastructure, and similar activities. Their
enthusiasm for comprehensive economic planning also
leads them to assume that a prerequisite for
achieving significant changes in income and its distribution is the ability to trace through in a
quantitative way the complex and interrelated changes
in savings, factor ownership, factor supplies,
production and technology, investment, consumption,
exports, imports, demands for products and for
factors, employment and factor incomes and much else.
Thus in advocating a "social accounting matrix" (SAM)
to supplement national income accouts, they assert
that one of their "main recommendations is that work
on national data systems can and should be reorganis-
ed so that planning can be concerned with poverty
and inequality as well as growth" (Pyatt and
Thorbecke, 1976, p. 48). Inasmuch as there appear to
be many other unfulfilled statistical needs in
developing countries that merit higher priority than
developing a SAM, it is fortunate that people in
today's low-income countries can find some re-
assurance in the fact that Japan, Taiwan, the
People's Republic of China, and quite a number of
other countries have achieved considerable success in
reducing both poverty and inequality without the

guidance of a SAM.

Similar problems are to be noted in connection with the even greater emphasis that has been placed on benefit/cost analysis, estimates of internal rates of return, and similar techniques for project evaluation. These techniques clearly have an important role to play in evaluating specific projects. However, reliance on benefit/cost analysis or other project-oriented evaluations without careful attention to other types of evidence almost inevitably leads to suboptimization. One difficulty is that some of the benefits and costs that should be considered are difficult or impossible to quantify in any meaningful way.[8] An example, which anticipates my discussion of population programs, concerns the quantification of the benefits associated with reducing child mortality. How do we assign a value to, say, a reduction of the infant mortality rate in a country from 150 to 50 per thousand? What is the relationship between such an estimate and the hardy (if not foolhardy) attempts that were made by Stephen Enke and others to estimate the "value" of a birth prevented by a family planning program? Can we ignore the fact that high rates of child mortality not only impose serious psychological cost on the families affected but also appear to have high social costs as a major source of resistance to family planning?

That final question about a narrowly defined, quantified approach to assessing the benefits and costs programs to reduce child mortality points to a more general problem of suboptimization with project-oriented benefit/cost analyses. In concentrating on the benefits and costs of individual projects considered in isolation, interactions and complementarities are ignored even though such interrelationships are likely to be highly significant. One of the clearest lessons of experience is that the effectiveness of an agricultural development strategy depends on a satisfactory mix and balance among its components--research, extension, and other support services, investments in irrigation and other types of infrastructure, the distribution of credit and inputs, etc.

Finally, it should be noted that there are

significant interrelationships among the three
program areas considered in the remainder of this
section. In particular, the shortcomings in fostering broad-based agricultural development and in
promoting the spread of family planning have been
influenced strongly by the general neglect of
problems of organization and management. There are
also complex but important interrelationships between
socioeconomic progress and the changes in behaviour
which lead to a reduction of fertility; and rapid
population growth makes it more difficult to achieve
the significant and widespread increases in per
capita incomes and changes in related socioeconomic
variables which seem to facilitate the spread of
family planning.

PROBLEMS IN THE DESIGN OF STRATEGIES FOR
BROAD-BASED AGRICULTURAL DEVELOPMENT

A great many factors have accounted for the
failure of many developing countries to design and
successfully implement effective unimodal strategies
for agricultural development. I focus here on one of
those factors which illustrates our failure to learn
effectively from accumulating experience. Nearly
all of us who have been concerned with research
pertinent to the design of strategies for agricultural development have been remarkably slow to confront
the special problems of achieving widespread increases in productivity under rainfed conditions. The
experience in Japan, Taiwan, South Korea, and a few
other countries has demonstrated that an agricultural
expansion path based on gradual but widespread
increases in productivity and output among a country's small-scale farmers is economically efficient
as well as offering important social advantages
(Hayami and Ruttan, 1971; Johnston and Kilby, 1975).
Indeed this is an area in which there has been a good
deal of cumulative progress in understanding. In
his 1955 treatise, Lewis only very tentatively
suggested that small farmers might have advantages
as compared to large farmers in the context of a
developing country. An impressive body of empirical
evidence from developing countries is now available
which demonstrates that small farms are not only
more labor-intensive but also achieve higher output

per acre and are usually characterized by higher factor productivity. (See, for example, Berry and Cline, 1979).[9] Moreover, a considerable consensus has emerged with respect to the advantages of unimodal strategies which emphasize widespread increases in the productivity of the small farms which provide work and income for the bulk of the rural population in late-developing countries (World Bank, 1975, 1978; Asian Development Bank, 1978; India, 1978, Chapter 9; the Philippines, 1977, Chapter 5; Kenya, 1979, Chapter 2, 6; Mellor, 1976; Johnston and Kilby, 1975).

With the benefit of hindsight, it is now clear that achieving a unimodal pattern of agricultural development based on widespread increases in productivity is considerably easier under conditions of controlled water supply that under rainfed conditions. A powerful methodology exists for developing "biological-chemical innovations" which permit large and reliable increases in crop yields and output when irrigation can assure and adequate supply of water. However, because of technical as well as economic constraints, the great bulk of the agricultural land in many developing countries, including most of Sub-Saharan Africa, is and will continue to be dependent on rainfed production. And the task of generating a sequence of profitable innovations that are feasible for small farmers subject to a severe purchasing power constraint poses special difficulties under those conditions.

There are some examples of considerable success in developing high-yielding varieties of maize that perform well under rainfed conditions when the rainfall is reasonably ample and well distributed. Kenya and El Salvador are two particularly interesting examples of countries where national experiment stations, drawing on the work of international research centers, have developed high-yielding, hybrid varieties of maize that have been widely adopted by small-scale farmers (Gerhardt, 1975; Walker, 1980). In both countries, however, the rate of adoption is very low in areas where environmental conditions are relatively unfavorable.

This experience points up a highly

important conclusion. In many agricultural areas in today's low-income countries, the level of rainfall, its year-to-year variability, and its seasonal distribution limit significantly the magnitude of the yield increases that can be obtained simply by the introduction of high-yielding, fertilizer-responsive varieties and enlarged use of fertilizer. The challenge of increasing productivity of small farmers under rainfed conditions is especially great in the semiarid tropical regions where "more than 500 million of the poorest people in the world eke out a livelihood from the meager resources of land and climate in an unfriendly climate" (Ghodake et al., 1978, p. 1). Under rainfed conditions, biological and chemical innovations usually need to be supplemented by equipment and tillage innovations which permit improvements in soil and water management and in the timeliness of planting and weeding. Therefore, without concurrent attention to biological-chemical and mechanical innovations the potential of improved seed-fertilizer combinations cannot be realized. But unfortunately, the research efforts devoted to equipment and tillage innovations have been so limited that the research base for increasing productivity and output among small farmers in rainfed areas is extremely inadequate.

There are many reasons for the neglect of research on equipment and tillage innovations adapted to the needs of small farmers with limited cash income. The most obvious is the paucity of resources for research and the low priority that has been given to agricultural research. In addition, in the countries of tropical Africa it was long assumed that because of the relative abundance of land, farmers could and should shift directly from the hoe to tractor cultivation. It is now apparent, however, that because of the cash income and purchasing power constraint which characterizes the agricultural sector in a late-developing country, tractor cultivation is too expensive to be adopted by more than a small fraction of relatively large and affluent farmers. Governments in a number of African countries have attempted to circumvent that problem by heavily subsidized tractor-hire schemes. But these schemes have also benefited only a limited number of farmers. Their main consequence has been to divert resources and attention away from alternative and more appropriate solutions to the power and equipment needs of small farmers.

There is a strong presumption that promotion of a range of simple, inexpensive but well-designed animal-powered implements offers great promise as a means of increasing farm productivity and also of fostering rural-based industrialization in the contemporary developing countries. This is especially true of Africa where on the order of 80 percent of the cultivation is still carried out by hoe, and very little progress has been realized in fostering the development of rural-based manufacturing firms.

In considerable areas the presence of the tsetse fly and trypanosomiasis rule out that option, but even in the savannah areas where cattle are readily available there has been only very limited progress in expanding the use of animal draft power. In Madagascar, in some of the francophone countries of West Africa, and in Mazabuka District of Zambia there has been substantial adoption of the use of a considerable range of ox-drawn implements. Elsewhere, however, animal draft power is not used at all or is confined almost entirely to the use of a plow for primary tillage. And quite often in the semiarid regions this is a moldboard plow that is illsuited to a situation where moisture conservation is more important than covering weeds by a soil-inverting plow (Johnston, 1980b, 1981).

In a number of Asian countries, perhaps especially in Taiwan, local manufacture of an expanded range of simple farm implements has provided an important stimulus to the development of metalworking and other technical as well as entrepreneurial skills in rural areas (Johnston and Kilby, 1975, Chapters 6, 8). To date, however, the limited production of animal-drawn equipment in Sub-Saharan Africa has been confined to a few relatively large and fairly capital-intensive factories in urban centers.

If the potential benefits from expanded farm use and local manufacture of animal-powered equipment are great, why has so little progress been made? As previously suggested, I believe that part of the answer lies in the preoccupation with tractors. This has been related to their "modernity" and a failure to recognize that their technical superiority does not imply that they are economically efficient in late-developing countries where capital is scarce and the opportunity cost of labor is low (Binswanger, 1978).

In my judgment, another highly significant factor is the lack of an effective methodology for R&D activities to generate and diffuse farm equipment innovations. Moreover, some agricultural scientists and economists have argued that the scarce resources available for agricultural research should not be allocated to farm equipment programs. It is emphasized, for example, that in the U.S. local blacksmiths and machine shops spontaneously designed and manufactured farm equipment in response to the growth of an effective demand among farmers--and typically with considerable farmer involvement in the design and redesign process. The frequent failure of ad hoc, poorly conceived, and understaffed R&D programs has also been cited as evidence that publicly supported research on mechanical innovations is inefficient as compared to "induced innovation" in the private sector. (See, for example, Ruttan, 1980). I believe however, that it is wrong to apply the U.S. analogy to contemporary developing countries because of the importance of accelerating the process of identifying promising items of farm equipment for particular soil-climatic conditions. Moreover, the program at the International Rice Research Institute (IRRI) for the testing and design of improved equipment and promotion of its local manufacture appears to have achieved considerable success. It has, however, also demonstrated the need for a sustained effort and a systematic methodology for evaluating promising areas for product development and for establishing design parameters based on analysis of a potential market and the technical and economic environment in which the equipment will be produced and used (Duff, 1980). The IRRI experience is, however, of little direct relevance to the countries of Sub-Saharan Africa and other areas where rainfed cultivation predominates because the work at IRRI has concentrated on equipment related to irrigated rice production.

A number of deficiencies that characterize
most R&D programs for farm equipment innovations
have been identified in addition to the limited and
sporadic nature of most of the programs. In
particular, it has become clear that agricultural
engineers working on'their own to test and develop
new equipment have not had much impact. This appears
to be partly the result of the penchant of engineers
to become so fascinated with design problems that
the limited resources available are almost totally
absorbed in endless design activity. More fundamental, however, is the need for a "systems approach"
by engineers, agronomists, economists, and other
scientists which takes account of the interacting
effects on crop yields of equipment design, tillage
methods, soil characteristics, moisture conditions,
and varietal improvements in fertilizer use (Monnier,
1975; Johnston, 1980b). Experience at the Institute
for Crop Research in the Semi-Arid Tropics (ICRISAT)
suggests that technological innovations involving a
combination of improved varieties, increased fertilizer use, and improved techniques of tillage and
water and crop management can lead to very significant increases in crop yields (Ryan et al., 1980).
But there is a need for considerable trial-and-error
learning to evolve effective methods of generating
such innovations under the diverse conditions found
in rainfed farming regions. The task of evolving
cost-effective techniques for promoting local
manufacture of animal-drawn equipment probably poses
even more difficult problems because of the lack of
relevant experience. Given the importance of
promoting the expansion of small-and medium-scale
manufacturing firms employing relatively labor-
intensive technologies and maximizing the use of
local raw materials, it seems likely that such efforts
should be given a rather high priority. In my
judgment, that conclusion is reinforced by the rapid
growth of the population of working age in Africa
and the need to accelerate the expansion of nonfarm
employment as well as income-earning opportunities
in agriculture. To cite an extreme example, it is
projected that Kenya's population of working age is
likely to increase sixfold between 1969 and 2024,
with a fourfold increase in the rural work force and

a sixteenfold increase in the active-age population in urban areas (Shah and Willekens, 1978, pp. 29, 38).

LACK OF PROGRESS IN SLOWING POPULATION
GROWTH IN LOW-INCOME COUNTRIES

In the past few years considerable attention has been given to the fact that a "turning point" has been reached and that the rate of population growth in less developed countries has begun to decline. That reversal has been influenced strongly, however, by the dramatic reduction in the rate of natural increase in the People's Republic of China, and by very substantial declines in fertility in Taiwan, South Korea, and a number of other middle-income countries. More modest but significant reductions in fertility have apparently also been realized in India and Indonesia, and the reductions in those two countries account for much of the decline in fertility in the low-income developing countries between 1960 and 1978. For the 38 low-income countries the decline in the crude birthrate was from 48 to 39 per thousand as a population-weighted average. But the reduction as an unweighted average was only from 47 to 45 per thousand, reflecting the fact that most of the low-income countries had virtually no reduction in fertility by 1978.

There has been a veritable explosion of demographic research focused on less developed countries during the past fifteen years. It is striking, however, how little that research has added to the insights contained in Lewis's 1955 analysis of the problems of population growth and of reducing fertility. Indeed several of the "contributions" which have received considerable attention have, in my opinion, been counterproductive. I have argued elsewhere that the "conclusion" derived from the Adelman-Robinson Korean model and from ILO's BACHUE model for the Philippines that over a 30-year period a slowing of population growth would lead to a deterioration in income distribution is a consequence of questionable assumptions built into models (Johnston, 1977, p. 886). I also argue there that a demographic simulation model developed by Julian Simon is even more misleading in claiming to demonstrate that moderate population growth is better for developing countries than slow population growth. Sanderson (1978, pp. 98-99) has subsequently pointed out in detail that this "conclusion" of Simon's is based on some extremely dubious assumptions.

With appropriate and refreshing candor, Lewis (1955, p. 311) states with respect to the decline in fertility in European countries: "We do not know what caused this decline". He notes that it is pretty safe to assume that the decline in fertility which completed Europe's demographic transition was due to a change of attitude toward childbearing and not merely to new techniques of birth control. He goes on to suggest that "probably the most important reason (for the change in attitude toward childbearing) is simply the fall in the death rate" (Lewis, 1955, p. 311). This is consistent with the "child mortality hypothesis" which has received much attention and provoked considerable controversy during the past decade and a half. His analysis is also similar to the "analytical framework" emphasized by Easterlin (1975, 1977) in emphasizing the importance of a transition from premodern to modern fertility determination. Before the threshold is reached which marks that transition, the "potential supply" of children, in Easterlin's terminology, generally falls short of the number that is desired. But the decline in child mortality, often accompanied by changes in attitudes toward the desired number of children, leads to the emergence of an "excess supply" situation and to what Easterlin refers to as the period of modern fertility determination in which it becomes usual for family size to reflect conscious decisions by individual parents. Lewis mentions changes in the status of women, the increasing cost of rearing children, and the effects of urbanization as relevant factors. He also notes that "Economic growth means that there is a larger income to enjoy, and such enjoyment takes time" (Lewis, 1955, p. 312). Thus he anticipates a major theme of "the new household economics" as developed by Becker and others who have elaborated a demand analysis of the determinants of parents' desires concerning the number and "quality" of children.[10]

There seem to be two main reasons why the large body of research on the determinants of fertility has provided such limited policy guidance. First, much of the research has emphasized demand factors, to the neglect of factors influencing the "potential supply" of children. Much of this research which has used the concepts of the new household economics is also focused rather narrowly on certain economic variables that lend themselves to quantification. Thus Keeley (1975), in defending the new home economics as applied to demographic research, deplored attempts to consider threshold effects and changes in tastes. T. P. Schultz (1971, p. 151), a major contributor to this research, has acknowledged the importance of "non-pecuniary factors" but explains that his research has concentrated on the pecuniary benefits and costs of children because they are not as "difficult to observe, conceptualize, and evaluate". Second, many of the studies have focused on correlations between fertility change and a variety of socioeconomic variables without paying much attention to whether the variables selected for attention were appropriate objects of government policy.

There has also been a tendency for scholars engaged in demographic research to emphasize the importance of gathering large bodies of highly disaggregated data in order to test various linkages postulated by the economic theory of the household as to permit further refinements. Another difficulty is illustrated by a 1976 paper by T. P. Schultz which raises the important policy issue of comparing the social returns from direct incentive payments to parents to avoid births with the benefits of programs such as "promoting the health and nutrition of mothers and young children, accelerating the growth of educational opportunities, . . . facilitating the entrance of women into the labor force, and strengthening the legal status of women". He argues that in order to make choices among alternative programs for fertility reduction, there is a need for

> two advances in the social sciences . . .
> First, agreement must be reached
> on how to characterize a society's
> interpersonal and intergenerational

goals and their trade-offs.
Second, a much improved
understanding will be required
of how economic and demographic
variables influence and are
influenced by reproductive
behaviour (T. P. Schultz, p. 11).

To seek such advances in the social sciences may
well be appropriate in relation to the academic and
disciplinary concerns of individual scholars. But
research objectives defined in such ambitious and
academic terms cannot be expected to be of much
value to those concerned with the design and
implementation of programs to accelerate the reduction in fertility.

Lewis had already recognized the
possibility that the unprecedentedly rapid reductions
in mortality in the contemporary developing countries
might be followed by exceptionally rapid declines in
fertility. He also dismissed the debate about family
planning versus development as a means of reducing
fertility as "a sham controversy" (Lewis, 1955,
pp. 314, 315). Unfortunately, that debate has continued to bedevil discussions of population policy.
However, in a sequel to their major study reviewing
evidence relevant to changes in fertility in the
developing countries, Mauldin and Berelson emphasize
that the best results in slowing population growth
are achieved when appropriate changes in socioeconomic
conditions are combined with a strong family planning
program. And they suggest that among the socioeconomic conditions that are relevant, "health and
education seem to be of particular importance"
(Mauldin and Berelson, 1978, p. 288).

Probably the most important development
during the quarter century since Lewis addressed the
issue of population growth is the progress that has
been made in evolving new and more effective strategies for promoting improvements in nutrition and
health. In spite of the rapid progress in reducing
overall mortality in most developing countries by
factors such as improved transportation and mass
campaigns against malaria and smallpox, infant and
child mortality rates have remained shockingly high

in many developing countries. A few countries, notably Taiwan, South Korea, the People's Republic of China, Hong Kong, Singapore, Sri Lanka, and Costa Rica have achieved especially large reductions in mortality and have dramatically reduced the risk that children will not survive to maturity. For example, in Taiwan in 1970 the risk of a child dying before age 5 was only about one-tenth as great as in India or Pakistan. And in the former countries the reductions in mortality have been followed by a dramatic decline in fertility. It is also noteworthy that in Taiwan, South Korea, China, and, to a lesser extent, Sri Lanka and Costa Rica, the broad involvement of the rural population in the process of agricultural development has meant that the great majority of households were affected by the socioeconomic changes which seem to lead to changes in attitudes toward childbearing.

Some rural health projects in India and in a number of other countries also seem to demonstrate the importance of an integrated approach to health and family planning in promoting reductions in fertility independent of more general changes in socioeconomic conditions. These projects are of great interest in demonstrating the cost-effectiveness of rural health programs which emphasize preventive activities such as nutrition and hygiene, immunization programs, and promotion of simple curative techniques such as oral rehydration. This type of health strategy which recognizes the inevitable trade-off between coverage and "quality standards" was first emphasized in a book edited by Maurice King (1966). And Gwatkin et al. (1979) and Pyle (1979, 1981) review a number of interesting examples. These projects have been particularly effective in reducing infant and child mortality. Because of the great importance of the two-way interactions between nutritional status and infection among infants and small children, the effectiveness of these projects is influenced greatly by a judicious combination of nutrition and health activities. General education about the principles of good nutrition seems to have very little impact on behavior. But very specific training focused on child-feeding practices and on the nutritional needs of pregnant and lactating women can be very effective (FAO/WHO, 1976, pp. 39-40).

This type of health strategy places major reliance on health auxiliaries and community-level health workers. The methodology that has been evolved has been particularly significant because the costs are low enough to permit effective coverage of rural as well as urban populations even in low-income developing countries. Moreover, by emphasizing a "composite package" of health, nutrition, and family planning services they have the potential to simultaneously reduce infant and child mortality and to promote increased awareness that the risk of child loss has been reduced significantly. The presumption that this linking of health and family planning activities can facilitate the change in attitudes, motivation and behavior required for reduced fertility is supported strongly by evidence from some of the projects in India. For example, in the Jamkhed Project the percentage of eligible couples practicing family planning rose sharply from 2.5 percent in 1971 to over 50 percent in 1976. The Miraj Project, also in the state of Maharashtra, concentrated on "target families" with three children or more. Coverage was increased nearly threefold to 89 percent between January 1974 and January 1977, and in all instances sterilization was the method of contraception (Pyle, 1979, attachment 11 and personal communication).

Although the potential contributions of this type of health strategy in promoting interrelated improvements in health and reduced fertility are clearly highly significant, it has not yet been demonstrated that it will be feasible for such projects to be implemented effectively on a national scale in today's low-income developing countries. The Rural Health Scheme and Community Health Worker Program initiated in India in 1977, for example, is encountering great difficulty in replicating the success of small demonstration projects within a large government program. Difficulties have arisen because of the opposition of many physicians to this type of health strategy. The greatest challenge, however, appears to be to achieve sustained progress in overcoming problems of organization and management in order to correct mistakes and shortcomings and to gradually achieve a satisfactory level of effectiveness and efficiency.

NEGLECT OF PROBLEMS OF ORGANIZATION
AND MANAGEMENT

The mainstream of development literature
has given remarkably little attention to questions
of organizational design and managerial procedures.
Yet a decade and a half ago, S. C. Hsieh and T. H.
Lee argued that "the main secret of Taiwan's
development" was "her ability to meet the
organizational requirements" (Hsieh and Lee, 1966,
pp. 103, 105). These issues of organization are
especially critical in providing public goods which
will not be made available at socially optimal levels
without interventions by publicly-supported
organizations. Success in fostering widespread
increases in productivity and output among small-
scale farmers is clearly very dependent upon effective support institutions for agricultural research,
extension, and for the construction and management
of irrigation facilities and other types of infrastructure. The East Asian countries of Japan, South
Korea, and the People's Republic of China as well as
Taiwan are notable in the attention that has been
given to creating a network of organizations capable
of providing those support services. Social service
programs to provide broad access to nutrition,
health, and family planning also partake of the
character of public goods. And, as was noted above,
success in realizing the potential contribution of
such programs is also dependent on serious and
sustained attention to problems of organization and
management.

The neglect of problems of organization is
probably mainly a consequence of the tendency of
economists to abstract from such "details". In
addition, I know that I have tended to shy away from
serious attention to such issues because of a feeling
that organizational performance depends so much on
idiosyncratic factors that I was skeptical whether
research and systematic analysis could yield useful
generalizations. It has been an agreeable surprise
to discover that I was wrong.[11]

It is useful to regard organization as a
means of providing a framework for "calculation and
control" whereby collections of individuals determine

what each is to do and seek to assure that each does what is expected of him (Dahl and Lindblom, 1953). A variety of social techniques are used for calculation and control, including the informal face-to-face bargaining that is so important in local community organizations, the hierarchical techniques which characterize a "facilitator organization" such as an agricultural extension service and other government bureaucracies, and exchange techniques such as price and market mechanisms. Economics has with good reason emphasized that prices and markets provide a powerful means of harmonizing the decisions of large numbers of producers and consumers. But because the provision of what are essentially public goods--research and other supporting services for agriculture and social programs for education, health, nutrition, and family planning--have such an important role to play in rural development, the performance of governmental organizations and also small local-level organizations is critical.

Although research and analysis of organizational problems can lead to useful generaliz-ations, it is not possible for these summary comments to do justice to those generalizations. This is in part because of the range and variety of existing organizational structures. The problems which arise in connection with small community organizations at the local level are very different from those which require attention in considering the "facilitator organizations" which link rural people and their local organizations with a regional or national government. The difficulty of offering a brief summary of these issues is also a consequence of the importance of the historical dimension of social organization. Organizations are organic entities which grow and develop over time. Strengthening of organizational capacities involves visible changes in organizational structure and obviously a growth in administrative skills. But it also involves less evident changes in cultural values and expectations because an existing organization represents a complex, dynamic system of linkages which is only partly understood by participants and observers.

Redesigning and reorganizing existing patterns of linkages is a tricky business, and any notion that policymakers and analysts have a "clean slate" on which to write their organizational prescriptions is naive. Drastic reorganizations are likely to damage historically evolved capacities to resolve social problems. In most cases the need is for a sequence of steps to mitigate the more serious failings of existing organizations.

Although facilitator organizations have certain common features, especially their reliance on a hierarchy of full-time bureaucrats, it is important to make a distinction between facilitator organizations concerned with "managing the predictable" and those organizations which need to be especially concerned with "managing a learning sequence". The highly structured approach to reorganizing agricultural extension programs according to the "Training and Visit System" analyzed by Benor and Harrison (1977), for example, is a case of "managing the predictable" because of the extensive experience that has been acquired in administering agricultural extension programs in developing as well as developed countries.

The problems referred to earlier with respect to the design and implementation of rural health programs are an especially significant example of a need for a learning approach. For most development organizations it is inappropriate to rely on a "blueprint approach" which views organizations simply as means of assisting planners and senior administrators to implement their preconceived plans (Korten, 1980). However, the need for an approach which promotes a mutual learning process involving local people, field staff, specialists, and higher level administrators seems to be especially pronounced in relation to the continuing trial-and-error process of designing, implementing, and redesigning rural health programs.

Furthermore, participation by local organizations such as a village health committee appear to be especially important in the design and implementation of health, nutrition, and family planning programs. The success of such programs depends on changes in behavior and in community norms, precisely the sort of changes that are facilitated by active local participation. Although it has become

94

fashionable in recent years to emphasize the importance of participation, most of the discussion has not gone beyond the level of rhetoric. For example, there is a tendency to treat participation as a free good. But obviously participation in a local organization requires an investment of time and energy for the participants. And it is an investment which cannot be commanded by administrators; it must be induced.

Recent experience in the Philippines is of considerable interest in relation to implementation problems which involve participation by local organizations. B. Bagadion and F. Korten (1980) have provided an extremely interesting account of how the National Irrigation Administration has approached the task of learning how to organize viable local organizations for managing small-scale irrigation systems. These so-called "communal" systems, in contrast with "national" systems, serve approximately half the irrigated land in the Philippines. The way in which pilot projects and a "learning laboratory" approach were used to facilitate the task of bringing farmers into the processes of planning projects for constructing or improving these small-scale irrigation systems and of managing the systems appears to be of broad relevance (D. Korten, 1980).

Cogitation alone cannot possibly provide answers to the difficult problems that must be overcome in dealing with difficult organizational programs such as evolving an effective community-oriented health program. An interactive "acting-out" approach and applied research are clearly needed to learn from the success and failures of ongoing experience. There also appears to be a need for studies to learn as much as possible about key problems such as securing the professional legitimization and acceptance of the new health strategies, fostering effective community participation, sustaining the motivation of village-level workers, and devising methods of financing which include contributions from the local community and probably private payments to cover the cost of drugs except in the case of the poorest families.

This need for sustained efforts and applied

research and an adaptive approach to problems of
management applies to many development programs.
Although the majority of agricultural extension
programs involve "managing the predictable", evolving
effective organizational arrangements and management
procedures for identifying and diffusing farm
equipment innovations must cope with the task of
managing a learning sequence because of the lack of
relevant experience and of understanding of how to
attain those objectives.

ENVOI

        In this paper I have examined three program
areas from the perspective of policy analysis.
Choice of some of the particular issues was fairly
arbitrary. Choice of the three program areas was
not. Production programs emphasizing broad-based
agricultural development and accelerated expansion
of nonfarm employment, consumption programs with
special attention to health, nutrition, and family
planning services, and organization programs
constitute the three "prongs" of a three-pronged
strategy for rural development which Clark and I have
emphasized in our essay on "Redesigning Rural
Development: A Strategic Perspective" (Johnston and
Clark, forthcoming, Chapter 6).

        I believe that it is highly probable, given
the structural-demographic characteristics of late-
developing countries, that it is a "hard conclusion"
that broad-based agricultural development with
positive interactions between agricultural and
industrial development is a necessary condition for
satisfactory progress in attaining the multiple
goals of development. And for a great many countries,
dealing more effectively with the special problems of
fostering increased productivity among small farmers
under rainfed conditions is essential. The evidence
is also quite clear, I believe, that it would be
desirable to promote wider and more efficient use of
a range of inexpensive animal-powered equipment
associated with tillage innovations adapted to a
variety of conditions of climate, soil, and topo-
graphy. And it seems equally desirable for
governments to take purposive action to stimulate

the growth of rural-based metalworking shops based
in part on growing farm demand for such equipment.
Whether it is also feasible for governments to
undertake R&D programs to achieve those two
objectives is more problematic. On the basis of my
limited experience in Kenya in 1974/75 and development since that time, I am optimistic (Westley and
Johnston, eds., 1975; Muchiri, 1980; Johnston, 1981).
Perhaps I am too optimistic.

There is really little doubt about the
desirability of slowing rapid population growth.
"It needs no elaborate argument", as Lewis remarked
(1955, p. 308), "to establish the proposition that
if death rates fall from 40 to 10, the world will
soon be in a mess unless birthrates fall to much
the same extent". There is room to quibble about
how soon is "soon" but not about the general
proposition. I am also persuaded that it is
desirable, even and perhaps especially in low-income
countries with limited resources, for governments
to attempt to accelerate the reduction in fertility
by undertaking integrated health, nutrition, and
family planning programs designed to further the
interrelated and mutually reinforcing objectives of
improving the nutritional status and health of the
population and reducing the rate of population growth.
Under what conditions that will prove to be feasible
is something that we can learn only from experience
with the design and redesign of organizational strategies and management procedures to implement such
programs with an acceptable level of effectiveness
and efficiency.

Finally, the importance of improving the
performance of development bureaucracies and of
strengthening the problem-solving capabilities of
local organizations is clearly an important concern.
Indeed, success in the two program areas that I have
just discussed depends in large measure on such
progress. Here again it remains uncertain to what
extent research and analysis can (or will) provide
policy guidance for such efforts.

Unfortunately, there is another question
which seems to be especially critical in many of the
contemporary developing countries. To what extent

will political conditions and the state of governance
in various countries be congenial to the design and
implementation of effective strategies for rural
development? I am not referring to the problems of
"urban bias" which Lipton (1977) has stressed so
eloquently and which are surely important in many
developing countries. Rather I am referring to
"The primary function of government (which) is to
maintain law and oder" (Lewis, 1955, p. 377). Many
additional functions are now, as Lewis notes, quite
properly assigned to governments. The harsh fact,
however, is that in a considerable number of
countries that primary function of maintenance of
the law and order required for economic and social
progress is not being fulfilled. Of all the ills
that Uganda suffered under Amin, the breakdown of
law and order was unquestionably the most fundamental.
Whether one is inclined to applaud or condemn the
ideology of the Ethiopian regime which replaced
Haile Selassie, it seems difficult to avoid the
conclusion that it has not yet been able to establish
a regime of law and order. I have insufficient
knowledge of the situation in El Salvador to argue
the case for or against the present regime of
President Duarte. But is seems hard to avoid the
conclusion that the civil strife and the extreme
polarization of opinion and politics is currently
making it extremely difficult to implement any
coherent, effective strategy of development. I
argued in section 11 that "inefficiency and lack of
consensus" in the development debate has been an
important factor limiting progress in attaining
development goals. It would be naive to suppose that
"good policy analysis" is capable of avoiding the
sorts of problems that now plague countries such as
Uganda, Ethiopia, or El Salvador. But as economists,
development planners, or whatever we can perhaps play
our additional role as policy analysts in ways which
will limit rather than exacerbate the ineffectiveness
and lack of consensus which contribute to the
emergence of such situations.

1. Production for export to cater to world demand
for agricultural imports can, of course, qualify
that statement. But there appear to be very few
historical examples in which successful agricultural
development has been achieved without the stimulus
of growing domestic commercial demand even though
agricultural exports have sometimes been a very
significant supplement to the growth of the farm
cash incomes.

2. This section draws heavily on a joint book with
William C. Clark, Redesigning Rural Development: A
Strategic Perspective. This book is the final
product of collaboration which we initiated in 1979
when we were both visiting research scientists at
the International Institute for Applied Systems
Analysis (ILASA). The ideas presented in this
section are essentially a very condensed paraphrase
of Clark's chapter on "Policy Analysis and the
Development Debate" in our joint book.

3. This view of organization as a means of
calculation and control derives from Dahl and
Lindblom (1953).

4. Wildavsky (1979) uses this phrase from Milton as
the title of his excellent book, Speaking Truth to
Power: The Art and Craft of Policy Analysis.

5. The 38 low-income countries with 1978 per capita
GNP ranging from $90 to $360 had a total population
of 1.3 billion in mid-1978 (World Bank, 1980, p. 110).

6. The influence of these three factors is
conveniently summarized in the well-known identity
which shows how the rate of increase (or decrease) in
the agricultural labor force (L_a') is determined by the
rate of growth of the total labor force (L_t'), the
rate of growth of nonfarm employment (L_n'), and the
initial share of agriculture in the total labor force
(L_a/L_t):

$$L_a' \equiv (L_t' - L_n') \frac{1}{L_a / L_t} + L_n'$$

7. The same undoubtedly applies to much of Latin America. I have only examined the evidence for Mexico. In spite of the fact that Mexico is a middle-income developing country and has witnessed a reduction from 55 to 39 percent in the share of its total labor force engaged in agriculture between 1960 and 1978, the rural population has grown substantially and there is persuasive evidence that rural poverty has increased (Johnston, 1980a).

8. Another difficulty is the common tendency for donor agencies to require increasingly complex procedures for the evaluation of projects which place excessive and inappropriate demands on the limited planning and analytical resources available in developing countries (Johnston, 1977, pp. 885, 890-91; Chambers, 1977).

9. In Mexico large farms typically obtain higher yields than small farms, but this appears to be mainly a consequence of the concentration of irrigation in the northern regions where large farms predominate (Johnston, 1980a).

10. In attempting to explain fertility changes in the U.S., Easterlin (1973) has also presented a demand analysis of fertility which is quite different from the "analytical framework" which he elaborated for examining determinants of fertility change in less developed countries.

11. The paragraphs that follow are merely some brief comments on Clark's extended treatment of the issues of organizational structure and managerial procedures in our joint book (Johnston and Clark, forthcoming, Chapter 5). We have benefited greatly from recent work by D. Korten (1979, 1980), Chambers (1974), Leonard (1977), Hunter (1978a, 1979b), Lele (1975), and Uphoff and Esman (1974).

REFERENCES

Anthony, K.R.M., Johnston, B.F., Jones, W.O. and
    Uchendu, V.C. *Agricultural Change in Tropical Africa.*
    Ithaca, New York: Cornell University Press 1979.

Arthur, W.B. and McNicoll, G. "Large-Scale Simulation
    Models in Population and Development: What Use to
    Planners?" *Population and Development Review,* Vol. 1,
    No. 2, 1975.

Asian Development Bank. *Rural Asia: Challenge and Opportun-
    ity.* New York: Praeger, 1978.

Bagadion, B.U. and Korten, F.F. "Developing Viable
    Irrigators' Associations: Lessons from Small
    Scale Irrigation Development in the Phillipines",
    Agricultural Administration, Vol. Vll, No. 4, 1980.

Benor, D. and Harrison, J.Q. *Agricultural Extension: The
    Training and Visit System.* Washington, D.C.: World
    Bank, May 1977.

Berry, R.A. and Cline, W.R. *Agrarian Structure and
    Productivity in Developing Countries.* Baltimore: John
    Hopkins University Press, 1979.

Binswanger, H.P. *The Economics of Tractors in South Asia: An
    Analytical Review.* New York: Agricultural Develop-
    ment Council and Hyyerabad, India: International
    Crops Research Institute for the Semi-Arid Tropics,
    1978.

Chambers, R. *Managing Rural Development: Ideas and Experience
    from East Africa.* Uppsala: Scandinavian Institute
    of African Studies, 1974.

_____. "Simple is Practical: Approaches and
    Realities for Project Selection for Poverty-
    Focused Rural Development." Paper Prepared for a
    Seminar on the Implications of the Employment and
    Income Distribution Objectives for Project
    Appraisal and Identification. Kuwait, 5-6 April
    1977.

Clark, W.C., Jones, D.D. and Holling, C.S. "Lessons

for Ecological Policy Design: A Case Study of Ecosystem Management," *Ecological Modeling*, Vol. Vll, 1979.

Dahl, R.A. and Lindblom, C.E. *Politics, Economics and Welfare.* New York: Harper & Brothers, 1953.

Dovring, F. "The Share of Agriculture in a Growing Population," *FAO Monthly Bulletin of Agricultural Economics and Statistics*, Vol. Vlll, Nos. 8/9, 1959.

Duff, R. "Providing Assistance in the Mechanization of Small Farms." Paper prepared for presentation at the Seminar on the Mechanization of Small-Scale Peasant Farming. Sapporo, Japan, July 7-12, 1980.

Easterlin, R.A. "Relative Economic Status and the American Fertility Swing," in *Family Economic Behavior: Problems and Prospects*, ed., E.B. Sheldon. Philadelphia: J.B. Lippincott Co., 1973.

_____. "An Economic Framework for Fertility Analysis," *Studies in Family Planning*, Vol. Vl, No. 3, 1975.

_____. "The Economics and Sociology of Fertility: A Synthesis," in *Early Industrialization, Shifts in Fertility and Changes in Family Structure*, ed., C. Tilly. Princeton, New Jersey: Princeton University Press, 1977.

Fei, J.C.H. and Ranis, G. *Development of the Labor Surplus Economy: Theory and Policy.* Homewood, Illinois: Irwin, 1964.

Food and Agriculture Organization of the United Nations (FAO). "Special Feature: FAO Indices of Food and Agricultural Production," *Monthly Bulletin of Statistics*, Vol. 11, 1979.

Food and Agriculture Organization for the United Nations/World Health Organization (FAO/WHO). *Food and Nutrition Strategies in National Development.* Report of the 9th Session Joint FAO/WHO Expert Committee on Nutrition. FAO Nutrition Meetings Report Series No. 52 and WHO Technical Report Series No. 522. Rome: FAO; Geneva: WHO, 1976.

Gerhart, J. *The Diffusion of Hybrid Maize in Western Kenya--Abridged by CIMMYT.* Mexico City: Centro Internacional de Mejoramiento de Maize y Trigo, 1975.

Ghodake, R.D., Ryan, J.G. and Sarin, R. *Human Labor Use in Existing and Prospective Technologies of the Semi-Arid Tropics of Peninsular India.* Progress Report, Economics Program-1, Village Level Studies Series 1.3. Hyderabad, India: International Crops Research Institute for the Semi-Arid Tropics, December 1978.

Gwatkin, D.R., Wilcox, J.R. and Wray, J.D. "Can Interventions Make a Difference? The Policy Implications of Field Experiment Experience." A Report to the World Bank. Washington, D.C.: Overseas Development Council, March 1979.

Hayami, Y. and Ruttan, V.W. *Agricultural Development: An International Perspective.* Baltimore and London: Johns Hopkins Press, 1971.

Hsieh, S.C. and Lee, T.H. *Agricultural Development and its Contributions to Economic Growth in Taiwan.* Economic Digest Series No. 17. Taipei: Joint Commission on Rural Reconstruction, 1966.

Hunter, G. "Report on Administration and Institutions," Asian Development Bank, *Rural Asia: Challenge and Opportunity,* Supplementary Papers, Vol. 1V, *Administration and Institutions in Agricultural and Rural Development.* Manial: Asian Development Bank, 1978a.

_____. ed. *Agricultural Development and the Rural Poor: Guidelines for Action.* London: Overseas Development Institute, 1978b.

India, Government of, Planning Commission. *Draft Five-Year Plan 1978-83.* New Delhi: 1978.

Inter Agency Working Group. "Proposals for a Programme of Action for the Development of Food and Agriculture in Africa 1980-85." Prepared for consideration by the OAU Extraordinary Economic Summit. Rome: FAO, February 1980; the Inter Agency Group included representatives of FAO, the World Food Council and the Economic Commission for Africa.

Johnston, B.F.   "Food, Health and Population in
     Development," *Journal of Economic Literature*, Vol. 15,
     No. 3, 1977.

_____.   "Agricultural Production Potential and
     Small Farmer Strategies in Sub-Saharan Africa,"
     in *Two Studies of Development in Sub-Saharan Africa*.
     Staff Working Paper No. 300. Washington, D.C.:
     World Bank, October 1978.

_____.   "The Design and Redesign of Strategies
     for Agricultural Development: Mexico's Experience
     Revisited." Paper presented at the Seminar on
     Economic and Social Relations Between the United
     States and Mexico. Stanford University, November
     12-15, 1980a.

_____.   "The Socio-Economic Aspects of Improved
     Animal-Drawn Implements and Mechanization in
     Semi-Arid East Africa," in *Proceedings of the Inter-
     national Workshop on Socio-economic Constraints to
     Development of Semi-Arid Tropical Agriculture, 19-23
     February 1979, Hyderabad, India.* Patancheru, A.P.,
     India: ICRISAT, 1980b.

_____.   "Farm Equipment Innovations and Rural
     Industrialization in Eastern Africa: An Over-
     view." Working Paper prepared for the World
     Employment Programme Research, Technology and
     Employment Programme. Geneva: International
     Labour Organisation, February 1981.

Johnston, B.F. and Clark, W.C. *Redesigning Rural
     Development: A Strategic Perspective.* Baltimore:
     Johns Hopkins University Press, forthcoming.

Johnston, B.F. and Kilby, P. *Agriculture and Structural
     Transformation: Economic Strategies in Late-Developing
     Countries.* New York: Oxford University Press,
     1975.

Johnston, B.F. and Mellor, J.W. "The Role of Agricul-
     ture in Economic Development," *American Economic
     Review*, Vol Ll, No. 4, 1961.

Jorgenson, D.W. "The Role of Agriculture in Economic
     Development: Classical versus Neoclassical Models

of Growth," in *Subsistence Agriculture and Economic Development*, ed., C.R. Wharton, Jr. Chicago: Aldine Publishing Company, 1969.

Karanjia, R.K. *The Mind of Mr. Nehru*. London: George Allen and Unwin, 1960.

Keeley, M.C. "A Comment on 'An Interpretation of the Economic Theory of Fertility'," *Journal of Economic Literature*, Vol. Xlll, No. 2, 1975.

Kenya, Republic of. *Development Plan for the Period 1979 to 1983*. Nairobi: 1979.

King, M., ed. *Medical Care in Developing Countries*. Nairobi: Oxford University Press, 1966.

Korten, D.C. "Toward a Technology for Managing Social Development," in *Population and Social Development Management: A Challenge for Management Schools*, ed., D.C. Korten. Caracas, Venezuela: Instituto de Estudios Superiores de Administracion-IESA, 1979.

_____. "Community Organization and Rural Development: A Learning Process Approach," *The Public Administration Review*, Vol. XL, No. 5, 1980.

Lele, U. *The Design of Rural Development: Lessons from Africa*. Baltimore and London: Johns Hopkins University Press, 1975.

Leonard, D.K. *Reaching the Peasant Farmer: Organization Theory and Practice in Kenya*. Chicago and London: University of Chicago Press, 1977.

Lewis, W.A. "Economic Development and Unlimited Supplies of Labour," *Manchester School*, Vol. XXll, No. 2, 1954.

_____. *The Theory of Economic Growth*. Homewood, Illinois: Richard D. Irwin, Inc., 1955.

_____. "Unlimited Labour: Further Notes," *Manchester School*, Vol. XXVl, No. 1, 1958.

_____. *Development Planning: The Essentials of Economic Policy*. New York: Harper & Row, 1966.

Lindblom, C.E. *Politics and Markets*. New York: Basic Books, 1977.

Lindblom, C.E. and Cohen, D.K. *Usable Knowledge: Social Science and Social Problem Solving*. New Haven: Yale University Press, 1979.

Lipton, M. *Why Poor People Stay Poor: A Study of Urban Bias in World Development*. London: Temple Smith, 1977.

Mauldin, W.P. and Berelson, B. "Reply" to R.B. Dixon, *Studies in Family Planning*, Vol. lX, Nos. 10/11, 1978.

Mellor, J.W. *The New Economics of Growth: A Strategy for India and the Developing World*. Twentieth Century Fund Study. Ithaca: Cornell University Press, 1976.

Michael, D.N. *On Learning to Plan--and Planning to Learn*. San Francisco: Jossey-Bass Publishers, 1973.

Monnier, J. "Farm Mechanization in Senegal and Its Effects on Production and Employment," in *Report on the Meeting of the FAO/OECD Expert Panel on the Effects of Farm Mechanization on Production and Employment*. Rome: FAO, 1975.

Morgan, M.G. "Bad Science and Good Policy Analysis," *Science*, Vol. CCl, No. 4360, September 15, 1978.

Muchiri, G. "Farm Equipment Innovation for Small Holders in Semi-Arid Kenya: A Conceptual and Empirical Analysis." Working Paper prepared for the World Employment Programme Research, Technology and Employment Programme. Geneva: International Labour Organisation, October 1980.

Perlman, M. "Some Economic Growth Problems and the Part Population Policy Plays," *Quarterly Journal of Economics*, Vol. LXXXlX, No. 2, 1975.

Phillipines, Republic of. *Five-Year Philippine Development Plan, 1978-1982*. Manila: September 1977.

Pyatt, G. and Thorbecke, E. *Planning Techniques for a Better Future*. Geneva: International Labour Office, 1976.

Pyle, D.F. *Voluntary Agency-Managed Projects Delivering an Integrated Package of Health, Nutrition, and Population Serivces: The Maharashtra Experience.* New Delhi: prepared for the Ford Foundation, March 1979.

_____. "From Project to Program: The Study of the Scaling-Up/Implementation Process of a Community-Level, Integrated Health, Nutrition, Population Intervention in Maharashtra (India)." Ph.D. dissertation, Massachusetts Institute of Technology, February 1981.

Ruttan, V.W. "Institutional Factors Affecting the Generation and Diffusion of Agricultural Technology: Issues, Concepts and Analysis." World Employment Programme Research, Technology and Employment Programme, WEP 2-22/WP 67. Geneva: International Labour Office, October 1980.

Ryan, J.G., Sarin, R. and M. Pereira. "Assessment of Prospective Soil-, Water-, and Crop-Management Technologies for the Semi-Arid Tropics of Peninsular India," in *Proceedings of the International Workshop on Socio-economic Constraints to Development of Semi-Arid Tropical Agriculture, 19-23 February 1979, Hyderabad, India.* Patancheru, A.P., India: ICRISAT, 1980.

Sanderson, W.C. *Economic-Demographic Simulation Models: A Review of Their Usefulness for Policy Analysis.* Memorandum No. 218. Stanford: Stanford University Department of Economics, 1978; also available as Technical Paper 4, ES:DP/INT/73/P02, Rome: FAO, 1978.

_____. *Economic-Demographic Simulation Models: A Review of Their Usefulness for Policy Analysis.* RM-80-14. Laxenburg, Austria: International Institute for Applied Systems Analysis, 1980.

Schultz, T.P. "An Economic Perspective on Population Growth," in National Academy of Sciences, *Rapid Population Growth: Consequences and Policy Implications.* Baltimore: Johns Hopkins Press, 1971.

_____. "Determinants of Fertility: A Micro-Economic Model of Choice," in *Economic Factors in*

Population Growth: Proceedings of a Conference held by the International Economic Association at Valescure, France, ed., A.J. Coale. New York: Wiley, 1976.

Sen, A.K. "Peasants and Dualism With or Without Surplus Labor," *Journal of Political Economy,* Vol. LXXlV, No. 5, 1966.

Shah, M.M. and Willekens, F. *Rural-Urban Population Projections for Kenya and Implications for Development.* Laxenburg, Austria: International Institute for Applied Systems Analysis, 1978.

Simon, H.A. "Designing Organizations for an Information-Rich World," in *Computers, Communications, and the Public Interest,* ed., M. Greenberger. Baltimore: Johns Hopkins Press, 1971.

Tinbergen, J. *Economic Policy: Principles and Design.* Amsterdam: North-Holland Publishing Company, 1956.

_____. *The Design of Development.* Baltimore: Johns Hopkins Press, 1958.

_____. *Development Planning.* New York and Toronto: McGraw-Hill Book Company, 1967.

Uphoff, N.T. and Esman, M.J. *Local Organization for Rural Development: Analysis of Asian Experience.* Special Series on Rural Local Government RLG No. 19. Ithaca: Rural Development Committee, Center for International Studies, Cornell University, 1974.

Vyas, V.S. "Some Aspects of Structural Change in Indian Agriculture," *Indian Journal of Agricultural Economics,* Vol. XXXlV, No. 1, 1979.

Walker, T.S. "Decision Making by Farmers and by the National Agricultural Research Program on the Adoption and Development of Maize Varieties in El Salvador." Ph.D. dissertation, Stanford University, 1980.

Westley, S. and Johnston, B.F. eds. "Proceedings of a Workshop on Farm Equipment Innovations for Agricultural Development and Rural Industrialization." Occasional Paper No. 16. Nairobi:

University of Nairobi, Institute for Development Studies, 1975.

Wildavsky, A. *Speaking Truth to Power: The Art and Craft of Policy Analysis*. Boston and Toronto: Little Brown and Company, 1979.

World Bank. *The Assault on World Poverty: Problems of Rural Development, Education and Health*. Baltimore and London: Johns Hopkins Press, 1975.

_____. *World Development Report, 1978*. Washington, D.C.: World Bank, 1978.

_____. *World Development Report, 1980*. New York: Oxford University Press, 1980.

BASIC NEEDS AND THE NEW
INTERNATIONAL ECONOMIC ORDER

by
Paul Streeten

INTRODUCTION

Sir Arthur Lewis has written illuminatingly about the importance of meeting the basic needs of poor people, and about the evolution of the international economic order.1 It is therefore not inappropriate for me to choose the relationship between these two concepts as the theme for my contribution to this volume in his honor.

In a paper contributed to a meeting of the International Economic Association at Bled, Yugoslavia, in 1970, entitled "Objectives and Prognostications" Sir Arthur Lewis starts by saying the central objective of development policy is to "raise the level of living of the masses of the people in L.D.C.s as rapidly as is feasible..."2

Sir Arthur Lewis saw two constraints on what was feasible: (1) a constraint on growth, identified with constraints on the savings ratio (or the growth of that ratio), and (2) technical constraints--assuming that the savings ratio was adequate. Under the first heading, Sir Arthur said that there were three problems. First, there was the choice between present and future consumption; second, the choice between independence and neo-colonialism; and third, between growth and equality. Under the first choice, between present and future consumption, Sir Arthur dealt with three factors counselling restraint in accelerating growth: (1) one might try to relieve current poverty, even at the cost of reduced saving for the future; (2) one might want to avoid the political dislocation of rapid growth by spreading its benefits more widely, even at the expense of reducing the rate of growth.

The third factor is of most interest to those concerned with a basic needs strategy. "It emphasizes that a high rate of growth of <u>commodities</u> is not all that important in the public's sense of

well being. If asked what they most need from the
economic system, those at the bottom of the ladder
seem almost everywhere to concentrate on a few simple
needs: (a) continuous employment, (b) a somewhat
higher income, (c) more or better schooling for the
children, (d) better medical services, (e) pure water
at hand, and (f) cheap transport. This list does
involve greater output of some commodities, whether
for direct use by their producers, or indirectly to
supply the men who produce the services; but an economic plan which gave more emphasis to the wants listed
here would devote relatively less resources to
commodity production. It would have less saving, more
taxes and a relatively lower rate of growth, as
national income statisticians measure growth."[3]

This brief paragraph is a good statement of
the objectives of a basic needs approach to development, which was given some publicity by the 1976 World
Employment Conference, and has been much discussed
since. One feature that distinguishes the basic needs
approach from an income approach, which aims at raising the earning opportunities of the poor, is greater
emphasis on social services, like education and health,
whose contribution to human welfare can exceed their
valuation at factor cost. Housing is not included,
because Sir Arthur regards it as an acquired taste,
but employment is included (in contrast to Sidney Webb
who considers leisure as a basic need).

One important merit of this approach is that
it specifies particular goods and services needed and
wanted by particular groups of people, and therefore
looks behind abstractions like income. One may differ
on the items included in a list of basic needs, which
will also differ between societies and time periods.
For some societies energy (in the form of fire wood or
kerosene) will have to be added. Some would want to
emphasize the importance of non-material needs like
participation and autonomy. But whatever these
differences in the items on the menu, the concrete
specification of needs and of methods to satisfy them
is a step forward from earlier, more abstract, more
aggregative approaches.

Basic Needs has entered the North-South
dialogue and misconceptions have grown around the
concept. The relations between basic needs (BN) and

the New International Economic Order (NIEO) can be discussed at several levels. At the level of <u>logic</u> one would ask about the relationship between the two concepts and would find that the NIEO is concerned with international, BN with domestic issues; that, in spite of apparent inconsistencies, the concepts are complementary, because if the NIEO leads to more resources for the developing countries, this can contribute to BN satisfaction, and BN objectives can be seen to be those for which support for international cooperation can be mobilized.

At the level of <u>economics</u> it would have to be shown how the various NIEO measures contribute to meeting basic needs: which countries and which groups within countries would benefit from which provisions, on what conditions. One would want to know how government revenue from taxation or aid receipts are spent, who benefits from trade liberalization, from commodity schemes, from debt relief, etc. And one would investigate how domestic efforts to eradicate poverty can be internationally supported.

At the level of <u>international politics</u> one would wish to analyze the motives, fears and apprehensions of the negotiating partners and devise ways of clarifying issues and designing institutions and procedures that would eliminate these fears. Finally, at the level of <u>domestic group interests</u>, one would wish to examine the resistance from vested interest to the implementation of basic needs approaches and the NIEO, and the extent to which the objections of the international negotiators are, on the part of the South, obstacles and inhibitions by particular groups to doing more for the poor, and, on the part of the North, masked attempts by vested interest to protect themselves.

THE LOGIC

On superficial inspection there appears to be a conflict between the two concepts. The NIEO aims at revising the rules of international economic relations between nations and is of particular concern to <u>governments</u>, whereas BN is concerned with the needs of <u>individuals</u> and households. The NIEO deals with issues such as commodity price stabilization and support, indexation, the Common Fund, the Integrated Commodity Program, debt relief, the SDR link, trade liberalization, trade preferences, technology transfer, transnational firms, etc., whereas BN deals with food, water, health, education and shelter. The NIEO aims at unconditional, automatic or semi-automatic, concealed transfers of resources (or at correcting past reverse transfers), whereas basic needs implies a highly selective approach, aiming directly at the alleviation of deprivation of particular groups. The NIEO would eliminate conditions imposed on resource transfers, a BN approach would wish to make transfers conditional upon their reaching the poor. The schemes proposed in the NIEO are likely to benefit the middle-income countries, and some very small (already relatively over-aided) countries, in whose economy foreign trade plays an important part, rather than the large, poor countries of Asia; and, within these countries, the proposed schemes may benefit the middle and higher income groups, such as exporting industrialists (possibly multinational corporations), large farmers, plantation owners, and banks, rather than the urban and rural poor. But the logical conflict between BN and the NIEO can be avoided. The differences between the two approaches point to the need to advance on both fronts simultaneously. The NIEO is concerned with formulating a framework of institutions, processes and rules that would correct what developing countries regard as the present bias of the system against them. This bias is thought to be evident in the structure of certain markets, where a few large and powerful buyers confront many weak, competing sellers; in the tariff structures and the nature of vertically integrated firms that discriminate against processing in developing countries; in discrimination in access to capital markets, and to knowledge, in the present patent law and patent conventions, in the thrust of Research and Development and the nature of modern technology, in the power of the transnational corporations, in shipping, in international monetary arrangements, etc. A correction in the direction of a more balanced distribution of power would enable developing countries to become less dependent and more self-reliant. But the NIEO by itself would be no guarantee that the governments of the developing countries would use their new power to meet the needs of their poor.

The BN approach, by focusing on the goods and services needed by deprived people, households and communities, highlights the importance of the needs of individual human beings.

A BN program that does not build on the self-reliance and self-help of governments and countries is in danger of degenerating into a global charity program and can be counterproductive by pauperising the poor. A NIEO that is not committed to meeting basic needs is liable to transfer resources from the poor in rich countries to the rich in poor countries.

It is easy to envisage a situation in which the benefits of international BN assistance are more than wiped out by the damage done by protectionist trade and foreign investment, by transfer pricing practices of multinationals, by the unemployment generated by inappropriate technology, or by restrictive monetary policies. The global commitment to BN makes sense only in an international order in which the impact of all international policies other than aid--trade, foreign investment, technology transfer, movement of professionals, money--is not detrimental to a self-reliant strategy of meeting basic needs. Insofar as the NIEO makes more resources available to the developing countries, BN can be met sooner.

The situation is similar in some respects to the rise of trade unions in nineteenth century England. Concern with the fate of the poor remained relatively ineffective until the poor were permitted by law to organize themselves, bargain collectively, strike, and have their funds protected. On the other hand, there has always been the danger that trade unions would turn into another powerful estate, less concerned with the fate of the poor than with protecting the privileges of a labor aristocracy; and that the strong unions reap gains at the expense of the weaker ones and the unorganized workers.

The NIEO is a call for a revision of the rules and institutions, regulating the relations between sovereign nations, and BN is one important objective which this framework should serve. There are those who maintain that integration into any

international economic order in which advanced
capitalist economies dominate is inconsistent with
meeting the basic needs of the poor. Pointing to the
People's Republic of China, until recently, they
advocate "delinking," in order to insulate their
society, or a group of like-minded societies, from
the detrimental impulses propagated by the international system. Policies derived from such a view of
the world order do not, of course, depend on wringing
concessions from rich countries, but can be pursued
by unilateral action.

Those, on the other hand, who think that the
international system has benefits to offer if the
rules are reformulated and the power relations recast,
will not opt for complete delinking, but for restructuring. Such restructuring has implications for
domestic policies in both developed and developing
countries and for international policies. If the
industrialized countries really want to help the
developing countries to pursue a basic needs approach,
they must assist their own workers in the labor-intensive industries to shift to better, more remunerative types of employment and make room for better
access of labor-intensive imports which generate
employment and incomes for the poor in the low-income
countries. The receipts from these exports will be
used to import capital-intensive products like
fertilizer, steel and synthetic fibres from the
industrialized countries, enabling their workers to
raise their earnings also.

THE ECONOMICS

In principle, NIEO and BN are complementary
concepts. But much would depend, of course, on which
measures of the NIEO are adopted and on how they are
implemented. There is remarkably little research on
the domestic impact on poverty groups of the various
NIEO proposals. Some work has been done on the
country distribution of commodity schemes and trade
liberalization, but hardly any on its impact on
domestic income distribution and poverty alleviation.
A commodity program that imposes restrictions on
production in order to raise prices would benefit the
large plantation owners, if small farmers have to

restrict their output, and small farmers if the large producers had to restrict. Debt relief may benefit banks in industrial countries, the S.D.R. link treasuries. The distribution of the benefits from trade liberalization would depend on who exports the additional products, at what remuneration, how they are produced, etc. Even if the rich benefit in the first round, taxation would make redistribution possible. But equally, if the poor benefit in the first round, redistribution upward may take place later. The largest benefits of the NIEO would arise from .the 0.7 per cent aid target, and the link between this achievement and basic needs would depend on how governments spend aid funds.

If the emphasis is on concessional finance going to the poorest countries with governments determined to tackle poverty, the impact on basic needs would be strong. If, on the other hand, the emphasis is on market access and better terms for technology transfer, both the country and the domestic impact would be in favor of middle incomes. Many measures would increase government revenues, whether directly like official development assistance, or indirectly through taxation of extra profits and incomes. If these governments adopt the appropriate policies the impact of these measures will be favorable to basic needs. The economics of the relationship between the NIEO and BN is at the heart of the matter and remarkably little thought has been given to ways in which possible conflicts can be avoided.

Many NIEO proposals are intended to speed up industrialization. Industrialization is entirely compatible with meeting basic needs, but it does not inevitably do so.[4] Much depends on the type of industrialization, whether it is capital-intensive or labor-intensive, and on the types of product produced for the domestic market.

The ideal combination would be for a national government to commit itself to a policy of meeting the basic needs of its people, such as a campaign to eliminate hunger and malnutrition, and for the international communtiy to underwrite such a program in the form of additional commitments of financial and technical assistance.

"Basic Needs" (like "appropriate technology") has acquired a bad name in the North-South dialogue. At international meetings delegates from the developing countries have rejected vehemently the BN concept. There has been concern over the potential hypocrisy of such a strategy and suspicion about the intentions of aid-giving governments and international agencies. This concern and suspicion are justified because some donors have misinterpreted and abused the concept. Misconceptions have taken the following forms.

(1) A BN approach has been interpreted as a substitute for growth, modernization, industrialization, and self-reliance. Industrialization has brought wealth and power to the North, and it is felt that the rich now wish to prevent the developing countries from following the same path, sometimes behind the cloak of ecological concerns.

(2) The slogan of BN has been used to justify reduced foreign aid for lack of projects and of "absorptive capacity" in the poorest countries.

(3) Middle income countries have feared that BN will be used to reduce aid to them under the pretext of concentration on the poorest countries.

(4) A BN approach can be used to slow down or prevent the rapid growth of manufactured exports from the developing countries and to serve as a thinly disguised protectionist device of the established, inefficient manufacturing lobbies in advanced countries.

(5) The introduction of BN criteria lends itself to the violation of

national sovereignty and of the autonomous setting of development priorities.

(6) In addition, the slogan can also be used as a cloak behind which to introduce irrelevant or controversial political, social or economic performance criteria.

(7) Above all, it was felt that BN has been used to divert attention from the New International Economic Order.

At the heart of this debate lies the controversy over whether poverty in the midst of global plenty is the result of intended or unintended exploitation or neglect on the part of the rich countries and of the rules of the international system, or whether it is the result of the power structure, the attitudes, institutions and policies of the developing countries.

Two points are worth noting. First, governments of developing countries have other objectives, as well as meeting basic needs. These include military objectives, independence, Northern style industrialization, meeting non-basic needs of the upper classes, in some cases democratic government, etc. Secondly, in spite of the hostility to BN in international discussions, BN and similar objectives figure prominently in national planning and policy-making.[5]

For instance, the new (1979-83) development plan for Kenya states that the "...alleviation of poverty is not only an objective in our development efforts, it is also a major instrument for ensuring that our development is rapid, stable and sustainable. ... Improvements of the well-being of the people remain our dominant aim."[6] Similarly, the Five-Year Philippine Development Plan (1978-82) indicates that "...the conquest of mass poverty becomes the immediate, fundamental goal of Philippine development." Development over the next decade "...will be a massive effort to provide for the basic needs of the majority of the population..."[7]

India's new draft plan for 1978-83[8] suggests "what matters is not the precise rate of increase in the national product that is achieved in five or ten years, but whether we can ensure within a specified time-frame a measurable increase in the welfare of the millions of poor." The three principal objectives of this plan are listed as the removal of unemployment and underemployment, the rise in the standard of living of the poor, and the provision by the State of certain "basic needs," namely drinking water, literacy, elementary education, health care, rural roads, rural housing and minimum services in urban slums. The Plan puts forward a revised "Minimum Needs Program" which substantially increases allocations for water supply, basic education, rural roads and other identified basic needs. At the same time, at a meeting of the UN's Committee of the Whole, the Indian delegate indicated that his government was "...strongly against any attempt to direct the attention of the international community to alternative approaches to development cooperation, such as the basic needs approach."[9]

The new Sixth Plan of Nepal (1980-85) lists as its first two objectives the "gradual elimination of absolute poverty through employment opportunities" and the "fulfillment of minimum basic needs." Meeting basic needs is seen as a way to "enhance the efficiency and productivity" of low income groups in backward areas. These minimum needs are listed as being "...potable water, minimum health care, primary and skill-oriented education, family planning and maternity child-health care services, irrigation facilities" as well as basic transport and agricultural extension services.[10] How these principles will be carried into the final plan document and its resource allocations, however, is not yet clear.

Korea is known as a country which already has made substantial progress on basic needs. Yet Korea's Fourth Plan (1977-82) significantly increased allocations for social development while maintaining a heavy emphasis on industrial development and export-led growth. In Indonesia, the Third Plan (1979-84) states its "essential goals" are "...to raise the living standards and levels of knowledge of the Indonesian people, to strive for a more equitable and just distribution of welfare..." Equitable distribution is an objective in "...access to means of fulfilling basic human needs, especially food, clothing and shelter..." as well as in access to health and education facilities, jobs, incomes and in regional development.[11]

Since 1975, Ethiopia has made significant progress in providing the poor with basic health services, primary education, etc. While the government does not use the term "basic needs" as such, its annual plan reveals its long-term objectives to be the "raising the standard of living of the broad masses of the people, abolishing poverty, ignorance, disease and unemployment..."[12] Standards of living will be increased "through an adequate provision of the daily necessities such as food, grain, clothing, etc."[13]

Not all countries have made an explicit shift to BN. In Tunisia, the new five year plan (Fifth Plan of Economic and Social Development) increases the emphasis on employment and income distribution, but does not give priority to a basic needs strategy. The current (1976-80) plan for Malaysia emphasizes poverty alleviation by increasing productivity, reducing population pressure, and increasing employment, as well as by the provision of essential services such as water supply, education, electricity. But the Malaysian Plan was drafted largely before "basic needs" had become a banner. Many countries have already made a heavy commitment to social development, and therefore have not felt the need to shift priorities. Such countries include Sri Lanka, Burma, Tanzania, Madagascar, and Algeria, among others. Many countries are still in the process of formulating new development plans. There are indications that many of their new plans, such as those being developed for Mexico, Niger, and Afghanistan, are likely to place more emphasis on basic needs and income distribution and employment issues. In Egypt, past development efforts have given high priority to social development, but this has been centered principally on urban areas. The new development plan for Egypt shifts the allocation of resources to the rural areas, and increases the amount of rural participation in planning decisions. In some countries (Sudan, Morocco, Peru), plans to expand social sector expenditures and poverty-oriented programs have been delayed because of resource constraints. In still other countries (Ivory Coast, Colombia), no shift in development priorities appears probable. On the whole, however, a large number of countries have given, or are about to give, their development strategies a greater poverty and BN orientation.

Rhetoric embodied in development plans does not, necessarily, mean a serious commitment. In many cases, however, the new plans reviewed here show increased allocations for the social sectors in support of a basic needs strategy. This is true specifically of Korea, Indonesia, Kenya, Malaysia, and the Philippines. In the Philippines, social sector expenditures will increase from 23.5% of total expenditures in 1977 to 28.1% in 1982, while in Kenya, the development budget plan increases their share from 21.7% (FY74-78) to 27.4% (FY79-83). In India, the allocations for the social sectors actually decline as a share of the total development expenditures while the commitment to basic needs is increased. Commitment to basic needs cannot be measured by total resource allocations to the social sectors generally, since much can be accomplished by a reallocation within the sectors. This also suggests that for those countries already allocating significant resources to the social sectors, reallocation can be used to meet basic needs without reducing investment in non-BN activities or decreasing non-BN consumption. A change in Plan allocations does not, of course, necessarily mean that resources will eventually find their way into these sectors. Historically, the social sectors have generally been considered "soft" and prime candidates for reductions in allocations in times of financial austerity. On the other hand, there is growing recognition that there are political risks involved in continuing to ignore the basic needs of the majority of a country's population, while continuing to provide services for the urban elites.

It is therefore evident that the developing countries' opposition to BN, at least in their declarations, is not so stark as it is often made out to be. Planning and Treasury officials speak with a different voice and from a different tradition and training from Foreign Office officials, and the objections may be more to the places than to the substance of the discussions. On the other hand, it is fairly clear that the domestic rhetoric is not always matched by a willingness to implement the declarations.

Let us return to the seven suspicions and look briefly at each of them.

(1) Meeting basic human needs is not at the expense of growth; on the contrary, growth is an indispensable prerequisite, (or, rather, result), though it is growth that is differently composed and distributed from the dualistic and concentrated growth that has failed to benefit the poor. Nor does it follow that a basic needs approach must confine itself to low or "intermediate" technology. Some highly modern technology may be required, such as satellites for aerial photograph and remote sensing. Private and public investment, and administrative resources, have to be redirected from high-income to low-income sectors so as to raise the productivity and incomes of the latter in the service of both efficiency and equity; the work of the poor has to be made more remunerative, public services have to be radically redesigned so as to cover more people more cheaply, and the private incomes of the poor have to be adequate to give them access to the free public services. All this cannot be done without modernization, industrialization and economic growth.

(2) A global commitment to BN requires more, not fewer, international resources. And international cooperation for basic needs performance is practical only if the international community provides additional resources.

Provisional estimates indicate that a basic needs program aiming at providing minimum acceptable diets, safe water, sewerage facilities, public health measures, basic education and upgrading existing shelter would call for substantial investment and additional recurrent expenditures. Assuming the OECD countries concentrate their effort on the poorest countries and contribute about 50% of the additional costs of these programs, this would call for a very large increase in ODA flows over twenty years. A figure of $20 billion p.a. at 1976 prices for the period 1980-2000 has been calculated.

In 1978, total ODA flows amounted to over $22 billion a year. Of this, the poorest countries receive only about $10 billion. Only a part of this assistance is at present devoted to meeting BN. It might be asked why the whole of the assistance should not be switched to what is agreed to be a priority objective, so that additional requirements could be greatly reduced. If, moreover, some ODA now going to middle-income countries could be redirected to the poorest countries, requirements could be further reduced.

Such redirection would, however, be neither desirable nor possible. Middle-income countries have a higher absorptive capacity and tend to show higher returns on resource transfers. They, too, have serious problems of poverty. Moreover, a re-allocation of ODA flows is politically much easier if it is done out of incremental flows than if existing flows to some countries have to be cut. The legacy of past commitments and the expectations that they have generated cannot be discarded in a few years.

There are three reasons why substantial additional resources are needed in order to make a convincing international contribution to BN programs in the poorest countries. First, twenty years is a very short time for a serious anti-poverty program. It calls for extra efforts both on the part of developed and developing countries. The domestic effort, economic, administrative and political, required from the developing ocuntries is formidable. At the same time, while an additional $20 billion p.a. average over 20 years for ODA seems large, the acceleration (from the present 0.34 per cent of G.N.P.) is certainly within the power of the developed countries and if the task is to be taken seriously by both sides, an increase of this magnitude appears to be a reasonable basis for mutual reassurance.

The second reason for additionality is the fact that the transition from present policies to a basic-needs approach creates formidable problems of

transition. Investment projects that have been
started cannot suddenly be terminated. An attempt
to switch to basic needs programs while the structure
of demand and production has not yet been adapted
to them is bound to create inflationary and added
brain drain as social groups anticipating being
hurt attempt to safeguard their interests. There
might be strikes from disaffected workers in the
organized industrial sector. Unless a government
has some reserves to overcome these transitional
difficulties, the attempt to embark on a BN program
might be nipped in the bud.

The third reason for additionality is
tactical and political. It is well known that the
developing countries are suspicious of the BN
approach. One reason for their suspicion is that
they believe that pious words conceal a desire to
opt out of development assistance. And there is no
doubt that some people in the developed world see
BN as a cheap option. If the international priority
commitment to meeting basic needs within a short
period is to be taken seriously by the developing
countries, the contribution by the developed country
must be additional and substantial. The essence of
the international dialogue is tha both developed and
developing countries should reach a basic understanding to meet the human needs of the poor within a
reasonable period of time. Such a dialogue would be
a sham if it did not involve substantial additional
capital transfers and technical assistance.

(3) While the bulk of incremental development aid should be devoted to the poorest countries
committed to a basic needs approach, some extra aid
should be available for middle-income countries
with pockets of poverty, which commit themselves to
their eradication. It is an essential feature of
the BN approach that, because basic needs may be
unmet at quite high income levels, adequate income is
not enough to eliminate deprivation. In addition,
better access to capital markets, more liberal trade
opportunities and loans at commercial interest rates
are the appropriate forms in which the international
community can contribute to increasing the resources
and thereby the ability of meeting basic needs in the

less poor developing countries.

(4) As the examples of Taiwan, South Korea and Singapore show, labor-intensive exports can be a powerful instrument to create jobs and therefore to combine high growth rates with BN fulfillment. The emphasis on agriculture and the rural sector is not in conflict with export-led industrialization; on the contrary, it is a necessary condition for it.

(5) It is possible to combine full sovereignty and autonomy with a targeted approach to BN by evolving buffer institutions or buffer processes, acceptable to both recipient and donor countries, that ensure the achievement of both sovereignty and donors' BN priority, by channelling funds in the right direction and by monitoring BN performance. Multilateral institutions are particularly suited for this role. Developing countries themselves could monitor each other's implementation of BN programs, financed by industrial countries, as was done in the Marshall Plan for Europe.

(6) Similarly, the way to avoid the intrusion of irrelevant criteria into aid transactions is to channel aid through multilateral institutions, on which developing countries are fairly represented.

(7) The main apprehension about basic needs by the developing countries is that a basic needs approach adopted by donors implies sacrificing features of the New International Economic Order. (And skeptics among the developed countries regard both the NIEO and BN as emotionally highly charged words without clear policy implications).

We have seen that the NIEO is concerned with larger transfers of resources from the North to the South, and reforms in the international distribution of power. The call for it arises from the belief among developing countries that there are a variety of distortions in international markets, as a result of which their development efforts are stunted and their development prospects are limited. We have also discussed the misinterpretations and abuses that have caused apprehension in the developing countries. The remedy is to insist on the correct interpretations.

Assuming these obstacles have been cleared out of the way, how then is an international BN approach to be implemtnted in a manner consistent with the spirit of the NIEO? The governments of developing countries are anxious to preserve their full sovereignty and autonomy and do not wish to have their priorities laid down for them by donors. They dislike strings attached to aid and close scrutiny of its use. Donors, on the other hand, wish to make sure that their contributions reach the people for whom they are intended.[14] The solution is to be found in the strengthening of existing, and the evolution of new institutions and procedures that are acceptable to both donors and recipients, and that ensure that international aid reaches the vulnerable groups. Such buffer institutions and buffer processes would combine full national sovereignty with BN priority. They would be representative, independent and genuinely devoted to the goals of international cooperation.

It is clear that only multilateral or extranational institutions can meet these conditions. But reform may be required on several issues. The distribution of votes must be such that the developing countries feel that they are fairly represented. The selection, recruitment and training of members of the international secretariat must be of a kind which transcends narrowly national loyalties, but is sensitive to the social and cultural issues in developing countries. Both narrow technocracy and an excessive politicization of issues would have to be avoided. It may be though that this amounts to a prescription for perfection. But international institutions and their secretariats have in some instances approximated these ideal canons. Unless they do, there is little hope of implementing BN in the framework of the NIEO.[15]

VESTED INTERESTS

We have seen that conflict between the NIEO and BN can spring from either of four sources: There can be conflict at the definitional level, but we have argued that clarification of the concepts shows them to be complementary. Second, there can be conflict in the economic implications. Here, more research and thought on appropriate policies is needed. Third, there can be conflict at the level of international negotiations, because misinterpretations have been used for political purposes. But finally, conflict can be due to the fact that particular organized interest groups, either in the developed or in the developing countries, resist implementation because they would get hurt. Resistance to the NIEO can be due to industrialists in advanced countries wishing the developing countries to refrain from competing with their products and to remain pastoral societies that export primary products. Resistance to BN by the ruling classes of developing countries can spring from the absence of the desire to do anything for their poor. The beneficiaries from concentrated and uneven growth are unwilling to share the fruits of this growth with the poor in their own countries. For them, opposition to BN and insistence on the NIEO serve as a convenient smokescreen. This is particularly true of some of the middle income countries in which total resources would be adequate to meet basic needs but the extremely unequal income distribution and the interests of the rich stand in the way. Since the world is organized in sovereign nation states, foreign pressures or persuasion may not be very productive, but there is no reason why such regimes should qualify for any of the additional resources made available specifically for meeting the basic needs of the poor.

NEGATIVE RESPONSES TO BASIC NEEDS IN
RICH COUNTRIES

As we have discussed at some length the objections to basic needs raised by the developing countries, it may be useful to end this essay by briefly discussing some of the objections raised by rich donor countries. For the enthusiasm for a basic needs approach is by no means universal among the advanced countries.

The principal reasons for opposition to the

implementation of a basic needs approach to development among officials, politicians and academics in donor countries and agencies can be summarized under the following headings:

(1) The approach would sacrifice investment, output, productivity and growth, for the sake of current consumption and welfare transfers, which only rich countries can afford.

(2) Donors respond to developing countries requests and the response of these countries to BN is, at best, lukewarm; at worst, hostile.

(3) There is nothing new except the label; we have done it all the time under the banner of poverty-orientation, employment creation or rural development.

(4) An implementation of BN is constrained by political obstacles inside the developing countries, and there is nothing the international community can do about this.

(5) BN is used as the Trojan horse of Communism (Maoism, Socialism), and most of the countries with which we cooperate do not wish to adopt these ideologies and forms of government.

(6) BN is often interpreted to require state intervention in the market, and the numerous defects of bureaucratic interference are too well known to need rehearsing; consumers are

the best judges of their
needs, markets are quite
efficient instruments of
allocation, and the
paternalism implied by
BN is unacceptable.

(7) BN has paid inadequate
attention to the
problem of transition;
inflation, capital flight,
strikes and even coups
d'etats are liable to
prevent a government from
achieving BN.

(8) BN has no analytical
content and is largely
rhetoric or polemics; no
one can dispute the
desirability of the
objective, but implementation is either fuzzy, or,
where spelt out, inefficient,
unsuited to achieve the
declared objective, and
possibly counterproductive.

Brief replies would be along the following lines:

(1) This criticism is not valid. The
logical precedence of ends over means in no way
implies that means can be neglected; on the contrary.
Although there is a welfare component in BN, to
meet BN on a sustainable basis calls for considerable
investment and growth, although differently composed
and distributed (and measured) than much past growth.
Growth is also required to meet the rising standards
of BN, as income per head grows, and to achieve
objectives other than BN.

At the same time, BN is a way of doing more
and doing better with fewer resources: replicable
preventive medical services for all, instead of high-
cost curative services for a few; low-cost village
primary education instead of high-cost urban tertiary
education for the privileged.

Economy in the use of existing resources, and augmentation of these resources through productivity increase, fertility decline and mobilization of local underutilized resources are important resource-saving and resource-augmenting aspects of BN.

(2) Donors can select for assistance those countries that are themselves eager to embark on a BN approach. Even where there is resistance, some degree of solicitation of requests can shift development programs in the direction of greater emphasis on BN. Recipient governments are rarely monolithic, and aid and dialogue can support those internal forces that are anxious to meet BN within a short time.

(3) While BN comprises a good deal of accumulated experience and knowledge, it does contain some distinctive and novel features. They can be best summarized as the need for redesigned public services, complementing improved earning power, for more attention to activities inside the household, and for greater emphasis on self-management and local mobilization of resources. There is also the positive, operational and concrete focus on meeting specific needs of vulnerable groups, which has tended to be neglected by previous, more aggregative and more abstract, approaches.

(4) It is clearly true that some of the most severe constraints are political. Even these should not be regarded as irremovable. The encouragement of reformist alliances, both by country selection and dialogue, can remove some of these obstacles. But politics is not the whole answer. There are gaps in our experience and we face administrative difficulties in implementing a BN approach. Such an approach makes a heavy demand on managerial and administrative skills, though these are not of the highest order. These skills are scarce in most developing countries. The busting of these administrative bottlenecks and the exploration of appropriate technologies and delivery systems are quite distinct from the problem of overcoming political resistance. Even where the political forces have been favourable, basic needs programs have failed

because of organizational defects.

(5) It is perfectly true that inequality indexes and poverty measures are lower in socialist than in capitalist countries. Revolutionary land reforms and public ownership of all means of production make it easier to pursue a BN strategy (though inequalities of power and access to power may be increased by the existence of a centralized bureaucracy). But the success of a number of nonsocialist countries in meeting basic needs suggests that socialism is not a prerequisite for meeting basic needs. And, as Cambodia has shown, it certainly does not guarantee that they are met.

(6) The question as to how much "supply management" in the form of market intervention is necessary should be treated as an empirical one and should be answered pragmatically, not ideologically. The deficiencies of bureaucratic controls are well known. At the same time, market imperfections in the widest sense have often prevented market responses to private purchasing power, even where this was fairly evenly distributed.

BN is not derived from a paternalistic ideology, although it acknowledges that consumers are subject to all kinds of pressures, from advertisers, consumption patterns of groups they wish to emulate, etc., against which countervailing pressures can legitimatley be mobilized. Ultimately, it is the felt needs of human beings in society that should define the content of BN.

(7) Examples of attempts of radical reforms that failed demonstrate that careful thought has to be given to the political and economic problems of the transition form a society in which large inequalities in the distribution of assets, income and power prevail and deprivation is widespread to one in which basic needs are met. Inflation, capital flight, brain drain, or disruption of production by disaffected groups are dangers that can frustrate a BN approach before it has got very far. These threats point to the need to work out carefully the macroeconomic implications, both domestic and international, of the transition to BN strategies.

(8)   The criticism that BN lacks analytical
content is probably of greater concern to academic
economists, who justify their existence by saying
the non-obvious, than to people concerned with
getting things done.   It also happens to be untrue,
for BN calls for a complex analysis of externalities
in cross-sectoral linkages, both to reduce costs and
to improve the impact on meeting needs.   It is
true, however, that some of the most important
unsettled issues lie in the area of politics and
administration, rather than in economic analysis.

It may, of course, turn out that some of
the approaches that are intended to meet basic needs
will be inefficient or even counterproductive.
"Trickle-up" and "government failure" or "bureaucratic failure" (corresponding in the public sector to
"market failure" in the private sector) are bound to
occur in delivery systems and some trade-offs with
more conventional objectives may have to be accepted.
But in view of the lack of success of many previous
approaches in reaching the deprived, experimentation
with new methods should be welcomed.

FOOTNOTES

1. Lewis W. A. The Evolution of the International Economic Order, Princeton University Press, 1977.

2. Ranis G. (ed) The Gap between Rich and Poor Nations, Macmillan 1972.

3. Ibid, p. 412.

4. Singh, A., " The 'Basic Needs' Approach to Development is the New International Economic Order: The Significance of Third World Industrialization " - World Development, Vol. 7, No. 6, June 1979.

5. See Norman L. Hicks "Basic Needs and the new International Economic Order" World Development Report 1980. Background paper, mimeo, 1979. The following paragraphs draw on this paper.

6. Government of Kenya, Development Plan 1979 - 1983, pp. ii-iii.

7. Government of Phillippines Five Year Phillippine Development Plan 1979-1983, p. 1-1.

8. Government of India - Planning Commission Draft Five Year Plan, 1978-1982, Vol. 1, p. 8.

9. U. N. General Assembly A/AC 191/21, April 28, 1978, p. 4.

10. National Planning Commission Secretariat (Nepal) Basic Principle of Sixth Man (Katuandu, April 1979) pp. 17-19.

11. Government of Indonesia, Repelita III: The Third Five Year Development Plan (English translation) p. 2.

12. Provisional Military Government of Socialist Etheopia "First Year Program of the National Revolutionary Development Campaign" (May 1979).

13. Ibid, p. 10.

14. A. K. Sen has rightly pointed out that, if there is a moral claim of the poor on the rich in the world community, not only must it be shown that the resources raised by rich countries reach the poor in poor countries, but also that not giving such aid (and e.g. reducing taxes) would benefit the poor in the rich countries. "Ethical issues in Income Distribution: National and International" - Paper presented to the symposium "The Past and Prospects of the Economic World Order" at Saltsjobaden, August, 1978.

15. For some imaginative ideas on how to combine international institutions devoted to basic needs with respect for national sovereignty, see Harlan Cleveland, "A Third Try at World Order", New York, 1976.

UNEMPLOYMENT AND POVERTY IN THE COMMONWEALTH CARIBBEAN*

by
Jack Harewood

DEMOGRAPHIC BACKGROUND

The problems of unemployment and poverty
have plagued most of the countries of the Commonwealth Caribbean during the past half-century. This
remarkable transformation of the Region from low
density and labour shortage to 'over-population,
labour surplus and poverty owes much to our population history'. The first important population policy
of the European colonizers for the Region was to
build up the population, in particular the 'working'
population as rapidly as possible. This was to
enable the sugar plantations to have the abundance of
cheap labour necessary for the high profits sought by
their proprietors. Since the population density in
the Region was then very low and there was no prospect of obtaining the rapid population growth needed
through natural increase, recourse was had to
immigration. At some times, when continued immigration seemed very doubtful, some efforts were made
to encourage an increase in fertility, as during the
last years of slavery. But the result was never
significant.

Over an extended period of two and a half
centuries, therefore, all the European countries
concerned brought in people from wherever they could
be obtained and under whatever conditions seemed most
economical. Because the plantations demanded a very

---

*Partly because data are more readily
available to the author about the Commonwealth
Caribbean, but also because this is the part of the
Region to which Sir Arthur Lewis belongs and on which
he has had the greatest influence, this chapter deals
with the Commonwealth Caribbean only. Unless otherwise specified, the term "Caribbean" should be
interpreted as "Commonwealth Caribbean".

large, unskilled work force, and given the attraction of the vast areas of available agricultural land to free immigrants, the plantations found it best to obtain their labour in the form of unfree immigrants - African slaves in the case of all countries, and indentured immigrants mainly from India in the case of those countries which remained 'under-populated' at the end of slavery. This large scale importation of unfree labour continued, in the case of countries receiving indentured workers, until the second decade of the present century.

It is now clear, however, that the planters used the unfree immigration to build up, not an adequate, but a surplus labour supply to ensure themselves of a low-cost, servile work force. Furthermore, since there is need for a much larger work force during the sugar cane crop season, the obtaining of a surplus of labour even at crop time meant that there was a very considerable problem of seasonal unemployment even during the period of immigration. Thus, Laurence (1971) points out that there was evidence of unemployment among Africans in Trinidad, Guyana and Jamaica by the end of the first decade of the present century.

This imported unemployment, including the seasonal unemployment and under-employment, were aggravated by the well-known, periodic problems facing the sugar industry of the Region, and resulted in appreciable poverty and distress among the non-indentured population. This accounts for the 'push' of emigrants from most of the English-speaking Caribbean (except notably Trinidad and Tobago) during the last decade of the last century and the first two decades of the present century. During this period there was large-scale emigration from the Region to: Panama, with the construction of the Canal; Central America to work on the developing banana plantations; Cuba with the expansion of the sugar industry there; and the United States of America in response to removal of some of the restrictions on migration from the West Indies to that country. In addition, there was some movement from the smaller neighbouring islands to Trinidad and Guyana which offered better employment opportunities.

Two demographic factors contributed to the worsening in unemployment and poverty during the late 1920's and the 1930's: first, partly, but not entirely, due to the world depression in the 1920's opportunities for emigration largely disappeared and, instead, many of the Caribbean territories experienced a significant re-migration; secondly, the 1920's saw the start of a substantial and consistent decline in mortality which has continued to the present time. The decline in mortality and the reversal in migration resulted in a rapid increase in the adult population. With the attendant economic depression, unemployment and poverty increased as we have already remarked. There ensued the famous riots and disorders in much of the Region around 1937.

During the 1940's and 1950's, the level of fertility increased appreciably in all countries of the Region except Barbados. Although there was an increase in the rate of population growth, this was kept down by the re-emergence of large-scale emigration, except from Trinidad and Tobago, mainly to the United Kingdom. The growing population was, therefore, accompanied by an increasing proportion of young persons under working age, and hence population pressure was less on employment and more on greater dependency at the family level. The changing age structure also necessitated the devotion of an increasing proportion of Government resources on providing for the welfare of children, particularly on education.

In the 1960's, the rate of fertility declined and emigration continued and, indeed, increased. For the first time Trinidad and Tobago joined in this net emigration. Migrants continued to go mainly to the United Kingdom until that country's Commonwealth Immigration Act of 1962 considerably restricted entry. Fortuituously, however, at this time restrictions on immigration of West Indians into the United States of America and Canada were greatly reduced and hence emigration continued to increase throughout the decade. Emigration continued at a high level in the 1970's while the birth rates fell more slowly and in some countries tended to level off. The resulting lower rate of population growth in these two decades has resulted in a lessening of the demographic pressures on unemployment and poverty.

SOCIO-ECONOMIC BACKGROUND

In the 1930's the vast majority of the working population in the English-speaking Caribbean were engaged in Agriculture. Only Trinidad with its petroleum and Guyana with its bauxite had mineral resources of some importance for their economies. Agriculture, for the Region, consisted principally of the production of export crops, the most important of which was sugar cane and its products. Also important in some countries was bananas which in fact, exceeded sugar in value in Jamaica for a long period. Other important crops in the Region, but not of course in all of the countries, were cocoa, spices, coconuts, coffee, citrus, rice, cotton and lime. Sugar was grown predominantly on the plantations and thus offered employment to agricultural employees. A small proportion of the sugar cane cultivation was, however, carried out by small farmers and so also was a large proportion of the production of bananas and other crops.

There was little manufacturing industry in the Region at that time, except for industries which had to be carried out on the spot (e.g. electric generation, ice production etc.) and industries concerned with 'processing' of agricultural products, particularly sugar. It is worth noting, here, that the English-speaking Caribbean countries, which now form the Commonwealth Caribbean, were, at that time and up to the early 1960's, all colonies of Britain with varying but strictly limited levels of local authority. Economic thought in the 'mother country' at the time saw these territories as essentially producers of agricultural products for export and were in fact opposed to the notion of industrializing the colonies.

All the agricultural industries, and sugar in particular, went through periods of extreme hardship for one reason or another. The causes of these hardships were myriad. In the case of sugar, for example, there were periods of competition from beet sugar and from cane-sugar produced by other countries but the 1930's was a period of expansion thanks to a substantial preferential assistance for 'British West Indian' sugar in Great Britain and Canada, and significant improvement in technical efficiency and hence greatly reduced costs of production. The International Sugar Agreement of 1937, however, restricted further expansion through a system of quotas, though this ceased to operate with the out- break of World War 11. Many of the other crops suffered at one time or another because of limited markets, variable prices, crop diseases, hurricanes and so on.

But the problem with agriculture was more fundamental. As Lewis (1950) pointed out, while population has been increasing, land is limited and at the same time technical progress has been leading to a progressive substitution of capital for labour on the land. This mechanization was seen as "the inevitable answer of the planters to the continuous tendency for wages to rise". Moreover, Lewis saw a further drastic reduction in agricultural employment (he thought it needed to be halved) as essential if agriculture was to provide a reasonable standard of living to persons engaged in it.

In the above circumstances, the availability of work was very limited, with ensuing high levels of unemployment and under-employment, the latter being particularly important among small farmers and pedlars and other small-scale own account workers. In the absence of effective unions, wages were generally very low so that even for those with jobs the level of living was sub-standard for the majority. With social and other assistance being negligible, there was appreciable poverty. Social conditions were also generally poor, with over-crowded, sub-standard and insanitary homes, inadequate schooling, health and other facilities being the norm in most of the coun- tries.

Over and above the appalling social and economic conditions, there was growing resentment against the political system in which the majority of the population were without effective representa- tion in the government in most countries in the Region and, in addition, final authority rested with Britain.

It was in these circumstances that riots, spearheaded by the labour movement, spread across much of the Region in the late 1930's. As Craig (1974) asserts: "The 'disturbances' therefore expressed the need to transform that social order, to reorganize the economy of the region away from the dependence on traditional staples for export, to open up the system of representation and to move for self-government (Independence)".

DEVELOPMENT STRATEGIES

The Royal Commission (Moyne), set up in 1938 in response to these uprisings, saw the "problem of the West Indies (as) essentially agrarian". The recommendations with respect to economic conditions, therefore, related mainly to agriculture, especially the sugar industry. Little prospect was seen for industrialization. In these conditions, and taking into account the increasing rate of population growth, there was not much hope for a significant impact on the unemployment problem. As regards the problem of poverty, emphasis was placed on welfare and on some improvement to the social services. As Craig (1974) states, "the emphasis was not on structural change but on agricultural diversification with estates intact". This colonial view, that there were strict limitations to industrialization in the West Indies and hence that in response to the problems of unemployment and poverty there must be increasing emphasis on social welfare, continued in the post-war period.[1]

When the colonial system started to give way, first to internal self-government and later to full independence in the post-war period, the national governments were understandably anxious to keep these two potentially explosive problems of unemployment and poverty under control. Necessarily, the national governments abandoned the colonial concept of the West Indies as perpetual producers of raw materials and importers of manufactured goods for the benefit of the 'mother country'. It was recognised that unemployment and poverty were merely symptoms of

140

underdevelopment and that, particularly with respect
to unemployment, any attempted solution must involve
efforts at rapid economic developments with special
emphasis on industrialization.

This break from colonial thinking was
largely due to the considerable influence of the
'development economics' of Arthur Lewis who, in
addition to his many and important general writings
on development economics, has been directly concern
with the economic development of the Caribbean
through his special writings on the Region and hav
served as adviser in one form or another on many
important occasions. His strategy for the develop
ment of the Caribbean has been set forth in three
important papers - 'An Economic Plan for Jamaica'
(*circa*. 1945), an analysis of 'Industrial Develop
in Puerto Rico' (1949) and prescriptions for 'The
Industrialization of the British West Indies' (19
His appointments to government-related posts in
Caribbean include: consultant to the Caribbean
Commission (1949), Special Adviser to the Prime
Minister of the West Indies Federation (1961), a
later Chairman of the Caribbean Development Bank
(1971-1974). In addition, along with Teodoro Mo
of Puerto Rico, he was instrumental in drafting
first development plan for Trinidad and Tobago
(1958-1962) at the invitation of the People's
National Movement (PNM) when it first formed th
government of that country. (Craig *op. cit.*).

It is outside the scope of this pape
attempt, in detail, either a review or a criti
Lewis' work. But since development planning
Region since the 1950's has been so greatly i
fluenced by him that the approach is often re
to as the 'Lewis strategy', and since, as sta
above, emphasis on development planning large
out of the need to find new approaches to the
of unemployment and poverty, we draw attenti
few of his critical ideas. For this, to a l
extent, we refer again to Craig (*op. cit.*).

For reasons already discussed, Le
urged that industrialization was not, for t
West Indies, an *alternative* to agricultural
ment. Instead, he claimed, "agriculture ca

141

put on to a basis where it will yield a reasonable
standard of living unless new jobs are created off
the land", i.e. through industrialization. As
regards the markets for the new industrial goods to
be produced in the Caribbean, Lewis pointed out that
while "production generates its own demand", this
could not be entirely relied on in the Caribbean
because of the high level of poverty and the fact
that "a poor people spends a very high proportion of
its income on food and shelter, and only a small
proportion of manufactures". It was therefore
necessary to put great emphasis on improving the
level of living of the population, again through
industrialization, but, in addition, if industrialization, and through it employment were to be increased
rapidly, then the Region must export manufactures
to outside destinations. Given the limitations on
agriculture in the Region, this meant that the
Caribbean must export manufactures to pay for its
importation of food. This, then, was a complete
reversal of the traditional colonial approach.

        As to the technique of industrialization,
greatly influenced by Puerto Rico's attempt, at the
end of the 1940's, to create employment by inviting
U.S. capital industries there for export, Lewis
(op. cit.) argued that "getting industries started in
an undeveloped area may involve considerable
sacrifice". In fact, he claimed that "the islands
(would not) be industrialized to anything like the
extent that (was) necessary without a considerable
flow of foreign capital and capitalists, and a
method of wooing and fawning upon such people". To
this end, he saw as imperative the setting up of a
special Industrial Development Corporation (for the
Region) after establishing a customs union. The
incentives to businessmen which he foresaw included:
provision of suitable factories at public expense, the
provision of adequate public utility services, protection in the local market, e.g. by restriction on
imports by tariff or by licence, and by an assurance
that other industrialists would not be allowed to
set operations in the same line within a given
period, subsidies possibly disguised in the form of
peppercorn rents and loans at nominal rates of
interest etc., holidays from direct taxes and the
remission of indirect taxes especially customs duties

142

on imported raw materials and machinery. In all
cases Lewis saw the necessity for ensuring that the
interest of the country and its people were not
jeopardised. The possibility of the governments
engaging in some industrial activities was also
envisaged though not given much prominence.

Despite the general concern with unemployment and poverty, then, the Lewis approach did not
envisage a direct attack on these problems, but
sought to affect them indirectly through rapid
economic growth. Barbados and the smaller islands of
the Region continue to adhere to the Lewis model but,
in due course, as it became clear that economic
expansion in terms of increasing national output was
not being accompanied by any significant impact on
unemployment, the Lewis approach was modified in the
larger countries to what might be termed 'employment-
oriented' strategies of development in which much
more attention was paid to the specific problem of
reducing unemployment. Thus, particular attention
was paid to the possibility of adopting labour-
intensive techniques of production as far as possible,
which required that in the transfer of technology
from the developed countries, efforts had to be made
both to derive modifications suitable for the
developing countries and to convince investors to
change the capital-intensive technologies with which
they were accustomed and which had proved successful
in the developed countries. Another and quite different attempt to reduce unemployment was to provide
employment on public works in some form of 'crash
programme'.

As will be seen, the employment-oriented
strategies have not been successful, either, in
reducing the level of unemployment and, moreover,
there is a growing awareness that efforts to improve
income distribution through the provision of greater
employment opportunities, still do not affect the
principal poverty groups in most developing countries.
Lisk (1977) has given as a reason for this that "the
poor are mainly outside the 'organized' sectors of
the economy - self-employed peasant farmers in rural
areas and members of the rapidly growing urban
informal sector who cannot find adequately remunerative work". *Best et al* (1979) have referred to these

groups outside of the organized sectors of the economy as persons whose income comprises the "amorphous category of mixed incomes which accrue to the poorly organized, unorganized, or disorganized residentiary sector".

For these reasons, there has been growing effort towards a re-orientation of development policy towards dealing specifically with the problems of income inequality and poverty. Such efforts, in the Region, range from those merely aiming, by action in some selected areas, to reduce the level of income inequality and poverty, to what are called 'anti-poverty' strategies concerned with eradicating major pockets of poverty by raising the average income of the very poor. It is generally acknowledged that for this purpose the provision of employment opportunity is not enough, and hence both the employment-oriented and the anti-poverty strategies also include a variety of measures aimed at changing the social, economic and institutional structures which appear to cause and perpetuate poverty among certain sections of the population. Thus, from time to time, and with different degrees of dedication and success, the countries of the Region have attempted to: (a) change the pattern of land ownership and tenure; (b) improve access to basic education, vocational training, health facilities, development finance and other productive assets; (c) foster the development of small-scale farms and business; (d) improve family welfare by providing and encouraging the use of contraception to reduce family size and the birth rate and (e) provide for consumption transfers through measures such as food subsidies, social welfare payments and pensions, free school meals and other such actions intended to support the poorest sections of the society.

Moving further in the direction of emphasis-ing the purpose of development as improving the level of living of the population, particularly of the very large numbers of under-privileged persons, the *basic needs approach* to development has come into prominence since the mid-1970's. According to ILO (1976) basic needs include two elements: "First, they include certain minimum requirements of a family for private consumption: adequate food, shelter and clothing are obviously included, as would be certain household equipment and furniture. Second, they include essential services provided by and for the community at large, such as safe drinking water, sanitation, public transport, and health and education facilities". Employment is seen both as a means and as an end, since in addition to contributing to output and providing an income to the employed, it "gives a person the recognition of being engaged in something worthwhile". Guyana is the one country of the Region that has formally adopted this approach and this is discussed in some detail later.

LEVELS AND TRENDS IN UNEMPLOYMENT AND POVERTY

UNEMPLOYMENT

There are no meaningful statistical measures of unemployment or poverty in the Region in the pre-World War 11 period. The Moyne Report (1939) which contains the most comprehensive review of economic and social conditions in the 'British West Indies' in the 1930's could speak in only general terms of the level of unemployment, referring to it as "a question of increasing importance .. (the) extent and effects (of which) are already very formidable in most of the West Indian colonies". The Report, also, had only very limited indirect information on the level of poverty, including data on wage rates and mortality, but again relied on qualitative assessments of the inadequacies in housing and other social conditions.

In the post-war period, some data are available on the level of unemployment in all of the countries as derived in the censuses of population, and in some countries at special sample surveys in the inter-censal periods. These enquiries have all adopted the *labour force* approach, which was originated in the United States of America as the basis for measuring unemployment during the depression of the 1930's and has since been modified and recommended by the ILO. This approach sub-divides the population above some specified age (see below) into the *employed*, the *unemployed*, and those *not in the labour force*, the *labour force* being the *employed* plus the *unemployed*.

145

An essential first step is to define *employment* . Two different concepts of *employment* have been in common use, though they are generally considered to be identical in result. According to the Eighth International Conference of Labour Statisticians (ICLS) of 1954, all persons should be classified as *employed* who, during some specified period, *performed some work for pay or profit*. This may, for convenience be termed the *social* concept of work. In 1966, the UN Statistical Commission defined the *employed* or *economically active population* as all persons "who furnish the supply of labour for the production of economic goods and services" during the specified reference period, the definition of *economic goods and services* being the same as that used in the UN system of national accounts. This second concept may, for convenience, be termed the *economic* concept of work. According to the social concept, work (employment) must provide an *income* , while according to the economic concept, it must yield an *output.* .

Both concepts sub-divide the employed population into four *types of worker* or *occupation status groups* . These are: (a) paid employees; (b) employers; (c) own account workers; and (d) unpaid family workers. From the social point of view, these may be arranged in two sets, the first, comprising (a), (b) and (c) being those who worked for pay directly; and the second, (sub-group (d)), being those who earned an income indirectly by engaged in a household business from which they benefit without receiving direct income. According to the economic concept, the sets may be more meaningfully: (a) those who were self-employed either with paid assistance (employers) or without paid assistance (own account workers); and (b) those who worked for others either as paid employees or as unpaid family workers who contributed some output to a family business. The international definitions recommend that unpaid family workers should be included as employed only if they worked, during the reference period, for at least one-third of the normal working time but this limitation has not generally been adopted in the Caribbean or, indeed, in many developing countries.

From the above definitions, it is clear that certain important types of *work* are excluded from the

definition of *employment*. In particular, household
duties performed for the benefit of one's own family
- e.g. the work at home of a wife and mother - is
excluded. Also, voluntary work is excluded though,
in the case of the economic approach, this is a
convention rather than a strict following of the
definition of work since the voluntary worker may be
contributing to output.

Given the definition of the *employed*, the
unemployed are defined as persons who during the
specified period were available for and willing to
accept employment, but could find no suitable employment. Those persons above the agreed minimum age
who were neither employed nor unemployed are classified as *not in the labour force.*

As we have indicated above, the labour
force approach classifies persons according to their
activity during a *specified period.* This is in
contrast to the earlier *gainful worker* approach which
classified persons on the basis of their *usual
activity*, based on the idea that each person has a
more or less stable functional role as a worker, a
housewife, a retired person, a student, etc., which
is largely independent of, and more important than,
his activity at any given time. Some writers, now
use the term *labour force* to relate to activity during a specified *short* period of a day or week (say),
and the term *gainful worker* to activity during a
long period such as a year. We prefer to retain the
term gainful worker for *usual activity* as originally
used, and to use the term labour force to cover both
short and long reference periods. In the recent
censuses of population in the Region, the distinction
is, therefore, made between the *week's* labour force
and the *year's* labour force.

As we have also indicated earlier, the
labour force classification is made with respect to
the general population above some specified age. In
the Censuses of Population of 1946 and 1960 the
minimum age limit was taken as 10 years, so that
persons 10 years and older were classified by labour
force status. In the 1970 and 1980 censuses as well
as in the sample surveys for obtaining labour force
data in the Region, some countries, including Trinidad

147

and Tobago (referred to as Trinidad hereafter) have used the population 15 years and older, while others, including Jamaica, have used 14 years and older.

While the definitions of employment and unemployment given above appear to be straightforward, in practice there are serious problems with the actual measurement of unemployment, in particular. One important reason for this is, that in any given reference period, no matter how short, a person may be in more than one status situation. For example, during a reference week, an individual may have been employed for part of the week, unemployed for another part, and not in the labour force for the remainder. The labour force approach determines the status of such persons on the basis of a priority criterion which stipulates that employment, for however short a period, takes precedence over unemployment which, in turn, takes precedence over the *not* in the labour force status. A person who was employed for all or part of one day, therefore, and unemployed for the remainder of the week is classified as *employed*. This tends to over-state employment and under-state unemployment and emphasises the importance of including *under-employment* (see below) in any labour force analysis.

Another serious problem in the measurement of unemployment, and one which has been important in the Caribbean as elsewhere, is how to determine who, among those persons that are not employed, are *willing and able to work*. According to the Eighth ICLS definition, unemployment is determined principally on the activity of *seekign work*. In addition, persons on lay-off without pay as well as those with a job to take up after the reference period are included. It is now generally accepted, however, that particularly in developing countries where there is a high level of chronic unemployment, a significant number of persons who are without a job and willing and able to work would not actively seek work during the specified short period primarily because they are aware (or believe) that no suitable work is available - the *discouraged worker*. To meet this situation, persons who volunteer information that they want work but knew of no suitable vacancy are included with the unemployed. But this is not enough as many persons

148

will not volunteer this information. One approach adopted in the Caribbean to identify these *discouraged workers* is to ask them directly whether they want work and are available for work. This approach is used in Jamaica and was also used in Trinidad in surveys carried out by the Ministry of Labour in 1958 and 1959. Another approach, which has been used in Trinidad since 1963, is to ask all persons without a job when last they looked for work, and to include as unemployed all those who looked for work at any time during the preceding three months and are still willing and able to work.

These different approaches to the identification of the discouraged worker have meant that the unemployment measures in the various countries in the Region may not be comparable and, in the case of Trinidad, that the data for some surveys are not comparable with others. They also provide the basis for dissatisfaction with the unemployment data. Thus, G. Arthur Brown, then Governor of the Bank of Jamaica, is reported as questioning the meaningfulness of the estimate of unemployment obtained by the Jamaica approach on the ground that it was too high (Harewood (1972), pp. 24-25). Similarly, Eric Williams, former Prime Minister and Minister of Finance of Trinidad has indicated, in recent budget speeches that he believed that this country's estimate of unemployment was too high and, more particular, did not reflect the large drop in unemployment that was assumed to have taken place in the recent period of oil prosperity. On the other hand, Trevor Farrel (1978) has argued that the approach adopted in Trinidad and, indeed, the recommended ILO approach, gravely under-states the true magnitude of unemployment.

We mention, one further serious short-coming in the measurement of the labour force, generally, and unemployment specifically, and that is that information on both the activity (e.g. seeking work) and intention (e.g. wanting work) of individuals is in general given by one member of a household for other members. Clearly there is ample scope for differences between the responses that would be given by an individual about him (her) self and those given on his (her) behalf by a spouse, parent, brother/sister or non-relative.

Finally, the data obtained from censuses of population on the one hand and from sample surveys on the other in the Caribbean are not comparable, because while the sample surveys measure the labour force with reference to activity during a specified week, the censuses use the year preceding enumeration as the reference period. The longer period is acknowledged to be much less satisfactory for the measurement of unemployment. There are two reasons why it has been used, however, in the censuses of population. The first is that if comparisons are to be made of labour force data at ten-yearly intervals, it is unreasonable to make these comparisons on the basis of activity during as short a period of one week which could easily be, for some reason(s), quite atypical. The second, and related reason, is that for such long-term comparisions, it is more meaningful to study changes in the general labour force and manpower situation over time rather than put emphasis on the measurement of the smallest component - the unemployed, however important it may be. In these circumstances, there needs to be reliance on inter-censal household surveys to obtain meaningful unemployment statistics bearing in mind, too, that this can be done much more efficiently in a small, tightly controlled sample survey than in the large multi-purpose census of population.

For these reasons, although the censuses of population are the only source of unemployment data for *all* countries of the Commonwealth Caribbean in the post-war period, we shall refer to these data only very briefly below and shall not put much reliance on the unemployment data thus obtained. Our discussion of unemployment will be based mainly on the situation in Trinidad and Jamaica where, as indicated below, continuous sample surveys of households to obtain labour force data have been carried out since the 1960's.

At the 1960 Census, the Western Census Region, comprising Jamaica, the Leewards and Belize, included those 'wanting work' with the unemployed while the Eastern Region did not. In the 1970 figures below we maintain this difference so that the figures for all three censuses (1946, 1960 and 1970) are consistent for the Eastern Region, while

the last two are consistent within the Western Region,
but the two Regions' figures are not directly
comparable.

The census figures show an increase, in the
Eastern Region, in the unemployment rate as a
percentage of the labour force, from 6 in 1946 to 11
and 16 respectively at the next two censuses. The
figures for Trinidad and Tobago are 7, 11 and 22, the
figure for 1970 being extremely large and probably
exaggerated because of the 'Black Power' disturbances
in that country around census time. In all countries
of both Regions, there was a large increase in
unemployment between 1946 and 1960; in Barbados, for
example, the unemployment rate was 8 in 1946 and 12
in 1960. Between 1960 and 1970, in addition to the
special case of Trinidad and Tobago, there was also
a large increase in the unemployment rate in Jamaica
from 13 to 20 percent of the labour force, and a
smaller increase in Guyana from 11 to 14 percent. In
all other countries of the Region, however, the unemployment rate declined except in St. Vincent where
there was no change. In Barbados, for example the
rate fell from 12 to 7 and in Grenada from 16 to 4.
There seems to be justification for being suspicious
of these large declines in the level of unemployment
as well as for the large increases in Trinidad and
Tobago. In Barbados, for example, recent sample
surveys indicate an unemployment rate of 13 percent
in 1978 and 1979. In fact, population censuses at
10-year intervals are clearly not very reliable
vehicles for measuring changes in unemployment for
persons mentioned above.

Data from sample surveys of households
provide an opportunity for more precise and consistent
labour force and unemployement data, though this
approach has not been efficiently used in many countries of the Region. While labour force surveys have
been carried out at one time or another in all of the
larger countries, consistent data which permit an
indication of unemployment trends are available only
for Trinidad and Tobago (since 1964) and Jamaica
(since 1968), in both cases from a system of continuous household surveys. The data from the 1955-1957
surveys in Trinidad can also provide data comparable
to those obtained in the continuous survey and hence

enable an indication of trends over a longer period.
The data for the two countries are not, however,
directly comparable as the Jamaica definition includes the persons 'wanting work' along with those who
sought work during the past week as the unemployed,
while the Trinidad approach requires that persons
should have looked for work at some time during the
preceding *three months,* or have given some reason
(such as not knowing of any suitable vacancies) why
they did not look for work.

On the basis of the definition currently
in use, the unemployment rate in Trinidad in 1956-57
was about 10 percent of the labour force. This level
increased in the early 1960's and in 1965, when the
continuous sample survey started, was estimated at
14 percent and remained at this level till 1969.[3]
There was a slight fall to 12-13 percent in 1970-1971,
but by 1973 the rate had increased to 15 before
declining sharply with the growing effects of the oil
boom to 12 and 11 percent respectively in 1978 and
1979.

In the case of Jamaica, with its more
inclusive definition of unemployment, the unemployment
rate in 1968, the first year of the continuous survey,
was 20 percent and this fell to 17 in the following
year. There was no survey in the ensuing two years
and by 1972 the rate had risen to 23 percent but fell
slowly to 21 in 1975. Once again the unemployment
level increased to reach 25 percent of the labour
force in 1978 and, given the economic and related
problems in recent years, has undoubtedly risen further since then, though figures for later years are not
available to the author.

Because of the difference in definition of
unemployment and hence of the labour force already
referred to, the above figures do not provide a
comparison of the unemployment levels in the two
countries. Comparability can be obtained by restricting attention to those unemployed who were 'seeking
work' during the survey and modifying the labour force
accordingly. On this basis, the 'seeker' rate was
9-10 percent of the labour force in Trinidad and 12-
13 percent in Jamaica for the three years 1968, 1973
and 1978.[4]

We now describe some of the important
characteristics of the unemployed. While there are
some significant differences in the level of unemployment within the Region, the indications are that
the general patterns are very similar, as is seen
when we compare the situation in the two countries
being studied here.

Unemployment is much higher among females
than among males. In 1973, the unemployment rate for
males was 13 percent in both countries, but was 21
and 33 percent respectively for females in Trinidad
and in Jamaica. This also highlights the fact that
the persons 'wanting work' who took no action to
obtain employment, who are included in Jamaica but
not in Trinidad, consists mainly of women. In fact,
in 1973, 85 percent of this group were women.
Moreover the rate of unemployment among women in both
countries tended to change more rapidly than among
men. Thus, the unemployment rate for males in 1967
and 1973 remained unchanged at 13 in Jamaica, and
rose very slightly from 12 to 13 in Trinidad. On the
other hand, the rate for females increased from 30
to 33 for Jamaica and from 16 to 21 for Trinidad.
With the decline in unemployment in Trinidad between
1973 and 1978, however, both male and female rates
fell by 3 percentage points, the relative decline for
males therefore being larger.

In other cultures, this high level of
unemployment among females need not imply greater
hardship for this sex, since a large proportion of
them would, in fact, be dependents. In the Caribbean
this is not the case, since as is well known, a
significant number of women are heads of their households and the main bread-winner. In Trinidad in
1977, for example, one-fifth of the women in the
labour force were heads of households. And the
unemployment rate among these female heads of households was considerably higher than among male heads of
households - 33 percent for females as against 4 percent for males.

Unemployment is much more severe among
young persons under 25 years old than among older
persons. In 1973, for example, the rate was 39 in
Jamaica and 30 in Trinidad for persons under 25 years

of age, as against 15 and 9 respectively for older persons. As another indicator of the contribution of youth to the unemployment problem, at the October 1973 survey in Jamaica, 60 percent of the unemployed males and 46 percent of the unemployed females were under 25 years of age. In Trinidad in the second-half of 1973, the proportion was 60 percent for both males and females.

Unemployment has also been found to be especially high among persons with a middle level of education. In Trinidad in 1973, for example, among persons with no education or only pre-primary education, the unemployment rate was 6 percent, and among those with a secondary education or higher it was 3 percent. For the intermediate groups, however, those with primary education had a rate of 14-15 percent and those with incomplete secondary education 18 percent.

In both countries unemployment is quite low among persons in Agriculture and allied industries (4 percent in Trinidad and 6 in Jamaica). The rate was highest in Construction (24 percent in both countries). The rate in Manufacturing was intermediate - 16 in Jamaica and 13 in Trinidad.

As an indication of the duration of unemployment being experienced, Trinidad sought information on the interval since unemployed persons last worked, while Jamaica enquired about the number of months worked during the past year. In Trinidad, one-quarter of the unemployed had never worked comprising, of course, mainly of young persons. Forty-three percent had worked within the 3 months preceding the survey week, 15 percent having worked during the preceding month. The long-term unemployed, if we use this term to cover those who had last worked 12 months or more earlier, comprised 14 percent of the total, and another 7 percent had worked 6-11 months before the survey. In Jamaica about 63 percent had not worked at all during the preceding year, of whom one-half had never worked. Of those who did work during the year, about one-half had worked for less than 6 months and an equal number for 6 months or more.

154

We stated above that the characteristics of the unemployed and the incidence of unemployment among groups with different characteristics are similar for Jamaica and Trinidad and probably in the rest of the Region as well. In addition, the pattern has not changed appreciably over the period for which data are available; although we have, for the most part, referred to the statistics for 1973 in the two countries, the pattern would have been the same if we had selected any other year for discussion.

In a recent, pioneering study of the economic and social life of a small sample of unemployed persons in Trinidad, Brathwaite (1979) found that while unemployment is, in a number of cases, associated with economic deprivation, depressed standards of living, and high levels of poverty, the majority of the unemployed did not view their unemployment as 'problematic' because, among other reasons: (a) being unemployed did not mean much financial loss, either because respondents were used to working in low paid jobs, or because they got 'network' support from relatives and friends, or could make money on their 'hustle' from odd jobs and so on; (b) unemployment is common place and hence is no ground for embarrassment and (c) the feeling that they could overcome the difficulties related to their unemployment. He also found no evidence that conflict behaviour such as 'disorganization', 'breakdown', 'deviance' and 'non-conformity' were dominant features of life among the unemployed, except in the political sphere where there was a tendency to political disaffection, and in survival strategies where dependency emerged as the norm.

Studies on how the unemployed view their predicament and more generally on their attitudes and aspirations may prove useful additional information to those who seek to find solutions for this intractable problem.

UNEMPLOYMENT AND OUTPUT

The aspect of unemployment which has generally attracted most attention and concern in developing countries has been the fact that the unemployed are denied the opportunity of obtaining an income and hence unemployment is an important source of income inequality and poverty. Unemployment in this sense is primarily a *social* problem. Given the title of the present chapter - Unemployment and Poverty - understandably this is the aspect with which we have been especially concerned. There are, however, other important aspects of unemployment, and of the most important of these - the economic aspect - is that the economy is foregoing the contribution of the unemployed to the national output.

In the labour force approach where the income aspect of unemployment is of prime importance, the population is first divided into those who are employed and those *not* employed, the latter in turn being sub-divided into those who want to be employed (the unemployed) and those who do not want to be employed (persons outside of the labour force). From the point of view of output, it would be more meaningful to sub-divide those who are *not* employed into: (a) those who can make a meaningful contribution to the increasing of total output in the present circumstances (the *unutilized manpower*); and (b) those who for any reason cannot make such a contribution at the present time. If among the latter there are persons who want work it would be more appropriate, in the present context, to refer to them as *surplus labour* until a meaningful demand for their services can be created. Indeed, the term *surplus labour* would also apply to those persons who are employed, but whose level of productivity is so low that they are not making a meaningful contribution to total production.

We are suggesting, therefore, that the term *unemployment* not be used in this context partly to avoid confusion with the earlier connotation of the term, and partly because the terms now suggested may provide some greater insights into this other aspect of our human resources problem.

It is outside the scope of the present chapter to deal in any detail with this other aspect of unemployment. But as indicated above, the unutilized (and under-utilized) manpower are in fact the persons

for whom every effort should be made to provide
employment in so far as increasing output is the
concern. As regards the surplus labour, however, the
immediate approach may need to be to improve their
skills, on the one hand, and/or seek to provide
additional job opportunities realizing that this may
be a much longer term solution than for the under-
utilized manpower. (See Harewood (1978) for some
expansion of this theme).

UNDER-EMPLOYMENT

The problem of under-employment has not been
given as much publicity as that of unemployment though
the Governments of the Region have become increasingly
aware of its importance. The under-employed are
those persons with jobs who, on the basis of the time
they worked (hours per week or weeks/months per year
for example), or the utilization of their manpower
skills, on the one hand, did not have the opportunity
to contribute fully to production (the economic
aspect); or, on the other hand, on the basis of
earnings, they received an income below some accepted
minimum standard (the social aspect).

Lewis (1950) emphasised the importance of
this growing problem of under-employment (both
economic and social) by drawing attention to the
growth in unproductive jobs. In Barbados, at the 1946
Census, for example, 18 percent of the employed
population were engaged in domestic service. And this
leads to another point stressed by Lewis, that being
that women were the principal victims of under-employment in this instance. "Being unable to get productive jobs, women have poured into domestic service and
into petty trading".

Using the criterion of hours worked per week
to derive a measure of visible under-employment, it is
usual in the Region to classify persons who worked
for less than 33 hours as being under-employed,
provided they were willing and able to work more hours.
Surprisingly, neither Jamaica nor Trinidad have sought
information from those working short hours on whether
they wanted to work a longer period. For Jamaica,
therefore, we must use, as an indicator of visible

under-employment, the total number of persons with a job who worked for less than 33 hours in the survey week. In the case of Trinidad, a somewhat more refined measure can be obtained by deducting from the above, those persons with a job who did not work at all during the survey week for reasons other than the unavailability of work.

Of the persons with jobs in Jamaica, 15 percent were visible under-employed in 1968 and this proportion increased to 16 and 22 percent in 1973 and 1978 respectively. In Trinidad, the proportion visibly under-employed, using the modification just mentioned, fell by one-third from 24 percent in 1968 to 16 in 1973 and remained the same in 1978. The actual number of persons under-employed was lower than the number unemployed in Jamaica in each of the three years considered here. Thus, in 1968 visible under-employment was 12 percent less than unemployment but the deficit was very much larger in 1973 (43 percent) and 1978 (35 percent). In Trinidad, on the other hand, even with the more refined measure of visible under-employment, while the number under-employed was slightly lower (2 percent) than the number unemployed in 1973, in 1968 and 1978 it was higher by 47 and 28 percent respectively. Bearing in mind the differences in definition of unemployment and under-employment in the two countries, the figures here indicate that under-employment was less serious, numerically, than unemployment in Jamaica, but more serious in Trinidad.

But much more important for developing countries than visible under-employment, especially in the context of our present concern with poverty, is under-employment in terms of income (social under-employment).

A distribution of persons with jobs in Trinidad by income, for the second half of 1973, showed that of all workers except unpaid family workers, 10 percent received a monthly income of less than TT$50 while nearly 30 percent received less than TT$100. Assuming, on the basis of data available to us, that about two-thirds of the unpaid family workers should be grouped with other workers receiving under TT$100 per month, then 32 percent of all workers in

158

Trinidad at that time fell into this low-income category.

Harewood (1960), classified persons with less than TT$50 per month at that time as low-income under-employed, on the ground that this was the minimum income of *unskilled* workers in Government and large establishments (10 or more employees). On this basis, he found 44 percent of the persons with jobs to be under-employed, as compared with 26 percent according to the criterion of working less than 33 hours per week. By contrast, unemployment on the present definition in the country was 10 percent of the labour force. He found under-employment to be high among the same groups for whom the level of unemployment was seen to be high - females, young persons, workers in Agriculture etc. Harewood (1978) using a similar approach found that low-income under-employment in July- December 1973 (allowing for the general increase in wages and prices) was 39-43 percent of those with jobs, and hence remained un-cannily close to what it was in 1956-1957. Expressing these figures as ratios to the total labour force, unemployment was 17 percent and low-income under-employment was 36 percent of the labour force in 1973 and hence only 47 percent of the labour force were fully employed. The relevant data are not available for a similar assessment of the level of low-income under-employment in the recent period of prosperity.

In Jamaica in 1975, in accordance with a new law, the national minimum wage was fixed at J$20 per week. Using this as our standard income for that country, and assuming that two-thirds of the unpaid workers should be included in this low-income group, then 48 percent of persons with jobs were under-employed. Because of the operation of the National Minimum Wage law, the proportion under-employed fell to 34 and 30 percent respectively in April and October 1976. By 1978 the economic and employment situation was deteriorating, but in that year the minimum wage was increased to J$24 per week. Making a rough interpolation of the data by income group, which showed income groups of under $20 and $20 to under $50, it is estimated that low-income under-employment on the same basis as above had increased to 43 percent of those with jobs.

POVERTY

So far, little attention has been given, in the Region, to the measurement of poverty, despite a general awareness of the fact that this is a major problem. The fact that poverty is so generally associated, in popular thought, with unemployment, might largely explain this omission. Whatever the reasons, the only empirical study of the level of poverty in the Region is Henry (1975) dealing with Trinidad. Some more general studies of income inequality are available but again mainly for Jamaica and Trinidad. But first let us discuss the definitions of poverty.

Poverty might be measured either in absolute or relative terms. Absolute poverty is defined to encompass all the persons (or households) in a society that are unable, because of inadequate income, to satisfy the fundamental needs of life. These 'fundamental needs' necessarily vary very appreciably between and even within societies. Even the case of food, for which the requirements in terms of calories and protein have been given appreciable scientific attention, does not permit a standard list of items to be prepared for any society except in very general terms. For non-food items no standard exists.

The usual approach to the measurement of absolute poverty, therefore, is for the researcher of research group to subjectively decide on the 'basket of goods and services' which, in the given society, they consider to be 'fundamental'. The total cost of purchasing the agreed 'fundamental needs' at any given time is then taken as the 'poverty line' and persons with a total disposable income less than this figure are classified as poor.

Henry (1975) used this approach to study poverty in Trinidad in 1972. He included in his 'basket': *food requirements*, based on data compiled by the Caribbean Food and Nutrition Institute: as well as *non-alcoholic beverages, housing, light and fuel, clothing, transport and education.* He made no provision for medical care on the ground that this could be obtained free from state institutions by

160

poor persons; nor was provision made for recreation and other services. This is, therefore, in his own words, a 'very restrictive definition of poverty'. As indicated earlier, he then made subjective judgements of the *minimum* requirements of the above for households of different size and composition.

According to prices existing in Trinidad in the third-quarter of 1972, Henry (*op. cit.*) found that the 'poverty line' income for households ranged from TT$64 per month for single-person households to TT$140 for 4-person and TT$183 for 6-person households. On this basis, and using data from the 1971/72 Household Budgetary Survey on incomes, he concluded that more than one-third (35 percent) of all households in the country were living in poverty, despite the very conservative basket of goods and services used. The known under-reporting of income in these surveys (see for example CSO (1965) has probably accounted for some over-statement of the level of poverty as here defined.

Pending similar and additional studies of poverty using data from the 1975/76 Household Budgetary Survey, Henry (1981) has made a provisional estimate of the cost of the same hypothetical requirements in the year 1976. Given increased retail prices, the poverty line on this simple basis would be TT$112 per month for a 1-person household, TT$249 for a 4-person household, and TT$350 for households of six persons or more. On this basis, 25 percent of all households in the country were living in poverty in 1976 as against the 35 percent estimated for 1972.

Returning to the situation in 1972, Henry (1975) found the incidence of poverty greatest among 1-person households, the proportion of this group classified as poor being 48 percent as against 40 percent of 7-person households, 36 percent of 2- and 6-person households, and 29-32 percent of households of other sizes. He attributed the high incidence of poverty among 1-person households to the significant number of elderly persons in this group, 62 percent of the poor single-person households being persons 60 years old and over.

The incidence of poverty was also very high

among households headed by women: 56 percent of these households were classified as poor as against 31 percent of those headed by men. Henry also drew attention to the large number of females among the poor single-person households (56 percent).

There was appreciable geographic variation in the incidence of poverty, the proportion being lowest (25 percent) in the two large municipalities (Port of Spain and San Fernando) and in the County of St. George which adjoins Port of Spain, and highest (55 percent) in Nariva/Mayaro on the east coast. In this connection, however, it should be noted that the measure of income in these surveys excluded home produced foodstuffs, and hence the level of poverty in rural areas would have been somewhat exaggerated.

By ethnic groups, the incidence of poverty was highest among persons of African orgin (46 percent) followed by those of Indian origin (42 percent). The incidence was considerably lower (8 percent) for persons of Mixed origin, and was negligible for other smaller ethnic groups. Since the consumption of home produced food could be expected to be higher among the Indians who are much more concentrated in rural areas than the African-descended population, the differential between these two largest ethnic groups would have been larger than the above figures indicate.

So far, we have based our assessment of the changing level of poverty on the *income* data from the household budgetary surveys of 1971/72 and 1975/76. These surveys were primarily concerned with the collection of detailed data on household expenditure, and while much effort has been put into obtaining accurate data on income as well, dissatisfaction has been expressed with the level of accuracy achieved in this regard. CSO (1965), for example, concludes that "there was considerable under-reporting of income in all income groups". Another major cause of dissatisfaction is that reported income is usually very significantly lower than reported expenditure. Moreover, the gap increased, with expenditure exceeding income by 19 percent in 1971/72 and 42 percent in 1975/76. It has however been pointed out[5] that the excess of expenditure over income may be due to definition since, using the National Accounting approach, for household durables purchased on credit, the actual price and not the down payment or the instalment in the period is recorded. During the period of prosperity and easy loans in 1975/76 this could mean that the much higher expenditure is associated with much higher debt. In view of these points, it therefore seems reasonable to study poverty in relation to expenditure as well. This, however, does not affect the general situation and is not dealt with here.

A preliminary measure of absolute poverty by Henry (1981), using the same poverty line as above, but with household expenditure instead of income, showed the level of poverty as 26 percent in 1971/72 as compared with 35 percent when based on income. In 1975/76 expenditure again indicated a lower level of poverty than income, the proportion poor being 25 and 33 percent when based on expenditure and income respectively. At both surveys, therefore, the proportion poor was lower when expenditure was used as the basis, while whichever basis was used the indications are that there was little change - a possibly very slight improvement - in the level of poverty between 1971/72 and 1975/76.

There have been no other studies of absolute poverty in the Commonwealth Caribbean. The alternative approach to the measurement of poverty already referred to - relative poverty - is based on the consideration that in a given society, poverty must relate to the general standards existing at a given time. One approach to the measurement of poverty in this sense has been to merely stipulate that all persons (households) in the lowest income groups, or comprising some given percentage of the total population are to be classified as poor. For example, one might define poverty to include all households which are among the 40 percent with the lowest incomes, as has been done in a number of studies. A related and more satisfying approach which has been suggested in a study of Canada is that the poverty line be drawn at some proportion (they suggested one-half) of the average living standard (Adams, Cameron and Penz (1971)). The detailed data for deriving a measure of relative poverty along the lines just mentioned are available to the author for the Trinidad Household Budgetary Surveys of 1971/72 and 1975/76 and this is attempted below, but first we discuss the available data on income inequality.

In any given country, there are a few people (families or households) with incomes that are considerably higher than the average, while at the other extreme, there are a relatively large number who have incomes that are appreciably smaller than the average, with a virtual continuum of incomes in between. It has been estimated that in developing countries, in which inequality is greater than in developed countries, the richest 10 percent of households receive, on average, 40 percent of total income, while the poorest 40 percent receive only 15 percent, and the poorest 20 percent receive about 5 percent of total income (ILO, 1976).

Figures from the three surveys carried out in Trinidad (1957/58, 1971/72 and 1975/76) indicate a worse level of inequality than the average just mentioned at the lower extreme, since the poorest 40 percent of households received 10-13 percent of income as against the average 15 percent in developing countries, and the poorest 20 percent of households received 2-3 percent of incomes as compared with the average 5 percent. Trinidad, however, has a more important middle class than the 'average' developing country for at the other extreme, the top 10 percent of households received 32-37 percent of total incomes as compared with an average 40 percent. We need, however, to be very cautious about drawing conclusions from data such as these in the light of the known serious shortcomings in both the quality and consistency of such data. (See Ahiram (1966), Henry (1975) and Harewood (1981) for some comments on these shortcomings).

A similar survey was carried out in Jamica in 1958 and Ahiram (1966) used data from this survey to compare the income distribution of Jamaica with that in Trinidad in 1957/58. He found the distribution in Trinidad much more equitable than in most developing countries, particularly with respect to the proportion of the total income in the hands of the richest 10 percent. In comparison with Jamaica, this group received 33 percent of all incomes in Trinidad as against 43 percent in Jamaica. Trinidad was also better than Jamaica at the other extreme, with the lowest 40 percent of households receiving 12.5 percent of all incomes in the former and only 8 percent in the latter country. Data for Guyana at around the same time (1956) showed that country as having a somewhat more favourable income distribution than Trinidad as regards the proportion accuring to the poorest 40 percent of households this being 14 percent for Guyana. (Harewood, 1977).

Considering changes in income distribution over time, Henry (1975) and Harewood (1981) have found that in Trinidad, income distribution worsened between 1957/58 and 1971/72, but then improved quickly in the period to 1975/76 with the result that the last situation was similar to that in 1957/58. Thus, the proportion of total income accruing to the poorest 40 percent of households fell from 12.5 to 10.0 and then increased to 11.5. As a summary measure of inequality, the *Gini Coefficient* increased from .45 in 1957/58 to .51 in 1971/72 before returning to .46 in 1975/76. Unpublished data for Jamaica also suggest a worsening in income distribution in that country between 1958 and 1972, the top 10 percent of households sharing 33 percent of total income in 1958 but 51 percent in 1972.

Turning now to relative poverty, we have decided, following Adams, Cameron and Penz (*op. cit.*) to use half the average household income as the *poverty line*, and to classify all households with less than this income as living in poverty. However, since the adequacy of any given income is so obviously dependent on the size of the household which must subsist on it, we have, like Henry (1975), obtained a separate poverty line on the above basis for each household size from 1-person to 10+ persons. On this basis, the proportion of households that are poor - the *head count ratio* - was 37 percent in 1971/72 and 33 percent in 1975/76. At both surveys, the head count ratio was highest for 1-person households (50 and 48 percent respectively) and declined, as household size increased up to households with 8 persons with the single but important exception, in each survey, that poverty was higher among 6-person households than among 5-person households.

In order to calculate summary indices of poverty, such as the *Gini Coefficient* of poverty, the households of different size had to be brought to a common basis. This was done by treating 1-person households as the standard for each survey and transposing the income of larger households to the 1-person equivalent by using a ratio (r_s) to multiply the income of the given household, where (r_s) is derived by dividing the poverty line for 1-person households by that for the given household size.

On this basis, and using the 1-person household income equivalent in each survey, the average income of the poor was TT$34 in 1971/72 and TT$63 in 1975/76. The *Gini Coefficient* of poverty fell significantly from .17 in 1971/72 to .12 at the later survey. Decomposing this summary measure into: (a) inequality among the poor, on the one hand, and (b) inequality between the poor as a whole and the non-poor (Hamad and Takayama (1977)), there was greater inequality among the poor - the *Gini Coefficient* of the poor being .28 and .21 in the two surveys respectively - than between the poor and the rich, the indices for which were .15 and .11 respectively. As these figures indicate, both indices fell by about one-half between 1971/72 and 1975/76.

The other commonly used index the *poverty gap ratio* [6] - fell from .52 in 1971/72 to .43 in 1975/76. All indicators therefore point to a reduction in the inequality of income both among the poor and between the poor and the non-poor, while there was also some improvement in the general level of relative poverty in the country in the short period under review.

Data are available, at present, which show, for 1971/72, the relationship between poverty and the characteristics of the household or the head of household. We now use the head count ratio to give a quick indication of the differential levels of poverty.

The proportion poor was very much higher in rural areas (49 percent) than in urban areas (30 percent) though, as we have stressed earlier, the fact that the value of home produced food is excluded from income would tend to overstate the difference between the two areas. Between 25 and 28 percent of the households in Port of Spain, San Fernado and St. George (county) were poor in 1971/72 as compared with 43-55 percent in the rest of Trinidad, and 43 percent in Tobago. The above comment about the exclusion of home produced food from income would again be relevant here.

Poverty was highest among 1- and 2-person households, the head count ratio being 50 and 44 percent respectively. Poverty continued to decline as household size increased to a minimum of 27 percent for 8-person and 10+ person households and slightly more for 9-person households. In fact, the head count ratio was greater for households consisting of 1 adult and 1 child (69 percent) than for single person households (50 percent). As before, poverty declined as the number of adults increased, whatever the household composition, from 37 percent for households with 2 adults (with or without children) to 12 percent for those with 5 adults or more. Among households with 2 adults, the proportion poor declined as the number of children increased, somewhat surprisingly, from 40 percent with no children to 31 percent for those with 3 children. Thereafter poverty was somewhat higher being 39 and 37 percent respectively for those households with 2 adults and 4 and 5+ children respectively.

Turning now to the characteristics of the head of household: Poverty was highest in households with female heads and with heads 65 years old and over as we have already indicated.

Understandably, the proportion poor was higher among persons engaged in Agriculture, either as an occupation (59) or as an industry (56) than among other persons in the working population. Poverty in other occupations ranged from 40 percent for sales workers and 33 percent for service workers to 6-8 percent for professional and technical workers, administrative workers and clerical workers. Among the non-Agricultural industries, poverty was highest where the head of households was in manufacturing (31) or transport (33) and lowest in mining and quarrying (6). Both in the classification by occupation and by industry, however, households in

167

which the head was not in the working population had
the highest level of poverty (65 percent).

Finally, we consider the relationship
between the poverty of the household and (a) the
ethnic origin and (b) level of education of the head.
Poverty was lowest among households in which the head
was of European descent (8 percent). It was very
much higher for households where the head was of
African or Mixed origin (33 percent) and higher still
where the head was Indian (45 percent). In the
breakdown by education, poverty was highest where the
head had no education (51), intermediate where the
head had primary education only (39), and lowest
where the head had incomplete secondary education
(17). Surprisingly, the residual group, which
includes those with completed secondary and higher
education as well as smaller numbers of persons not
classifiable in this pattern have a much higher level
of poverty (32) than preceding group. This may be
due to the fact that the highest group includes
miscellaneous persons not classifiable in the first
three, which may be distorting the position as regards
those with the highest education. This needs some
further examination.

UNEMPLOYMENT AND POVERTY

I have argued above and elsewhere (Harewood,
1978) that the available evidence does not confirm
that there is a very close relationship between unemployment and poverty in the Caribbean. Undoubtedly
there are very many cases in which as a result of
unemployment, individuals and households suffer
severe economic hardship and poverty. However, the
popular conception that the poor consist mainly of
the unemployed and that the incidence of poverty is
higher among the unemployed than among any other
group is not supported by the available information.

We can test these relationships by using
the data on relative poverty for Trinidad and Tobago
which we have been discussing above. An important
shortcoming of these and other available data, however, is that unemployment is essentially a measurement of the status of the individual while poverty

relates to the household. We can, however, derive some indication of the relationship between unemployment and poverty by studying a cross-classification of poverty by the employment status of the head of the household. This is not entirely satisfactory as we are ignoring the fact that the head of the household need not be the only or even the principal income earner in his household. Bearing this shortcoming in mind, let us examine the available data for 1971/72 for Trinidad.

As is seen in Table 1, first of all, the households in which the head is unemployed comprise only 13 percent of the poor households. Indeed, of the poor households in 1971/72, the head was employed in 55 percent of the cases: in one-third of the cases as a paid employee (Government 8 percent and non-Government 25 percent), and 22 percent as an own account worker.

TABLE 1. PERCENT DISTRIBUTION OF POOR HOUSEHOLDS AND THE INCIDENCE OF POVERTY BY EMPLOYMENT STATUS OF HEAD OF HOUSEHOLDS FOR (a) ALL HOUSEHOLDS, AND (b) ONE-ADULT HOUSEHOLDS 1971/72

Employment Status of Head of Household	All Households		One Adult Households	
	Percentage Distribution	Incidence of Poverty	Percentage Distribution	Incidence of Poverty
Total	100.0	37.0 (2,744)	100.0	55.5 (605)
Paid Employee: Government	8.4	13.0 (655)	3.3	11.5 (96)
Paid Employee: Non-Government	24.8	26.7 (939)	18.8	35.4 (178)
Employer	1.0	21.7 (46)	0.6	33.3* (6)

TABLE 1. PERCENT DISTRIBUTION OF POOR
HOUSEHOLDS AND THE INCIDENCE OF POVERTY
BY EMPLOYMENT STATUS OF HEAD OF
HOUSEHOLDS FOR (a) ALL HOUSEHOLDS, AND
(b) ONE-ADULT HOUSEHOLDS 1971/72 Cont'd

Employment Status of Head of Household	All Households			One Adult Households		
	Percentage Distribution	Incidence of Poverty		Percentage Distribution	Incidence of Poverty	
Self-Employed	21.8	52.6	(420)	18.4	69.7	(89)
Unemployed	12.9	73.2	(179)	17.3	86.6	(67)
Retired	7.8	61.2	(129)	5.1	77.3	(22)
Old Age Pensioner	13.3	81.3	(166)	21.4	96.0	(75)
Not Classifiable	10.1	48.6	(210)	15.2	70.8	(72)

*No. of cases inadequate.

The number of heads of poor households who were old age pensioners and who were unemployed were similar (13 percent), while 8 percent were retired and 20 percent were not classifiable by employment status.

The incidence of poverty was in fact very high among households with an unemployed head for three quarters of the households in which the head was unemployed were classified as poor. This compares with 13-26 percent of those households where the head was employed and nearly one-half where the head was not classifiable by employment status. The incidence of poverty was, however, higher among households headed by old age pensioners (81 per cent) than among those headed by unemployed persons, while the incidence among those with a retired head was also very high (61 per cent).

Poverty is, therefore, a very serious problem for households with an unemployed head, though it is even worse where the head is an old age pensioner. This approach, moreover, greatly overstates the relationship between poverty and unemployment, as it excludes precisely those households in which the unemployed person is a dependent, including the young unemployed, and is therefore not the principal income-earner in the household. According to the Continuous Sample Survey of Population (CSSP), in 1971 only one in five of unemployed persons was the head of a household. Unfortunately we are unable, at this stage, to identify all households in which at least one person was unemployed in the Household Budgetary Surveys.

From Table 1 it is clear, on the other hand, that poverty is much more widespread than unemployment, and hence the solving of the unemployment problem would not, of itself, greatly affect the level of poverty. Indeed, if we exclude the households with an unemployed head from the analysis entirely, the head count ratio of poverty would fall by only 2 percentage points from 37 to 35 percent. This latter figure can be taken as indicative of the level of poverty that would have existed in 1971 if unemployment among heads of households had not existed.

Although we are unable at this stage to classify households according to the number of persons unemployed in the household, we can identify households in which the main breadwinner is unemployed by restricting our attention to households with only one adult. The level of poverty among these one adult households is also shown in Table 1.

First, we should point out that poverty is much greater among households with one adult plus children than among single person households, the head count ratio for the former being 69 percent as against 50 percent for the latter. Moreover, among the former, *all* households which were headed by an unemployed person, a retired person or an old age pensioner were classified as poor.

Returning to the Table, it will be seen, that as in the case of all households together, households in which the head was unemployed comprised only a small proportion (17 percent) of all households. There was a larger number of poor households in which the head was an old age pensioner (21 percent) or an own account worker (18 percent). Here again, the incidence of poverty was very high among unemployed households (87 percent) but was very much higher yet among households dependent on old age pension, of whom only 4 percent were not classified as poor. The incidence of poverty was also high, though somewhat lower than among the unemployed, in households in which the single adult was retired (77 percent) not classifiable by employment status (71 percent) or self-employed (70 percent). About one-third of the single-adult households in which the adult was either a non-Government employee or an employer were poor, the numbers for the latter group being very small. Poverty was least (11.5 percent) among the single-adult households where the adult was employed by Government.

The restriction of this analysis to single-adult households has, as we have indicated, shown as unemployed households those in which there was no employed or other adult but the unemployed person. It, therefore, has tended to deal with cases in which unemployment is most likely to be associated with poverty. It confirms that the incidence of poverty is very high among the unemployed single adult households, but not as high as among such households dependent on old age pension only. Moreover, this comprises only a small proportion of the total problem of poverty.

PROGRAMMES AND MEASURES TO REDUCE UNEMPLOYMENT AND POVERTY

We shall now review and assess, in this section, some of the principal programmes and measures through which governments of the Region have attempted, during the past two decades or so, to reduce the incidence of unemployment and poverty and to mitigate the disadvantages of the unemployed and the poor. In the following section, we shall consider the impact of these programmes and measures. Although the circumstances and the programmes of the various

countries of the Region have been remarkably similar
in a number of important respects, there have been
sufficient significant differences to prevent a
general statement for the region as a whole. However,
it would be beyond the scope of the present study to
deal in any meaningful detail with each separate
country of the Region. We must, therefore, select
for consideration some of the more important measures
and their results, drawing attention where relevant,
to similarities and differences between countries.

As we have already indicated, as national
government took over political responsibility for
the various Commonwealth Caribbean countries, they
put especial emphasis on development strategies
which emphasized economic growth through industrialization as a means of solving the social and economic
problems and in particular unemployment and poverty.
In due course this approach has been modified, for
the reasons already mentioned, to include aspects of
the later employment-oriented and poverty-oriented
strategies. In at least one country in the Region -
Guyana - a basic needs approach has been espoused. In
this, and the following section, we shall rely largely
on the case of Trinidad and Tobago to exemplify the
Lewis strategy and the subsequent modifications along
the lines of the employment and poverty-oriented
strategies. We shall use Guyana as the single real
example of the basic needs approach. The choice of
these two countries has been primarily determined by
the availability of recent studies covering the area
in which we are interested.[7] The case of Trinidad is
however, fortuitous in that country has gone through
the stages of economic hardships that others have
experienced, though with its oil industry it has
always been somewhat more fortunate than many of the
others, but in addition it is now experiencing a
period of unprecedented prosperity based, again, on
its oil industry. We can therefore see how the
approaches mentioned fare both in times of economic
stringency and in times of economic prosperity.

Trinidad provides a useful indication of
how non-ideological factors have caused changes in
development strategy, since the country has had the
same political party and the same political leader[8]
in power during the past two decades and more. When

the People's National Movement first came into power
in 1956, Trinidad had been experiencing a long period
of prosperity. At the start of World War 11, there
was a diversified export agricultural sector including sugar, cacao, coffee, citrus and tonca beans,
and an increasingly important petroleum industry.
The setting up of US military bases in the country
led to further rapid expansion. In the post-war
period, through the 1950 *Aid to Pionner Industries*
Ordinance and other measures, early efforts at
industrialization were having some effect. The
P.N.M. Government took steps to increase the speed
and the scope of development.

        The post-war boom continued until 1961,
after which there was a slowing down in the economy
in the period 1962-1965 followed by a limited
improvement in the period 1966-1968. Another
economic reversal ensued starting in 1969 and lasting
until 1973, and this was considerably more serious
than the preceding ones. The national prosperity in
the post-war period was based upon the petroleum
industry and, more directly, on the production of
crude petroleum. In the period 1969-1972, however,
crude oil production fell by 30 percent and this
resulted in balance of payments and fiscal problems,
and serious inflation towards the end of the period.
Because of this worsening economic and social situation, there was political and social unrest which
reached its zenith in 1970 when there were 'black
power' demonstrations and disorders capped off by an
attempted military coup. The dramatic increases in
petroleum prices starting in late 1973, and the
fortuitous discovery and exploitation of vast new
marine oil reserves, have resulted in unprecedented
national proseprity and a most spectacular increase
in Government finances. From 1974, therefore, and
increasingly thereafter, money has not been an
important constraint on efforts to deal with unemployment and poverty.

        In its first five-year plan - 1958-1962 -
on which, as we have said, Arthur Lewis was a con-
sultant/adviser, the Government adopted the 'Puerto
Rican model' or the 'Lewis strategy' as it is also
called, and which was popularised in Lewis (1950).
This plan's approach to major development problems,
which remained unchanged for most of the 1960's,

saw Government's role as principally to create the conditions necessary for the more effective undertaking by the private sector of the task which it had already begun, of increasing the output of goods and services upon which any improvement in the general standard of living must depend. The Government's view was that once the right conditions were provided, including appropriate institutional structures and adequate incentives to industry along the lines set out in Lewis (1950) and briefly described earlier, the private sector in response would both transform the economy and generate the jobs necessary to alleviate the most critical social ills of unemployment and poverty.

The emphasis, then, was on *economic* development through which the jobs would be provided to solve the problem of unemployment which, in turn would contribute to the solution of poverty. For the short run, however, the Government sought to alleviate the situation of the lower income groups by providing social amenities like subsidised housing, education, health and the like.

In the second five-year plan - 1964-1968 - the approach remained one of relying on the private sector to provide the jobs while the public sector provided the social amenities. However, since the provision of adequate jobs in this way was clearly turning out to be impossible in the short run, a Government *Special Works Programme* was instituted. This programme was to be the instrument for undertaking some needed public work, e.g. road repairs, but its true objective was to contribute to lowering unemployment by providing relief work on a rotational basis, each participating worker being guaranteed five days' work per fortnight.

But this approach to development, by now dubbed 'development by invitation' was considerably modified in the third five-year plan (1969-1973). It was by then clear that the manufacturing sector was making negligible contribution to growth in employment and was having no impact on unemployment. There was, therefore, a shift away from reliance on the private sector and towards Government's direct intervention in productive activity including joint ventures with local and/or foreign firms, one of the principal objectives being to save or increase jobs. Another important and related objective was to shift the locus of decision-making from the metropole to the local environment. It was felt that jobs could be saved or increased partly because nationalization could make some otherwise threatened industries viable, and partly because the Government, as compared to the local private sector, could adopt the longer view and had more resources, and hence could give greater emphasis to eliminating unemployment. This heralded, therefore, a shift towards an unemployment-oriented strategy.

But, as indicated earlier, the year 1969 heralded the start of a period of serious economic reversal which lasted until 1973. Despite the economic, social and political problems that ensued, and indeed spurred on by them, the Government directed greater effort to improving the social conditions of the less privileged and especially to reducing the high level of unemployment. To this end, an 'unemployment levy' of 5 percent was imposed on all chargeable income (personal and corporation) in excess of TT$10,000,[9] and this fund was used to provide work, on a rotational basis, to the unemployed as well as to provide for their training and upgrading. This was in addition to the 'Special Works Programme' which had been started in the 1960's and which provided relief employment in local areas. The money obtained from this levy was used in housing, slum clearance, training, education and youth development, and for labour intensive works projects.

In addition, a National Insurance Scheme, weighted in favour of the poor workers, was launched in 1972, and a programme of bulk purchasing of rice, a staple in the diets of lower and middle income groups, was instituted.

In this period, also, the programme of subsidies that was initiated in the agricultural sector in the 1960's was extended. The subsidies cover fertilizers, high quality seedlings, planting material and livestock and other items, as well as for soil conservation, land preparation, bee-keeping, grass planting and the establishment of approved tree

crop orchards. These were all designed to improve
the lot of the small farmer in particular. At the
end of the Third Five-Year Plan, the Government
decided to discontinue the practice of planning in
five-year cycles and adopted, instead, a system of
project or sector specific plan formulation. The
reason given for this was that since the flow of
revenue was dependent on a highly fluid international
economic and political order, it was far more meaningful to plan in terms of very specific projects.

In this period of oil prosperity since
1974, with a view to eliminating structural unemployment for the future, the Government has placed much
emphasis on the development of industrial activities.
These activities concentrated in the Point Lisas area
in the central western area of the island of Trinidad,
include the establishment of an iron and steel
complex, expansion of electricity generation and of
cement production, establishment of ventures for the
production of fertilizer, of Methanol, and of Amonia
and the establishment of an aluminium smelter, all
to utilize the vast available natural gas as a source
of fuel. Action in the field of Agriculture included
further subsidies, the acquisition of old estates and
the distribution of their lands to small farmers, the
setting up of a fishing fleet and a fishing complex
and so forth, while consideration is being given to
rationalizing the sugar industry including the
transfer of lands from sugar to food production by
small production by small farmers.

To improve the welfare of the population, a
wide ranging set of programmes have been initiated
including: subsidization of a wide variety of foodstuffs, of the cost of cement, of gasolene and of the
operations of the public utilities such as water,
bus transport and electricity, all with a view to
keeping down the cost of living of the consumer;
provision of loans for home construction; increase in
old age pension and public assistance together with a
Food Stamp programme and free bus transporation for
the aged and needy; provision of free bus transportation for school children, introduction of a school
nutrition programme, free school medical and dental
services, a grant for books, the payment of examination fees and so forth all for primary and/or

secondary school children as applicable, while apart
from a large programme of scholarships to university,
the fees of all nationals attending the University of
the West Indies are met from public funds.

Turning now to Guyana, Standing (1979)
claimed that that country was one of the few in the
world in which "the Government is openly committed to
what could be described as a 'basic needs' strategy
of development", the Government having proclaimed,
in 1971, that "we must feed, clothe and house ourselves by 1976".[10]

The economy of Guyana is largely based on
three export crops - sugar, bauxite and rice - which,
between them, accounted for 38 percent of the GDP
and 87 percent of total export earnings in 1976.
Other important features of the economy, according to
Standing, are: (a) that the economy is very "open"
and its "openness" is increasing and hence the economy
is highly vulnerable to fluctuations in world trade
in primary goods; and (b) state control of the
economy has grown rapidly.

The Government has been anxious to diversify
production, notably by encouraging food production
and "has assumed greater control over national assets
by nationalizing the previously foreign-owned sugar
and bauxite industries". But the country remains
very dependent on imports. Moreover, factors such as
the precipitate fall in sugar prices after 1975 to
one-fifth of the peak level, and the greatly increased
national debt as a result of the nationalizations
mentioned have caused a serious shortage of foreign
reserves which is a serious threat to the country's
economic development strategy.

A unique feature of Guyana is that both
the Government party (the People's National Congress)
and the main opposition party (the People's Progressive Party) are publicly committed to the "socialist
principles of public ownership of the means of
production and to the eradication of poverty as their
highest socio-economic objective".

The country became independent in 1966 and
a 'Co-operative Republic' in 1970. The Government's

ideology is avowed to be 'Co-operative Socialism',
the co-operative being the means by which the small
man can play a dominant role in the economy, and
socialism providing the vehicle for the worker to
take control of the economic structure. As the
co-operative movement is not yet dominant, however,
reliance has been put, for the present, on
nationalization as a means of achieving control of
the economy for the people.

Elaborating on its basic needs strategy,
the *Guyana Development Plan 1972-1976* points out that
not only must the country be able to "feed, clothe
and house the nation", but "must itself determine the
pace and direction of its social and economic development". In this context, especial attention need to
be given to: (a) a substantial and continuing
improvement in income distribution; and (b) providing
employment opportunities for all adult nationals.

The country has had little success in
achieving these lofty ideals. Standing (*op. cit.*)
devotes much attention to demonstrating this failure
and seeking to find reasons for it. One of the
greatest failings of the Plan, according to Standing,
was that it made no provision for incorporating
workers into the economic and social decision-making
processes nor did it make local government a viable
vehicle for achieving community development. The
continued political division of the society on racial
grounds is also seen as a major reason for the lack
of success.

After analysing, from the often inadequate
information available on the level of and trends in
income distribution and of wealth, health and
nutrition, living conditions and economic participation, Standing concludes that "poverty and inequalities of various kinds remain serious". From a Labour
Force Survey carried out in 1976 an unofficial
estimate of unemployment indicated that the unemployment level was 19 percent of the labour force. There
was no direct information on household income distribution adequate to indicate levels of or trends in
income inequality and poverty. However, the indications were that the situation remained very unfavour-
able. For example, information on the factoral

distribution on income indicated "that in the recent past workers in Guyana were receiving a relatively small share of the total national income compared with many other countries", though "in the 1950's the share was even smaller". Land reforms and a substantial rise in public sector employment were thought to be responsible for the increased share of national income, but the low levels were thought to be the result of the capital-intensive nature of the production process particularly in bauxite.

There was evidence, however, that the Government's expenditure policies had probably made some contribution to an improvement in income distribution. Thus, total government expenditure as a proportion of GNP increased substantially since the early 1950's and more so since 1964. There has also been a shift in expenditure towards the social services - education, rural infrastructure development, and housing for example. Other financial measures that have probably improved income distribution include: a system of subsidies, price controls, and a national pension scheme.

A comprehensive nutrition survey conducted in 1971 (PAHO 1976), indicated a widespread incidence of malnutrition. Underweight was found to be a general phenomenon and was assumed to be one of the effects of malnutrition. Malnutrition was found to be more severe in rural areas and among the Indian population who were mainly rural dwellers. One of the reasons for malnutrition among Indians was thought to be the religious prohibitions against the eating of meat among Hindus and Muslims.

The 1970 Population Census suggested that there was overcrowding and poor quality in housing as well as a lack of access to potable water, adequate sanitation etc. For example, only about one-third of all households had water piped into their homes, the situation being considerably better in Georgetown than in the rest of the country.

As we have indicated earlier, the basic needs approach puts great emphasis on the economic participation and economic involvement of workers. Standing feels that "this is an aspect of Guyana's

development where government failure is most evident",
as the massive unemployment, racially segmented
labour force, and widespread insecurity of employment
continue as they did in the colonial period. This
partly reflects the country's historical legacy of
paternalism and the domination of the economy by
multinationals, but equally it indicates that the
"measures taken since independence to overcome that
legacy have been limited and demonstrably inadequate",

Standing is also very critical of the
achievements of co-operatives which have not, so far,
had much impact on either production or increasing
income equality. The development of co-operatives
is necessarily slow and it may be too early to dismiss
their small achievements as ineffectual rather than
a slow transitional build up as the Government believes.

In general, however, Guyana has been under-
going a long period of economic stagnation and neither
the Government's commitment to co-operative socialism
nor to a "basic needs" strategy of development have
been able to achieve any significant improvement in
unemployment or income distribution. The drastic
fall in sugar prices since 1975 coupled with the
rapidly escalating price of petroleum and, to a lesser
extent, price increases in other imported goods have
undoubtedly been a major contributor, and contrasts
with Trinidad's recent prosperity as a producer of
oil.

THE IMPACT OF GOVERNMENT PROGRAMMES AND
OTHER INFLUENCES ON UNEMPLOYMENT AND POVERTY

IMPACT ON UNEMPLOYMENT

As has been made clear in the earlier
discussion, the 'Lewis strategy' or 'industrialization
by invitation' as it has more recently been called,
has not contributed to the reduction in unemployment
in accordance with the very high hopes originally
placed in development through private enterprise. In
the case of Trinidad, apart from the post-1973 period
of oil prosperity, unemployment has not declined

significantly and in some instances has increased
appreciably during the last two decades. Even at
the present time the unemployment rate has not fallen
below about 10 percent of the labour force as
compared with about 15 percent before the period of
prosperity. In Jamaica there has been no decline.
Because of problems with census measures of unemployment already discussed changes in the other countries
are not assumed here to be meaningful.

Our concern in this section is to try to
determine the reason for the failure. The earliest,
simplistic view was that the total solution of the
unemployment problem involved the creation of new
jobs equivalent in *number* to the unemployed, with
little attention to: (a) the characteristics of the
unemployed and how this would affect the types of jobs
needed; or (b) how the creation of new jobs itself,
as well as other related factors, were likely to
affect the demand for jobs and hence the number of
unemployed.

One factor which contributed to an increase
in the demand for jobs was the growth in population
already discussed though since 1960 the rate of
population growth has been less than in the preceding
inter-censal period in the Region as a whole. Another
and very important factor has been that increased
industrialization has been accompanied, in most
countries of the Region by a decline in self-employment and in unpaid family work as paid employment has
increased. For example, in Trinidad own account workers comprised 19 percent of the total working population in 1965 but by 1975 this proportion had fallen
to 14 percent. In the same period, unpaid family
workers declined from 10 to 7 percent. On the other
hand, paid employees increased from 69 to 75 percent
of persons with jobs.

We now consider this situation in Trinidad
in some detail, contrasting the period 1965-1970,
which we take as indicative of the long period of
economic hardship, with the following period which
includes the period of oil prosperity.

In the 5½-year period from mid-1965 to end-
1970 (derived as the mean for the 12 months centered

on these dates), the number of Government employees
increased by 15,100 and the number of 'other'
employees by 11,000 - a total of 25,100: but own-
account jobs fell by 13,400 and there was a very
small decline also in unpaid workers so that the net
increase of jobs was only 12,300. The number of paid
employees, in this interval, increased by 13,300
among large establishments (including Government)
with 10 or more employees while the increase among
small establishments of under 5 employees was almost
as large - 12,500. It is notable, however, that the
increase in large establishments (including Government) was due entirely to the increase in Government
jobs and, in fact, employment in non-Government large
establishments actually fell by nearly 2,000 in this
period.

        In the following 5½-year interval, which
included the period of recent prosperity, the increase
in total jobs was very much larger - 32,100. But on
this occasion the increase in Government jobs (36,000)
exceeded the net total increase while there were
small increases as well among 'other' employees
(4,400) and among own account workers (4,200) while
the number of unpaid workers fell by 12,500. In this
latter period, the increase of 40,400 in paid
employees was the net result of an increase of 36,000
in Government, 9,600 in large non-Government
establishments and 3,000 in medium-sized establishments of less than 5 employees registered a decline
of 8,100 jobs. The increase in own account workers
in this period is significant and is due to the
growing trend, in the recent period of prosperity,
for persons to branch out on their own to provide
professional and personal services to business and to
households and individuals. Lewis (1972) acknowledged
that an increase in paid employment in the modern
sector might not have much impact on unemployment,
pointing out that while "the expansion of the modern
sector of the economy creates new jobs and raises
sharply the incomes of all who live by that sector ...
there is no guarantee that it will not destroy more
jobs than it creates, through its impact on the
traditional sector".

        Returning to the job opportunities provided
by new industries in the modern sector, the fact that

these industries tend to be highly capital-intensive
has meant that, as compared with the additional output they provide, they offer a disappointingly small
number of additional jobs. Moreover, the jobs
created in these 'modern' industries often require a
level of education and skill much higher than that
available among the existing unemployed. The result
has tended to be that better qualified persons who
were not previously in the labour force (e.g. house-
wives and retired persons) are likely to be drafted
into employment. But perhaps much more important
has been an increasing demand for highly trained
immigrant workers to meet the demands of the new
industries. In Trinidad in the 10-year period 1968-
1977, for example, 10,000 new work permits were
granted to bring in workers, three-quarters of these
being white collar workers. (Harewood (1981)).
Moreover, with that country's recent prosperity the
Government has, since 1979, decided to utilize
Government-to-Government arrangements to obtain
foreign expertise to assist in the large scale infrastructure and industrial projects which it is
seeking to implement with its petro-dollars. This
approach, which involves agreements with a number of
developed countries, has already resulted, in a large
influx of technical and professional workers from
developed countries and this number will greatly
increase in the future. (Harewood - *op. cit.*). It
is seen, therefore, that even a Government with as
much concern for reducing unemployment as that of
Trinidad has found itself pushing rapid development
by employing non-national white collar workers despite
the continuance of a relatively high level of unemployment among nationals.

A further important point which contradicts
the simplistic view that the number of unemployed is
an indicator of the number of new jobs needed is the
fact that when well-paid jobs in the modern sector
become available, a number of persons are willing to
offer themselves for such jobs who were not previously
classified as unemployed. Among these will be the
large number of involuntarily under-employed as well
as many persons, particularly women, who were not
formerly in the labour force. A special case of the
first point was given in Harewood (1960). This dealt
with the seasonal increase in 'well-paid' jobs in the
sugar cane crop season. He noted that between

November 1956 (out-of-crop) and March 1957 (crop season) the number of jobs as paid employees increased by about 10,000, the majority of these being 'well-paid' jobs. But this increase led to a reduction of only 2,500 in unemployment, although about 20,000 persons were unemployed and seeking work at the time. The remaining 7,500 jobs were filled by 1,000 persons not previously in the labour force and 6,500 persons who were in the labour force but not as paid employees, comprising 1,000 unpaid apprentices, 2,000 unpaid family workers and 3,500 small-scale own account workers - all presumably in the low-earning under-employed sector. This pattern of seasonal change has been considered to be likely to hold true also for secular change.

Given the large proportion of the unemployed who are young and untrained, the problem must, to a large extent, be a special problem of the young and as such, its solution may need much more attention to extending the provisions for education and training to ensure that these young persons who are seeking to enter the labour force are really equipped, both as regards training and attitude, to undertake productive and well-remunerated jobs and prospective employers must see them as such. To this extent, then, again the solution of the problem is not merely the indiscriminate provision of additional jobs. Furthermore, the provision of full time training for these young persons would result in an immediate reduction in the inflated unemployment rate and, at the same time, ensure a higher quality of worker with a much greater demand for his services when his training is complete.

In the early period of national efforts at economic development, the governments of the Region soon became aware that 'industrialization by invitation' was not having any substantial, immediate impact on the unemployment situation and hence, in order to put some brake on the rising unemployment levels, most governments turned to some type of 'crash programme' in public works as we have already indicated. Jamaica and Trinidad, the two countries which form the basis of much of our discussion, both put great emphasis on such programmes as far as funds were available.

But while the 'crash' programmes in the various countries have undoubtedly provided jobs to a number of persons, their impact on unemployment, too, has been disappointing. There are a number of reasons for this, some of which are merely special cases of points already made with respect to the failure of the 'development' approach to reducing unemployment. First, to a large extent, the 'crash' programmes which, in fact, paid relatively high wages, attracted a significant number of persons from Agriculture and other low-income jobs. The result tended largely to be, therefore, a shift in employment and, very probably, a real reduction in low-income under-employment. This does not mean that the unemployed did not share in the 'crash' programme jobs, but that the reduction in unemployment was considerably less than the increase in 'crash' programme jobs.

An important factor is that the idea of a 'crash programme' to reduce unemployment ignores the fact that a very large proportion of the unemployed were, as we noted earlier, young persons with middle levels of education and hence motivated towards lower and middle level white collar jobs rather than towards manual labour on the repair of roads and the like.

A point related to the 'crash programmes' that is conveniently interjected here is that these programmes have been blamed for a serious reduction in the 'work ethic' in a number of countries in the Region, precisely because they were conceived and accepted as programmes to provide persons with some income and with insufficient attention to production and productivity. Workers in these programmes are notorious for being on the job for only a few of the hours for which they are paid and for making little effort to be productive while they are at the work site. This approach is believed to have spilled over into other sectors of the economy and the 'crash programme' attitude is held responsible for what is believed to be a massive reduction in productivity over the past two decades. While serious reduction in productivity has undoubtedly occurred, it seems certain that 'management' in both the private and the public sectors must also share a large part of the blame. As regards the private sector, the 'Lewis strategy' incentives themselves are thought to have

permitted firms in the modern sector to be guaranteed
a profit despite their inefficiency largely by pass-
ing on the price of their inefficiency to the
consumer in the captured markets.

Finally, an important consideration to which
little attention has been given in the past, is the
attitudes and aspirations of the people for whom jobs
are being created in the various programmes aimed at
reducing unemployment. A number of factors, in
addition to those already mentioned, clearly indicate
that the mere creation of jobs - any kinds of jobs -
will not attract the unemployed. For example, despite
the high level of unemployment in the Region, certain
types of unskilled and semi-skilled jobs remain un-
filled. Many of the countries have had, therefore to
consider resorting to immigration for some of these
jobs among them being the cutting of sugar cane once
again. Lewis (1954) saw domestic service as one of
the most important sectors providing marginal jobs
and hence keeping down open unemployment in countries
with a surplus of labour. But despite the high levels
of unemployment in the Caribbean this sector is fast
dying out, and this at a time when increasing proportions of women from middle income groups are going
out to work and would therefore be both able and
happy to retain at least one domestic servant. Lewis
(*op. cit.*) also drew attention to the importance of
petty trading, in this regard, but here again this
sector has apparently been declining despite the high
levels of unemployment.

We have also already argued that the jobs
created in government 'crash programmes' may well be
unattractive to the young unemployed with a fair
education. We have shown that in general as the
socio-economic situation improves people tend to shift
away from self-employment towards jobs as paid employees, yet, in Trinidad since 1974, with its new prosperity, there has been a reverse trend.

There is evident need for much more attention and study to be given to attitudes and aspirations, as we have said, both with a view to modifying
development programmes and to attempting, where this
seems appropriate, to modify these attitudes and
aspirations in accordance with the country's best
interests. Improvement in the 'work ethic' and other

measures to improve productivity at all levels of
both management and labour could be a special aspect
of the latter.

IMPACT ON POVERTY

There has long been concern with income
inequality and poverty in the Commonwealth Caribbean,
and this concern has greatly increased in recent
years. As we have already indicated, poverty has
usually been seen as the result of, or at least
directly related to, unemployment. A clear enucia-
tion of this was made in Guyana's Second Development
Plan for 1972-1976 which stated that "the problem of
unemployment is associated with that of unequal
distribution of income which is intensified by the
larger numbers of unemployed adults to be found in
families with small incomes". The first two
objectives of the Plan, therefore, were: (a) the
creation of employment opportunities for all Guyanese;
and (b) the attainment of an equitable distribution
of income.

We have already dealt with the programmes
and measures taken with regard to unemployment and in
this sub-section, therefore, we shall be mainly
concerned with programmes and measures other than
these and which relate more specifically to poverty
and income inequality. First, however, we will
discuss very briefly the impact that the 'unemployment' programmes have had on poverty. As we have
indicated, the two principal approaches to the
problem of unemployment were the creation of jobs
through: (a) rapid industrialization; and (b) Government 'crash programmes'.

As regards 'industrialization by invitation',
Best et al have argued that in Trinidad the array of
incentives contributed to a shift of income towards
profits and hence a worsening of income inequality and
poverty. Furthermore the considerable loss of customs
duty and direct taxes through these incentives meant
that a disproportionate tax burden had to be borne by
the consumer in the form of import tax of consumer
goods to the detriment of the low income groups.
Finally, while large establishments in the staple and

quasi-staple sectors flourished and were forced, in their struggle with the trade unions, to make reasonable provision for workers in these industries, and while workers in Government as well as the professional services class also prospered, the workers in the "poorly organised, unorganised or disorganised residentiary sector" tended to suffer. These and allied factors would have contributed to the worsening of income distribution and poverty already discussed in the period preceding the oil boom in Trinidad. The same analysis will no doubt hold, with minor deviations, for the other countries of the Region.

The 'crash programmes' on the other hand, did succeed in increasing the income of the lower income groups and hence would have made some contribution to relieving poverty depending on the resources available to the Governments for this purpose.

The other measures which have been taken specifically to affect income distribution and poverty have taken the form primarily of welfare expenditures, while some fiscal reforms have also been carried out to this end. The extent to which such measures have been taken has depended most of all on the available government resources, the political ideology of the governments notwithstanding. We have, for example, described earlier the major welfare expenditures of the Trinidad government both prior to and since its period of oil prosperity and indicated that similar measures have been taken by the other governments in the Region within their available resources.

FOOTNOTES

1. See for example, Caribbean Commission (1948) and HMSO (1953).

2. Craig (1975).

3. In both Trinidad and Jamaica data are available for two periods each year, January to June and July to December, and the months of April and October for Jamaica. Unless otherwise stated, the figures used in this section related to the annual average in each case.

4. The Jamaica figures relate to the population 14 years and over; while the Trinidad figures are for persons 15 years and over.

5. By Leo Pujadas, Director of Statistics, Trinidad in a personal comment on this analysis.

6. The poverty gap ratio is the difference (gap) between the total income that would have been obtained by the poor if each poor household received the poverty line income and the total income actually received by the poor, this gap being expressed as a ratio of the former.

7. Harewood and Henry (1981) for Trinidad and Tobago, and Standing (1979) for Guyana.

8. Dr. Eric Williams, Prime Minister of Trinidad and Tobago and political leader of the P.N.M. died while in office on the 29th March 1981.

9. Raised to $20,000 in 1980.

10. Unless otherwise stated, all quotations re Guyana are from Standing (1979).

REFERENCES

ADAMS, I.W., PENZ, P. & CAMERON, B. (1971) - *The Real Poverty Reports*. Hurtington, Edmonton.

AHIRAM, E. (1966) - "Distribution of Income in Trinidad and Tobago and Comparison with Distribution of Income in Jamaica". *SOCIAL AND ECONOMIC STUDIES*. Vol. 15, No. 2, June.

BRATHWAITE, FARLEY S. (1979) - *Unemployment and Social Life: A Sociological Study of the Unemployed in Trinidad*. Ph. D. Thesis.

BEST, Lloyd *et al* (1979) - *International Co-operation in the Industrialization Process: The Case of Trinidad and Tobago*. A study prepared by the *TRINIDAD AND TOBAGO INSTITUTE OF THE WEST INDIES* under the direction of Lloyd Best, for UNIDO.

CARIBBEAN COMMISSION (1948) - *Industrial Development in the British Territories of the Caribbean*. Report prepared by the British member of the Industrial Survey Panel of the Commission. 2 Vols.

CRAIG, Susan E. (1974) - *Community Development in Trinidad and Tobago: 1943-1973: From Welfare to Patronage*. Working Paper No. 4 of the I.S.E.R., University of the West Indies, Jamaica.

CRAIG, Susan E. (1975) - *The Germs of an Idea*. Mimeo. I.S.E.R., University of the West Indies, Trinidad.

C.S.O. (1965) - *Consumer Price Index*. Unpublished Departmental Note on the 1957/58 Household Budgetary Survey. Central Statistical Office, Trinidad and Tobago.

FARRELL, Trevor M.A. (1978) - "The Unemployment Crisis in Trinidad and Tobago: Its Current Dimensions and Some Projections to 1985". *SOCIAL AND ECONOMIC STUDIES*. Vol. 27, No. 2, June.

GOVERNMENT OF GUYANA (*Circa* 1972) - *Draft Second Development Plan 1972-1976*. Ministry of Economic Development.

HAMADA, Koichi & TAKAYAMA, Noriyuki (1977) - "Censored Income Distributions and the Measurement of Poverty". International Statistical Institute Conference. New Delhi.

HAREWOOD, Jack (1960) - "Over-population and Under-development in the West Indies" *INTERNATIONAL LABOUR REVIEW*. Vol. LXXXll, No. 2.

HAREWOOD, Jack (Ed. 1972) - *Human Resources in the Commonwealth Caribbean*. Report of the Hunam Resources Seminar in 1970. I.S.E.R., University of the West Indies. Trinidad.

HAREWOOD, Jack (1977) - "Poverty and Basic Needs" in Harewood, Jack (Ed.): *Unemployment, CARIBBEAN ISSUES*. Vo. lll, Nos. 2 and 3.

HAREWOOD, Jack (1978) - "Unemployment and Related Problems in the Commonwealth Caribbean". *I.S.E.R. OCCASIONAL PAPERS*. Human Resources, No. 2.

HAREWOOD, Jack (1981) - "White Collar Migrant Labour - Some Observations on the Case of Trinidad and Tobago in the Last Two Decades". Paper prepared for the Symposium on *White Collar Migrant Labour*. International Union of Anthropological and Ethnological Sciences. Amsterdam.

HENRY, Ralph M. (1975) - "A Note on Income Distribution and Poverty in Trinidad and Tobago". *C.S.O. RESEARCH PAPERS*. No. 8.

HENRY, Ralph M. (1981) - "Poverty by Size of Household Based on 1971/72 Expenditure, 1975/76 Income, and 1975/76 Expenditure". Unpublished calculations.

HMSO (1953) - *Industrial Development in Jamaica, Trinidad, Barbados and British Guiana*. Report of a mission of United Kingdom Industrialists.

ILO (1955) - *The Eighth International Conference of Labour Statisticians, 1954.* Report of the Conference. International Labour Office, Geneva.

ILO (1976) - *Employment, Growth and Basic Needs: A One-World Problem.* International Labour Office, Geneva.

LAURENCE, K.O. (1971) - *Immigration into the West Indies in the Nineteenth Century.* CARIBBEAN UNIVERSITY PRESS.

LEWIS, W. Arthur (*Circa* 1945) - "An Economic Plan for Jamaica

LEWIS, W. Arthur (1949) - "Industrial Development in Puerto Rico". *CARIBBEAN ECONOMIC REVIEW.* Vol. 1, Nos. 1 and 2.

LEWIS, W. Arthur (1950) - "Industrial Development of the British West Indies" *CARIBBEAN ECONOMIC REVIEW.* Vol. 2, No. 1.

LISK, Franklyn (1977) - "Conventional Development Strategies and Basic Needs Fulfilment: *INTERNATIONAL LABOUR REVIEW.* Vol. 115, No. 2, March-April.

MOYNE (1945) - *West India Royal Commission Report.* (Moyne Report). HMSO, London, (CMD 6608).

STANDING, Guy (1979) - "Socialism and Basic Needs in Guyana" in: Standing, Guy and Szal, Richard: *Poverty and Basic Needs: Evidence from Guyana and the Phillipines.* International Labour Office. Geneva.

EDUCATION, UNEMPLOYMENT AND GOVERNMENT
JOB CREATION FOR GRADUATED IN LDCs

by
Ake G. Blomqvist*

INTRODUCTION

One of the most difficult and politically
sensitive policy problems facing LDC governments
during the last two decades, has been that of preventing a high rate of unemployment among graduates
of the rapidly expanding educational systems,
especially from the secondary and higher levels. The
underlying causes of the problem have been well described by Professor Lewis, writing in the mid-nine-
teen sixties (Lewis, 1966). During the 1950s and
early 1960s, both the stocks of educated nationals
and the capacities of most LDC educational systems to
add to the stock, were quite small. Wages and salaries of educated manpower were very high relative to
the wages of unskilled workers, and many of the jobs
in the educated categories were held by foreigners.

Starting around the early 1960s, however, a
very rapid rate of expansion of the higher educational
systems was begun in many LDCs. As a consequence, the
relatively short supply of educated manpower was
quickly changed into its opposite, and there began to
be downward pressure on the wages and salaries of the
educated. But the process diminishing the income
differential between the educated and the unskilled is
painful and slow, and does not take place without
"political trouble" (Lewis 1966, p. 91). In fact, the
process has not gone fast enough to prevent the
emergence of sizable amounts of graduate unemployment,
in part because of the added political difficulty of
letting real wages fall in a market where the government itself is the leading employer.[1]

The problem has also been aggravated by the
limited success of efforts at slowing the rate of inflow into the educational system and the expansion of
educational facilities. In the early sixties, it
certainly made sense to subsidize the cost of education, rather than letting the students themselves (or

194

their parents) pay the cost: with imperfect information, risk aversion, and imperfect capital markets, this seemed a necessary condition to ensure that access to education would not become a privilege of those coming from rich families with educated parents. On the other hand, once a subsidy system is in place, it may be hard to remove, especially in a situation where university students wield a fair amount of political power. Attempts at directly limiting the intake of students to post-secondary institutions, or preventing regional authorities from establishing their own universities, may also entail considerable political costs.

The combination of limited wage flexibility in the market for educated labor and the relatively restricted possibilities for government action designed to reduce the inflow of students into post-secondary education, certainly serve to explain the tendency toward a rising level of graduate unemployment. But the process is, of course, to some extent self-limiting: a high level of graduate unemployment will in itself represent a reduction in the expected returns to education: even if the wage for employed graduates is high, if one has to wait for a long time after graduation to get a job, the ex post return will be reduced. This will in the end decrease the rate at which students enter the system, and an equilibrium may ultimately be established at a positive (though possibly quite substantial) unemployment rate. It is interesting to observe that this reasoning is entirely analogous to that in the Harris-Todaro model, with education taking the place of rural-urban migration, and wage rigidity prevailing in the market for educated labor rather than in the market for urban "modern-sector" labor.

A situation in which the economic system tends towards an equilibrium where substantial unemployment for a factor of production continues to exist, but where the policy-makers consider themselves unable to directly remove the rigidities causing the unemployment, nevertheless suggests that certain second-best measures may be tried. For example, the existence of unemployment in a factor market may be interpreted as an indication that the shadow price it should be given in public-sector project evaluation, should be below its market price. Equivalently, it may be taken to suggest that public subsidization of the private employment of the factor would be socially profitable, or indeed, that direct "job creation" in the public sector would be beneficial.[2]

All these possible measures have been extensively discussed for the case of urban unemployment in the context of rural-urban migration models. The conclusions regarding their probable effects are somewhat ambiguous, however. While the basic result of Harris and Todaro (1970) was that an urban employment subsidy would be welfare-improving, it was also shown that the second-best subsidy would fall short of eliminating unemployment; in earlier work on a similar problem, Harberger constructed a model in which the appropriate shadow price of urban labor was equal to the market wage.[3] In his work on dynamic models of rural-urban migration, Todaro has consistently warned that urban "job creation" is likely to be an expensive and ineffective strategy to deal with urban unemployment.[4]

By contrast, the analytical literature on policy measures to cope with the problem of graduate unemployment has been relatively scarce, even though on reflection the problems appear quite similar. At the same time, it is difficult to avoid the impression that in practice, the simple approach of direct job creation, especially in the public sector, has been extensively used to deal with the problem. But if that strategy is likely to be expensive and ineffective as a way to cope with urban industrial unemployment, the question arises whether the same judgement would not be warranted when it is applied to graduate unemployment.

The purpose of the present paper is to construct an explicitly dynamic model of non-human and human capital formation (i.e., education) when there is wage rigidity in the market for educated manpower, and hence graduate unemployment. Within the framework of this model, I will then consider the question of second-best policy measures (such as employment subsidies or changes in the private costs of education). given that the wage rigidity cannot be directly removed. I will show that under certain conditions, the appropriate shadow price of labor may be equal to, or even exceed, its market wage even when graduate unemployment exists, and that the optimal level of employment subsidy may be positive or negative. I will also demonstrate that the problem of rigid wages may lead to a situation analogous to the one consider-by Bhagwati and others in the work on "immiserizing growth", in which attempts to raise the long-run level of consumption in the economy through additional capital formation, will in fact reduce long-run welfare.[5]

THE THEORETICAL FRAMEWORK[6]

The model underlying the analysis in the paper is a simple one in which one good only is produced using three factors, namely physical capital, raw labor and educated labor. (In a one-good model, one cannot explicitly consider international trade, of course. But if one interprets the one good as representing a composite of many goods being produced and traded, one may think of an aggregate production function as a relation between the economy's real income and the quantities of its productive factors, given that the opportunities for international division of labor are efficiently utilized. If this interpretation is taken, one should bear in mind that the elasticities of substitution between the various factors will tend to be high, because they will then represent not only the opportunities for substitution in the production of given goods, but also the indirect substitution that becomes possible via adjustments on the international trade side).

We denote by E and L repsectively the proportions of the labor force with and without education[7]. We have

(1) $L + E = 1$

Gross output per member of the total labor force in the economy is given by.

(2) $Q^G = F (L, H, K)$

where K is physical capital per head.

197

The quantity of employed educated labor per head is denoted by H; we have U = E - H where U is the quantity of unemployed educated workers.[8] All the firms in the economy are assumed to take factors prices as given and to maximize profits, which implies:

$$(3) \qquad w^{\ell} = \frac{\partial F}{\partial L} \equiv F_L \ (L, \ H, \ K)$$

$$(4) \qquad (r + \theta) = \frac{\partial F}{\partial K} \equiv F_K \ (L, \ H, \ K)$$

$$(5) \qquad (\bar{w} - s) = \frac{\partial F}{\partial H} \equiv F_H \ (L, \ H, \ K),$$

where w^{ℓ} is the wage rate for uneducated workers, r is the market rate of interest, θ is the exponential rate of depreciation of physical capital, $\bar{w}$ is the exogenously given wage rate for educated workers, and s is any public subsidy paid for the employment of educated workers. Since uneducated labor and physical capital are assumed fully employed, equations (3) - (5) imply that w^{ℓ} and r are endogenously determined; with $\bar{w}$ and s being exogenous, however, the third endogenous variable in this subsystem is H, the quantity of employed educated labor. To emphasize this, we may rewrite (5) as (5'):

$$(5') \qquad H = H \ (L, \ K, \ \bar{w} - s)$$

Total capital accumulation (i.e., of both human and non-human capital) per member of the labor force, is described by:

$$(6) \qquad \dot{K} + C\dot{E} \equiv W = \sigma Q^N - n \ (K + CE)$$

where C is the resource cost of converting an un-educated into an educated worker,[9] σ is the average propensity to save, n is the population growth rate, and where Q^N is the economy's net income per capita, given by:

$$(7) \qquad Q^N = F(L, \ H, \ K) - \theta K - \rho CE,$$

with ρ being the exponential rate at which human capital is assumed to depreciate due to deaths, retirements, and "technical obsolescence".[10]

Equation (6) relates to the constraint on the total amount of capital accumulation (i.e., of both human and non-human capital) which is imposed by the limitation on available savings. To close the model, a description is also needed of the mechanism through which total savings is allocated between the two types of investment. I do this by postulating that the rate of investment in education depends on the expected rate of return to human capital relative to the market interest rate, or equivalently, on the expected net present value of "getting a degree":

$$(8) \qquad \dot{E} = g(V) - (\rho + n)\, E \equiv Z,$$

where V is the expected net present value, and $g(V)$ is the gross rate of investment in human capital. In the steady-state analysis below, I will focus on the case where $g'(V) \to \infty$, so that the equilibrium condition $\dot{E} = 0$ for the steady state will correspond to the condition $V = 0$.[11]

I come now to the problem of the determination of the "expected net present value of a degree", i.e. V in (8). In postulating a formula for V, I will make three important simplifications. First, I will assume "unitary elasticity of expectations", i.e., that the expected future values of the variables determining it are the same as the current ones.[12] Second, I will assume that when there is graduate unemployment, the unemployed will always consist of graduates who have not yet found their first job.[13] Third, I will abstract from problems of risk aversion and of randomness in the time lag between graduation and unemployment, and simply assume that this time lag is treated as a fixed parameter in the formation of expectations for the present value. I may thus write:

$$(9) \qquad V = e^{-u\,(r + \rho)} \left[\frac{\bar{w}\,(1 - t)}{r + \rho} \right] - \left[\frac{w^{\ell}}{r + \rho} + \hat{C} \right]$$

where t is the tax rate on the earnings of educated workers,[14] $\hat{C}$ is the direct private cost of education (which may differ from the social cost C defined above if education is subsidized), and u is the expected time lag between graduation and employment. This time lag can be expected to depend, on the one hand, on the number of unemployed job seekers in the market, and on the other hand, on the number of jobs becoming available per unit of time.[15] In the steady state, when the stock H of educated workers per member of the labor force is constant, the flow of new jobs will simply be equal to $H(\rho + n)$, and we will therefore write:

$$(10) \qquad u = \frac{U}{(\rho + n)H} = \frac{E - H}{(\rho + n)H} = \frac{1}{(\rho + n)}\left[\frac{E}{H} - 1\right]^{[16]}$$

The formula (9) for V may now be interpreted as follows. The expression within the first set of square brackets simply represents the discounted value of life-time earnings after tax of an educated worker <u>at the beginning of his earning life</u>. Since he expects to wait u units of time before getting a job, the present value at the <u>time of graduation</u> is obtained by discounting this value u periods back, i.e., by multiplying by exp $(- u(r + \rho))$, as indicated. The expression within the second set of square brackets is the total cost of education, including an opportunity cost in the form of the present discounted value of the life-time earnings of an uneducated worker.

In the subsequent analysis, an important role will be played by the partial derivatives of V with respect to the state variables E and K, denoted by V_E and V_K, and, for the case where the effects of exogenous job creation are to be evaluated, by its derivative with respect to the quantity of graduate employment H, denoted by V_H.[17]

These derivatives may be written as:

$$(11) \qquad V_E = \left[V_{w^\ell} \frac{dw^\ell}{dE} + V_r \frac{dr}{dE}\right] + \left[V_u \frac{du}{dE}\right]$$

$$(12) \qquad V_K = \left[V_{w^\ell} \frac{dw^\ell}{dK} + V_r \frac{dr}{dK}\right] + \left[V_u \frac{du}{dK}\right]$$

$$(13) \qquad V_H = \left[V_{w^\ell} \frac{dw^\ell}{dH} + V_r \frac{dr}{dH}\right] + \left[V_u \frac{du}{dH}\right]$$

where

$$V_{w^\ell} \equiv \frac{\partial V}{\partial w^\ell} < 0, \; V_r \equiv \frac{\partial V}{\partial r} < 0, \; V_u \equiv \frac{\partial V}{\partial u} < 0.$$

The signs of the expressions within square brackets cannot be formally determined unless one imposes a complicated set of restrictions on the production function F. I will not attempt to find and interpret such conditions here, but will rely instead on intuitive arguments.

The expressions within the first set of square brackets in the formulae for V_E, V_K represent the effects on V of factor price changes resulting from changes in E and K. I will assume that the signs of these terms are determined by the "own-price" effects, i.e., by $(dw^\ell/dE) = - (dw^\ell/dL) > 0$ $dr/dK < 0$, where the directions of the inequalities follow from the assumption that the "factor demand curves" are downward sloping. With respect to the first term on the right-hand side of formula (13), which involves only cross-effects of a change in graduate employment on the returns of other factors, I will assume that complementarity effects dominate so that its sign is non-positive.

The expressions in the second sets of square brackets of (11) to (13) involve the "quantity effects" of changes in E, K and H, on the expected value of V via their impact on the graduate unemployment rate. We may write these expressions as follows:

$$(14) \qquad V_u \frac{du}{dE} = V_u \frac{\partial u}{\partial E} \left[1 - \frac{E}{H} \frac{dH}{dE} \right] < 0$$

$$(15) \qquad V_u \frac{du}{dK} = - V_u \frac{\partial u}{\partial E} \left[\frac{E}{H} \frac{dH}{dK} \right] > 0$$

$$(16) \qquad V_u \frac{du}{dH} = - V_u \frac{\partial u}{\partial E} \frac{E}{H} > 0,$$

where I have used the fact that

$$\frac{\partial u}{\partial E} > 0, \quad \frac{\partial u}{\partial H} = - \frac{E}{H} \frac{\partial u}{\partial E} < 0,$$

from (10).

The sign of (15) follows from assuming that physical capital and skilled labor are complementary to a sufficient extent so that $dH/dK > 0$. The sign postulated for (14) is equivalent to assuming that the initial impact of an increase in the proportion of the labour force in the educated category on the rate of graduate unemployment is less than completely offset by any resulting substitution of educated labor H for uneducated labour L when the latter decreases as a consequence of the transfer of workers from the unskilled to the educated category (recall that L = 1 - E).[18]

The above assumptions together imply the following inequalities:

(17) $V_E < 0, V_K > 0; V_H \gtrless 0.$

Under circumstances where the "quantity effects" (i.e., the effects of V via changes in the graduate unemployment rate) dominate the expressions, we will have $V_H > 0$.

EFFECTS OF EMPLOYMENT SUBSIDIES AND OTHER POLICIES

(i)   Preliminary Observations

In this section, I consider the effects of "job creation" for graduates through an employment subsidy, and also those of other policy changes such as an increase in the private cost of education or in the rate at which the earnings of educated workers are taxed. As was noted in the Introduction, I will also briefly discuss the possibility of wage rigidity in the market for educated labor giving rise to a phenomenon analogous to "immiserizing growth", along the lines discussed by Bhagwati and others.

The method to be used will be that of comparing steady states of the system; no explicit attention will be paid to questions of uniqueness and stability, and I will simply assume that the system converges to a unique steady state at which $\dot{K} = \dot{E} = 0$ for any set of parameter values. I will further generally assume that the wage of educated workers is sufficiently high so that there will be residual unemployment both before and after the policy changes under consideration. As the welfare criterion for

202

evaluating different states of the system, I will use the level of steady-state consumption per capita in the economy, denoted by Q. We have

(18) $\qquad Q = Q^N(1 - \sigma) = F(L, H, K) - \Theta K - \rho EC - n(K + CE)$

where the last equality follows from (6) at $\dot{K} + C\dot{E} = 0$

For future reference, it is also useful to define the <u>social rates of return</u> to non-human and human capital formation, given by the marginal changes in society's net income following an increase in the respective stocks of capital; they are given by:

(19) $\qquad \dfrac{\partial Q^N}{\partial K} \equiv \pi_C = (F_K - \Theta) + H_K F_H$

(20) $\qquad \dfrac{\partial Q^N}{\partial E} \equiv \pi_E \cdot C = -(F_L + \rho C) - H_L F_H$

Consider now (19). It is seen that the distortion caused by the rigid wage in the market for educated labor will lead to a differential between the market rate of interest r (= $F_K - \theta$) and the social rate of return π_C: an increase in the physical capital stock will in general change the employment of educated labor ($H_K > 0$), causing output to increase by an amount greater than the marginal product of the physical capital itself, so that the social marginal product is greater than the market rate.[19]

With wage rigidity prevailing in the market for educated labor, an addition to the stock of educated persons does not directly lead to a corresponding increase in the number of <u>employed</u> graduates, and the social rate of return to education is thus likely to be negative: it will essentially reflect the impact on net output of the removal of an unskilled worker from the employed labor force, plus a depreciation term. Hence, the term $-(F_L + \rho C)$ in (20) measures what this loss would be at unchanged employment of educated labor; the remaining term corresponds to the indirect effect on output via the associated change in the employment of educated labor. Depending on the relationships of complementarity or substitutability between the three factors, the indirect effect may either reinforce or attenuate the direct one, but I will assume that the total effect remains negative.

(ii) Impacts of Policy Changes

In this subsection, I turn to an analysis of the impact on steady-state consumption Q of changes in the various parameters, as discussed in the introduction. Treating Q as a function of the parameters and of the stocks of human and non-human capital, a general expression for the impact of any parameter change may be written as

$$(21) \quad \frac{dQ}{dx} = \frac{\partial Q}{\partial x} + \frac{dK}{dx} (\pi_c - n) + \frac{dE}{dx} \cdot C (\pi_E - n)$$

where π_c and π_E are the social rates of return discussed above, x is any one of the parameters of interest, and where dK/dx, dE/dx are found from total differentiation of the system (6) and (8) at $\dot{K} = \dot{E} = 0$, with respect to x.

For expositional reasons, I begin by considering the effect of an increase in $\hat{C}$, the private cost of education. In the Appendix, the following expression is derived:

$$(22) \quad \frac{dQ}{d\hat{C}} = \left[\frac{n(1 - \sigma)}{n - \sigma \hat{\pi}} \right] \left[\frac{-C}{CV_K - V_E} \right] (\pi_E - \pi_c)$$

where π is a weighted average of π_E and π_c, and V_K, V_E are the derivatives defined in (11) and (12) above.[20]

Equation (22) may now be interpreted as follows. The first term of the product on the right-hand side (within square brackets) can be interpreted as a multiplier corresponding to the increase in steady-state consumption following an autonomous increase in the economy's net income; I will henceforth denote its value by M (for multiplier). As observed in the Appendix, given the other assumptions in the model one has M > 0 if the system is stable.

The middle term in the product may be described as the negative of the number of units of steady-state capital which will be transferred from

physical to human capital following an initial unit
increase in the value of V, the "net present value of
a degree". When one multiplies it by the last term,
which corresponds to the (negative) social rate of
return differential between the two types of capital,
one obtains a measure of the re-allocation effect on
net income of transferring capital from one form to
the other. Defining this effect as:

$$(23) \qquad \frac{C}{CV_K - V_E} \; (\pi_E - \pi_c) \equiv R < 0,$$

one can rewrite (22) as

$$(22') \qquad \frac{dQ}{d\hat{C}} = M \cdot (- R) > 0^{21}$$

The magnitude of (the absolute value of) R depends on
the magnitude of the return differential, and on the
absolute values of the terms V_K and V_E. The latter
were discussed above.

The interpretation of (22) is thus quite
straightforward: in the presence of graduate unemployment, there will be an efficiency gain from
raising the private cost of education, because the
principal effect of such a measure is simply to reduce
the rate of unemployment and the amount of resources
spent in the educational system.

Other measures which affect the expected
private return to education without changing the incentive for firms to employ educated labor will have a
similar impact. Thus, the effect of increasing the
tax rate t on educated labor can be written as

$$(24) \qquad \frac{dQ}{dt} = M \cdot (V_t \cdot R) > 0,$$

where the sign follows from the fact that both V_t
($\equiv \partial V/\partial t$) and R are negative. It is also evident that
increases in the private cost of education or the tax
rate will continue to yield efficiency gains as long
as graduate unemployment continues to exist.

I turn now to parameter changes which affect
both the expected private return to education and the

incentives of firms to employ graduate labor. One such parameter in the model is the wage rate for educated labor, since it is taken to be exogenous. Even though it may not be meaningful to consider it as an unrestricted policy parameter, it is nevertheless subject to some policy influence, so that information about effects of changing it may be a relevant input into the overall process of formulating educational and labor market policy. Furthermore, a study of its impact on resource allocation provides a useful standard of comparison for assessing the consequences of "job creation" through an employment subsidy.

From the Appendix, we obtain the following expression for the effects of changing the wage rate:

$$(25) \qquad \frac{dQ}{d\bar{w}} = M \cdot \left[H_w \ (F_H + R \cdot V_H) + R \cdot V_{\bar{w}} \right] \quad,$$

where $H_w \equiv \partial H / \partial \bar{w}$ from (5'), V_H has been defined above, and where

$$V_{\bar{w}} = \partial V / \partial \bar{w} > 0.$$

Before interpreting this result, consider now the effects of a policy of job creation via a subsidy to firms for the employment of educated manpower. The impact of such a subsidy on steady-state consumption may be expressed as:

$$(26) \qquad \frac{dQ}{ds} = M \left[- H_w \ (F_H + R \cdot V_H) \right]$$

A comparison of (25) and (26) illustrates the fact that an exogenous increase in the wage rate for educated labor can be interpreted as, on the one hand, a tax (negative subsidy) on the employment of such labor, and, on the other hand, an equivalent subsidy to those educated workers who are employed. Ceteris paribus, the latter will have the effect of raising the expected return to education. It also follows directly that the effects on resource allocation of increasing the wage rate cannot be entirely offset by a subsidy for the employment of graduates alone: while a compensating subsidy may neutralize the effect of a wage increase on the incentives of firms to employ graduates, it will not offset the increase in the expected private return to education implied by a wage increase. Adding (25) to (26), the net result of a wage increase with an equivalent subsidy may be written as:

$$(27) \qquad \left[\frac{dQ}{d\bar{w}} + \frac{dQ}{ds}\right]_{\bar{w} - s = const.} = M \cdot R\, V_{\bar{w}} < 0.$$

It is worth noting that this result is analogous to the finding in Harris and Todaro (1970), where they discussed the possibility of offsetting the effects of an increased urban wage through an employment subsidy, in the context of their model of rural-urban migration: while the subsidy may be set at such a level that it offsets the impact on employers of imposing a rigid wage, there will still remain an increased incentive for individuals to migrate. The optimal subsidy level will have to take account of both effects, and the first-best solution is not attainable via a subsidy alone.

Let us now return to the question of the effects of job creation via an employment subsidy alone, given the wage rate. Utilizing the definitions of π_c and π_E, we may write the expression in parenthesis multiplying H_w in (26) as:

$$(28) \qquad F_H - R \cdot V_H = (\bar{w} - s) - \left[\frac{V_H}{CV_K - V_E}\right]\left[G(r^* + \rho) + w^{\ell *}\right]$$

where

$$(29) \qquad r^* = r + H_K\, F_K$$

and

$$(30) \qquad w^{\ell *} = w^{\ell} + H_L\, F_H$$

may be interpreted as the social discount rate and unskilled wage rate respectively. The expression $V_H/(CV_K - V_E)$, on the other hand, can be interpreted as the increase in the steady-state number of educated people in response to the creation of one extra job for educated workers. Now the equilibrium condition $V = 0$ can be rewritten (using (9)) as:

$$(31) \qquad \bar{w} - e^{u(r + \rho)}\left[(1 - t)^{-1}\left(\hat{C}\,(r + \rho) + \hat{w}^{\ell}\right)\right] = 0$$

The term within square brackets in (31) may be taken to represent a flow measure of the cost of education, including the opportunity cost and considering the tax t on an educated persons earnings as a cost, paid by an employed graduate earning the gross wage $\bar{w}$. When there is unemployment of graduates, a portion of this cost will accrue before the income stream begins, so that equilibrium requires that the wage rate be greater than this cost, with the factor of proportionality being given by exp $(u(r + \rho))$.

Now consider the effects of introducing a small employment subsidy, supposing that none exists to begin with. Combining (28) and (31), one finds the condition for dQ/ds > 0 at s = 0, namely:[22]

$$(32) \qquad \frac{e^{u(r + \rho)}}{V_H / (CV_K - V_E)} > \frac{(C(r^* + \rho) + w^{\ell *})(1 - t)}{\hat{C}(r + \rho) + w^{\ell}}$$

Given the value of the left-hand side, it follows that "job creation" is more likely to raise per capita consumption the higher is the private cost of education relative to the social cost, and the higher the tax rate on educated workers' incomes. It is worth observing, however, that the results discussed above indicate that in the presence of graduate unemployment, raising the private cost of education or the tax rate are in themselves welfare-improving measures. This suggests that "job creation" may in part be regarded as a complement, from an allocation point of view, to such policies.[23]

Consider now the expression on the left-hand side of inequality (32); to begin with, suppose that the proportion of educated people in the labor force is small. The terms V_H and V_E will then be dominated by the "quantity effects", i.e., the terms V_u (du/dE) and V_u (du/dH) respectively. From (14) to (16), setting dH/dE = dH/dK = 0, one obtains $V_H/(CV_K - V_E) = E/H$.

To simplify the numerator, one notes that for small values of the exponent, one may write:

$$(33) \qquad \exp (u(r + \rho)) \simeq (1 + u(r + \rho)).$$

Using this approximation, and the definition of u, one

may finally write the LHS of inequality (32) as:

$$(34) \qquad \frac{e^{u(r + \rho)}}{V_H / (CV_K - V_E)} \approx \left(\frac{r + \rho}{n + \rho} \right) \frac{\left(\frac{E}{H} - \frac{(r - n)}{(r + \rho)} \right)}{E/H}$$

As r approaches n, this expression approaches unity. Under these circumstances, the criterion for job creation to be welfare-improving takes a particularly simple form: <u>an employment subsidy will raise steady-state consumption if the private cost of education is higher than the social cost (adjusted for taxes)</u>.[24]

     Note that this result is closely related to the conclusion drawn by Harberger (1974) regarding the shadow price of urban labor in his model of rural-urban migration with a rigid urban wage and urban unemployment. In that model, his result was that the shadow wage should be equal to the (rigid) market wage, which in the context of our model is analogous to the conclusion that an employment subsidy would not be warranted. The argument there is that in an unemployment equilibrium, the creation of an extra urban job will cause more than one rural worker to move to the city, and under the implicit assumptions in Harberger's papers, the amount of extra migration is precisely enough to offset the difference between the respective marginal productivities of rural and urban workers. In the present model with the RHS of (32) equal to unity and positive unemployment, the marginal productivity of an educated worker is higher than the total cost of educating one worker. Comparing two equilibria, however, creation of one more job for a graduate will raise the number of educated persons by more than one, and under the assumptions necessary to render the LHS of (32) equal to unity, the cost of educating the extra people will precisely offset the return-cost differential, so that job creation will not pay.[25]

     The preceding result was obtained on the assumption that the proportion of educated labor in the total labor force was "small". If it is not, the approximation (34) will no longer be valid, and one has to take into account the effect of job creation not only on the unemployment rate of graduates but also on relative factor prices.[26] As discussed earlier, it is impossible to state in general whether this will have the effect of raising or reducing the value of the LHS of (32), i.e., whether it will make it more or less likely than "job creation will pay". However, an intuitive argument can be used to show that the answer to this question essentially depends on the degree of substitutability between educated labor and the other factors of production. Suppose that the elasticities of substitution are low in absolute value. This would tend to increase the absolute value of the term $(CV_K - V_E)$[27] and reduce the value of V_H.[28] Both of these effects would tend to increase the LHS of (32), other things equal, thereby increasing the likelihood that an employment subsidy would be welfare-increasing (or equivalently, raise the value of the optimal subsidy, i.e., that subsidy at which $dQ/ds = 0$; see (28). Thus, even when the social cost of education is equal to or higher than the private cost, job creation through an employment subsidy may be warranted if the degree of substitutability between skilled labor and the other factors of production is sufficiently low. Equivalently, the appropriate shadow price for educated labor in social project evaluation should then be below its market wage, even when account is taken of the fact that the employment of additional skilled labor will lead to an increased inflow of students to the (socially unprofitable) education activity. On the other hand, it is important to note that when the private cost of education is considerably below the social cost, and when there is a reasonable degree of substitutability between productive factors, the second-best policy may involve a tax on the employment of graduates (i.e., a negative value of s), and an appropriate shadow price in excess of the market wage. (Again, it is interesting that an entirely analogous reasoning could be used to show that under similar circumstances, a tax on urban jobs might constitute the second-best policy in a situation where rigid urban wages and rural-urban migration have combined to produce extensive urban unemployment. As far as I know, this possibility has not been raised in the extensive literature on the urban unemployment problem in LDCs).

(iii) Immiserizing Growth

        In a number of papers in international trade

theory, it has been demonstrated that the existence of various types of distortions in the economy may lead to a situation where the welfare loss of the distortion is accentuated by factor accumulation to such an extent that aggregate welfare may in fact fall when more of a factor becomes available.[29]

A similar possibility exists in the present model. As I have discussed above, in the presence of wage rigidity the social rate of return on funds allocated to human capital formation is likely to be negative. If the private rates of return are such that a large share of incremental funds (becoming available via an exogenous increase in the savings propensity, e.g.) are allocated to education, immiserizing growth may arise.

Formally, the conditions for immiserizing growth may be found by considering the effect on steady-state consumption of an increase in σ, the propensity to save. From the Appendix, we have

$$(35) \qquad \frac{dQ}{d\sigma} = \frac{\sigma(\hat{\pi} - n)}{n - \sigma\hat{\pi}} \cdot Q^N$$

As noted earlier, for the steady state to be stable, the numerator must be positive. A sufficient condition for an increased savings propensity to decrease steady-state consumption is thus that $\hat{\pi} < n$, i.e., that the weighted average social rate of return on human and non-human capital formation be less than the population growth rate. Since one may reasonably assume $\pi_c > n$, this requires that the weight of the (negative) rate of return to human capital formation be relatively large. This weight is given by $CV_K/(CV_K - V_E)$, so that for immiserizing growth in this sense to be possible, the private profitability of education must be relatively sensitive to changes in the stock of physical capital. The conditions under which this will be so may be analyzed using the expressions (11) and (12) above for the derivatives V_K and V_E.[30]

CONCLUDING COMMENTS

The starting point of the present paper was that the problems of wage rigidity and increasing

211

amounts of open unemployment for educated labor in LDCs, are similar in nature to those arising from wage inflexibility in the market for urban industrial labor labor, if one recognizes that education (like rural-urban migration) is an endogenous activity which responds to private economic incentives. It may be politically impossible, in both cases, to deal directly with the lack of flexibility in wages; in both cases, there have also arisen strong pressures on the policy-makers to relieve the unemployment problem via subsidies to private employers, or (especially in the educated-labor-market) via direct job creation in the public sector.

While the principal conclusion in the early paper by Harris and Todaro (1970) on the urban-industrial labor problems was that a positive amount of job creation would be welfare improving, the thrust of much of the later work by Todaro (1976, 1977) has been that the benefits of such a policy may be limited, and that alternative strategies (such as raising the opportunity cost of migration via an increased emphasis on rural development) may be more effective. Harberger's conclusion that even when the industrial wage is rigid and open unemployment exists, the appropriate shadow wage may nevertheless be identical with the market wage, certainly tends to support the notion that direct job creation is of limited effectiveness at best.

The results derived in this paper can be taken to indicate that, provided education is indeed properly to be taken as an endogenous activity, skepticism regarding any beneficial effects from job creation or employment subsidization is highly warranted in the case of the market for educated labor as well. When the private and social costs of education are the same, the results are similar to those from the analysis of the urban-industrial market. Thus, if the educated labor force is relatively small and educated labor is highly substitutable for other factors of production, the optimal subsidy for the creation of educated employment is small and the appropriate shadow wage for such labor in social benefit-cost analysis is close to the market wage. In the limiting case, job creation has a zero efficiency gain, and the market and shadow wages are identical, as in the case studied by Harberger. On the other hand, the more realistic case to consider is that where education is highly subsidized (even allowing for the higher taxes imposed on education labor), so that its social cost is higher than its private cost. In that case, job creation will pay (i.e., the optimal subsidy will be positive) only under circumstances when there is a relatively low degree of substitu-ability between educated labor and the other factors. If this does not hold, the paradoxical conclusion follows that the second-best policy, in spite of graduate unemployment, may be a tax on the employment of such labor, and its shadow wage will be in excess of its market wage![31]

The discussion in this paper, as in most analyses dealing with second-best problems, can be criticized for a certain lack of imagination when it comes to visualizing the real alternatives facing LDC decision-makers. Thus, the results on the optimal rate of employment creation are derived on the assumption that both the wage rate of educated labor and the degree of subsidy to education, were given. It may well be realistic to postulate that wages can-not be allowed to fall, at one go, to their market clearing level, or that the private cost of education cannot be brought into equality with the social cost in a single "reform package". Over time, however, policy-makers may be able to chisel away at those rigidities or imperfections; to the extent they succeed, it has been shown that the possible gains from employment creation will decrease, and since employment creation itself tends to introduce future rigidities (employment reduction being a great deal more difficult than creation), this may be seen as further weakening the second-best case for subsidiza-tion.

An obvious limitation on the policy rele-vance of the results derived here, finally, is the treatment of education strictly as a process of human capital accumulation, undertaken for no other reason than to increase the economic productivity of the labor resource. Treating education in this way, and computing the return on human capital, may be a good starting point for an economist charged with advising a government on its educational policy. But, as Professor Lewis reminds us, the economist who is

prepared to go a bit beyond that which can be easily
quantified, can do more, and probably give better
policy advice (1966, p. 110):

> "He can stress that a wide educational
> base is needed to find the best brains,
> which may make the crucial difference.
> He may welcome the fact that education
> raises aspirations, because low aspira-
> tions are one of the causes of low
> achievement. He can add that any kind
> of education must have some productivity,
> since it stretches the mind... Finally,
> he can remind the government that
> education does not have to be productive
> in order to justify itself; it is valu-
> able for its own sake, and, when compared
> with other consumption expenditures,
> giving young people more education is
> just as valuable as giving them
> gramaphones."

FOOTNOTES

*University of Western Ontario. The paper was written while I was visiting the Institute for International Economic Studies, University of Stockholm during 1979-80, and financial support from the Bank of Sweden, Tercentenary Foundation, is gratefully acknowledged. I would also like to acknowledge the research assistance of Refik Erzan. Helpful comments were received from participants at the IIES Conference on International Trade, held in August 1980, at which I presented an early version of the paper. I have also benefitted from comments by Avinash Dixit, Jonathan Eaton, June Flanders and Mark Gersovitz. Any remaining shortcomings in the paper are my responsibility:

1. An early analysis of this problem for the case of India is found in Blaug et al (1969); an abbreviated discussion is found in Blaug (1970). A more recent survey of the problem of educated unemployment in LDCs is contained in Edwards and Todaro (1974).

2. Edwards and Todaro (1974) contains a comprehensive discussion of second-best policies.

3. Harberger (1974), discussion on pp. 168-173.

4. See Todaro (1976), and (1977), especially pp. 196-198.

5. For a survey of the literature discussing this possibility, see Bhagwati (1971).

6. The model is similar to one I have previously used for analysis of the effects of migration of educated manpower (Blomqvist, 1980). In that paper, I assumed full employment of all factors, however.

7. For simplicity, I only consider one type of education, thought to correspond to post-secondary schooling.

8. I am assuming full employment of workers without an education.

9. I abstract here from the fact that education

takes time, and instead assume a zero "gestation lag" in the production of human capital.

10.   In a more realistic model, the assumption that all human capital depreciates at the same rate regardless of its age, must clearly be replaced by other ones where the rate is taken to vary with the age of the educated person, and possibly with other factors as well.

11.   While these assumptions may be reasonable in the context of a comparison of steady states, they should probably be modified for a short-run analysis of the system's behaviour. For example, the assumption $g'(V) \to \infty$ would lead to "bang-bang" behaviour in investment allocation, corresponding to a situation where either <u>all</u> investable funds, or none at all, would be devoted to human capital formation at a given time. Furthermore, the implicit assumption in the text that physical capital accumulation is a residual between total savings and the amount of human capital accumulation, neglects all problems arising from a situation where savers and investors in physical capital are different agents, i.e., one of the central problems in short-run macroeconomics.

12.   Again, this assumption may be satisfactory when attention is confined to a comparison of steady states. If one were to study the behaviour of the system outside its steady states, it should be modified in some manner.

13.   This is equivalent to assuming that once a graduate has found a job, he will never suffer involuntary unemployment.

14.   For simplicity, I have assumed that the earnings of unskilled workers are not taxed; an allowance for a positive tax could be made without much complication, however.

15.   For a discussion of a similar formulation in the context of a rural-urban migration model, see Blomqvist (1978). It has been pointed out to me that this formulation, together with the assumption of no risk aversion makes the model equivalent to a deterministic "queuing model", in which each graduate takes his place at the end of a queue, and has to wait (in a

state of unemployment) u periods until he is first in
line and becomes employed.

16. Outside the steady state, the value of H may
change over time, and the denominator of (10) should
then also include the time derivative of H. I will
abstract from this complication here, however.

17. In evaluating V_E and V_K, the value of H will be
treated as endogenously determined, whereas it will
be treated as a parameter when V_H is evaluated.

18. It is worth noting already at this point, however, that if educated and unskilled labor are highly
substitutable for each other, expression (14) may be
relatively small in absolute value. I will return to
this observation below.

19. This is an illustration of the general principle
that a distortion in the market for one factor will
in general affect the appropriate shadow prices of
other factors as well. See Srinivasan and Bhagwati
(1978).

20. Expression (22) is identical with (21) in
Blomqvist (1980). Because of the assumption of a
rigid wage for educated labor in this paper, however,
the interpretation is different.

21. The reason for the minus sign preceding R is of
course that an increase in the private cost of education $\hat{C}$ decreases the value of V, whereas R as discussed in the text measures the reallocation effect of
an initial unit increase in V.

22. Note that condition (32) is valid for $V_H > 0$, as
one would normally expect; see the discussion above.
When $V_H < 0$, it follows directly from (28) that
$dQ/ds \gtrless 0$.

23. A similar relationship might be demonstrated in a
dynamic version of the Harris-Todaro model if one were
to introduce an exogenous migration cost into it:
the social profitability of job creation would then be
raised by raising this cost.

24. Note that letting $r \to n$ implies that the timing
of graduate unemployment become irrelevant. If the

specification of the model had involved the assumption of randomly occurring unemployment, and the expression $\exp(-u(r + \rho))$ in the formula for V in (9) above had been replaced by H/E, the value of the numerator would have been exactly E/H regardless of the value of r.

25. In another context, I have shown that under certain circumstances, this result applies in the Harris-Todaro specification of a rural-urban migration as well; see Blomqvist (1979).

26. I.e., one can no longer neglect the first of the two terms on the right-hand sides of (11)-(13).

27. With a low degree of substitutability between educated and uneducated labor, the term $d\bar{H}/dE$ in (14) would tend to be negative, so that the absolute value of the term V_u (du/dE) would tend to be large and positive. Similarly, the terms V_u (du/dK) and V_r (dr/dK) would tend to be positive and relatively large. As long as the cross-effects dr/dE and dw^ℓ/dK are not "too large", one would thus expect a "large" value for $(CV_K - V_E)$.

28. With a low degree of substitutability, the terms dw^ℓ/dH and dr/dH would both be positive; since they are both multiplied by negative coefficients on the RHS of (13), this would tend to offset the positive terms V_u (du/dH), thereby decreasing the (positive) value of V_H.

29. The observation was first made independently by Bhagwati (1958) and Harry Johnson in the late 1950's, for the case where the "distortion" consisted of the failure by a "large" country to exploit its monopoly power in international trade. The analysis was subsequently extended to the case of distortions in the form of non-optimal tariffs (Johnson (1967)) and wage rigidities (Bhagwati (1968). For a survey, see Bhagwati (1971).

30. From the intuitive discussion in footnote (27) above, a high degree of substitutability between skilled and unskilled labor would tend to produce a relatively small absolute value of V_E, whereas a high value for V_K would depend on a low degree of substitutability between capital and skilled labor; those would thus be

conditions making it likely that immiserizing growth would apply.

31. Though, as noted above, this possibility has not been extensively analyzed for the case of urban industrial labor, it is possible to imagine circumstances where a similar policy (i.e., "negative job creation"), might be allocationally efficient in that case too. Suppose, for example that agricultural output is heavily taxed (as is sometimes the case for export agriculture), so that the private opportunity cost of leaving the countryside is less than the social opportunity cost. Or consider a situation in which physical capital is heavily subsidized in industrial uses, so that the social marginal product of industrial capital is below its private rate of return. In both cases, it is possible to visualize plausible models in which positive employment creation in urban industry may decrease allocational efficiency.

REFERENCES

Bhagwati, Jagdish (1958) - "Immiserizing Growth: A Geometrical Note," *Review of Economic Studies*, 25, June, pp.

_____ (1968) - "Distortions and Immiserizing Growth: A Generalization," *Review of Economic Studies*, 35, October, pp. 481-485.

_____ (1971) - "The Generalized Theory of Distortions and Welfare" in Bhagwati et al (eds.), *Trade, Balance of Payments and Growth, Papers in International Economics in Honor of Charles P. Kindleberger*, Amsterdam, North Holland, pp. 69-90.

Blaug, M., Layard, P.R.G. and Woodhall, H. (1969) - *The Causes of Graduate Unemployment in India*, London, Allen Lane.

Blaug, M. (1970) - "The Unemployment of the Educated in India" in Jolly, K., *et al* (eds.), *Third World Employment: Problems and Strategy*, Penguin (1973), pp. 203-211.

Blomqvist, Ake G. (1978) - "Urban Job Creation and Unemployment in LDCs: Todaro vs. Harris and Todaro," *Journal of Development Economics* 5 (1), pp. 3-18.

_____ (1979) - "Urban Unemployment and Optimal Tax Policy in a Small, Open Dual Economy," *Journal of Development Studies* 15 (2), January, pp. 147-164.

_____ (1980) - "International Migration of Educated Manpower and Social Rates of Return to Education in LDCs," Seminar paper 147, Institute for International Economic Studies, University of Stockholm.

Edwards, E.O. and Todaro, M.P. (1974) - "Education, Society and Development: Some Main Themes and Suggested Strategies for International Assistance," *World Development*, 2, January, pp. 25-30.

Harberger, A.C. (1974) – *Project Evaluation: Collected Papers*, Chicago, Markham Publishing Company, pp. 168-173.

Harris, J.R. and Todaro, M.P. – "Migration, Unemployment and Development: A Two-Sector Analysis," *American Economic Review* 60, March, pp. 126-142.

Johnson, H.G. (1967) – "The Possibility of Income Losses from Increased Efficiency or Factor Accumulation in the Presence of Tariffs," *Economic Journal* 77, March, pp. 151-154.

Lewis, W.A. – *Development Planning: The Essentials of Economic Policy*, London, George Allen and Unwin, 1966.

Srinivasan, T.N. and Bhagwati, J. (1978) – "Shadow Prices for Project Selection in the Presence of Distortions," *Journal of Political Economy* 86, February, pp. 97-116.

Todaro, M.P. (1976) – "Urban Job Expansion, Induced Migration and Rising Unemployment: A Formulation and Simplified Empirical Test for LDCs," *Journal of Development Economics*, Vol. 3, September, pp. 211-225.

_____ (1977) – *Economic Development in the Third World*, London and New York, Longman.

APPENDIX

The system (6) and (8) of two differential equations in the variables E and K can be approximated, at an equilibrium point, by:

(A1) $\dot{K} + C\dot{E} = \sigma(F_K - \theta + H_K F_K) - n\ dK + \sigma(-F_L - \rho C - F_H H_L) - nC\ dE$

(A2) $\dot{E} = g'(V)V_K\ dK + g'(V)V_E - \rho - n\ dE$

or, in matrix form,

(A3) $$\begin{bmatrix} \dot{K} + C\dot{E} \\ \\ \dot{E} \end{bmatrix} = \begin{bmatrix} B_{11} & B_{12} \\ \\ B_{21} & B_{22} \end{bmatrix} \begin{bmatrix} dK \\ \\ dE \end{bmatrix}$$

where the B_{ij}'s are defined by the bracketed terms. As discussed in the text, we assume $B_{21} > 0$, $B_{22} < 0$. To consider the sign of $|B|$, the determinant of the matrix of B_{ij}'s, first observe that (A3) can be transformed into a pair of equations with $\dot{K}$ and $\dot{E}$ respectively on the left-hand sides, by subtracting C times the second equation from the first. Local stability implies that the determinant of the matrix of this system is greater than zero. Since the value of the determinant of the matrix B is unaffected by the transformation, however, it follows that stability also implies $|B| > 0$.

Using (19) and (20) in the text, we have

(A4) $B_{11} = \sigma\pi_C - n, \quad B_{12} = C(\sigma\pi_E - n).$

The determinant $|B| = B_{11}B_{22} - B_{12}B_{21}$ can therefore be written as:

(A5) $|B| = (B_{22} - CB_{21})(\sigma\hat{\pi} - n)$

where

(A6) $\hat{\pi} = \dfrac{B_{22}\pi_C}{B_{22} - CB_{21}} - \dfrac{CB_{21}\pi_E}{B_{22} - CB_{21}}$

is a weighted average rate of return to human and non-human capital, with the weights being the proportions in which additional savings in the economy are allocated to the two forms of capital[1]. Given the assumed signs of B_{22} and B_{21}, $|B| > 0$ requires $(n - \sigma\hat{\pi}) > 0$. This verifies the text statement that the multiplier M introduced in (22') is positive.

To derive the comparative steady state results in the text, consider the effects of any parameter X which affects the economy's net income Q^N and the present value of a degree, V. Totally differentiating (6) and (8) at an equilibrium point, we have

(A7)
$$\begin{bmatrix} B_{11} & B_{12} \\ B_{21} & B_{22} \end{bmatrix} \begin{bmatrix} \dfrac{dK}{dX} \\ \dfrac{dE}{dX} \end{bmatrix} = \begin{bmatrix} -\sigma Q_X \\ -g'(V)V_X \end{bmatrix}$$

where $Q_X \equiv \partial Q^N/\partial X$, $V_X \equiv \partial V/\partial X$. One obtains

$$dK = \frac{-B_{22}\sigma Q_X}{|B|} + \frac{g'(V)V_X B_{12}}{|B|}$$

(A8)
$$\frac{dE}{dX} = \frac{B_{21}\sigma Q_X}{|B|} - \frac{g'(V)V_X B_{11}}{|B|}$$

Multiplying these expressions by $(\pi_C - n)$ and $C(\pi_E - n)$ respectively, using (A5) and the definitions of the B_{ij} in (A2) and (A3), we may rewrite (A8) as

$$(\pi_C - n)\frac{dK}{dX} = \frac{-B_{22}(\pi_C - n)\sigma Q_X}{(B_{22}-CB_{21})(\sigma\hat{\pi}-n)} +$$

$$\frac{g'(V)V_X \cdot C(\sigma\pi_E - n)(\pi_C - n)}{(g'(\overline{V})V_E - \rho - n - Cg'(V)V_K)(\sigma\hat{\pi}-n)}$$

(A9)
$$(\pi_E - n)\frac{dE}{dX} = \frac{B_{21}C(\pi_E - n)\sigma Q_X}{(B_{22}-CB_{21})(\sigma\hat{\pi}-n)} -$$

1. The interpretation of $\hat{\pi}$ can be verified by solving for $dK/d\sigma$, $dE/d\sigma$ using the method outlined below.

223

$$\frac{g'(V)V_X(\sigma\pi_C - n)C(\pi_E - n)}{(g'(V)V_E - \rho - n - Cg'(V)V_K)(\sigma\pi - n)}$$

These expressions may now be substituted into the expression for dQ/dX in (21), and they may be considerably simplified by recalling the definition of $\hat{\pi}$ in (A6), the fact that we assume $g'(V) \to \infty$, and taking account of the fact that $\partial Q/\partial X = \partial Q^N/\partial X$ for the parameters of interest here. One obtains

$$\frac{dQ}{dX} = \frac{\partial Q}{\partial X} + \frac{dK}{dX}(\pi_C - n) + \frac{dE}{dX}C(\pi_E - n)$$

(A10)

$$= Q_X(1 - \frac{\sigma(\hat{\pi}-n)}{(\sigma\hat{\pi}-n)}) + V_X(\frac{C}{CV_K-V_E} \cdot \frac{n(1-\sigma)}{(n-\sigma\hat{\pi})}) \cdot (\pi_E-\pi_C)$$

or, finally

(A11) $$\frac{dQ}{dX} = Q_X\left[\frac{n(1-\sigma)}{(n-\sigma\hat{\pi})}\right] + V_X\left[\frac{n(1-\sigma)}{(n-\sigma\hat{\pi})}\right]\left\{\frac{C}{CV_K-V_E} \cdot (\pi_E-\pi_C)\right\}$$

The expressions in square brackets are recognized as the multiplier M defined in the text. The expression in curly brackets represents the term R in the text.

The comparative steady state results in the text can now be derived as special cases of (A11). To obtain (22), one sets $Q_X = 0$, $V_X = -1$, while (24) results from $Q_X + $), $V_X = V_t$. Expression (25) is derived from setting $Q_X = H_WF_H$ and $V_X = V_{\bar{w}} + H_WV_H$, while (26) results from $Q_X = -H_WF_H$ and $V_X = -H_WV_H$. The result (35), finally, is obtained by letting $V_X = 0$, and replacing the term $(-\sigma Q_X)$ in (A7)-(A9) by Q^N and simplifying.

REVENUE AND EXPENDITURE RATIOS AGAIN

by
A. R. Prest

INTRODUCTION

It would seem appropriate that the chapter in this volume relating to public finance issues should take as its point of departure the well-known paper by Martin and Lewis (1956) published exactly twenty-five years ago.

After explaining in the first section that they were going to examine revenues and expenditures at all levels of government in a cross-section of sixteen developing and developed countries, the authors then emulated Adam Smith in the next section by discussing expenditure relationships before coming to matters of revenue. The relationship of expenditure to GNP was examine first and it was quickly concluded that such ratios were an increasing function of income per head. Detailed analyses followed of the composition of public expenditure, the relationship between capital expenditure and GNP and that between public saving and GNP. In Section 111, the relationship of total revenue to GNP and the relative importance of direct taxes, taxes on foreign trade and other revenue were brought out. Finally, in the last section, the various constituents of local authority expenditure and revenue were analysed.

Several features of this exposition should be noted. The first is that much of the data had to be extracted by hard manual labour from the original government budget papers; dishes had to be prepared, as it were, from staple ingredients rather than convenience mixes. Having assembled the data the authors confined themselves to fairly simple manipulations of the figures. But the comments made and judgements offered were far from rudimentary, with a number of bold and startling generalisations reflecting not just the tabulations in front of them but also practical knowledge and personal experience of the countries under discussion. Starting from the general aim of examining how the pattern of revenue and expenditure differs at various levels of development ranging from poor African and Asian countries to the USA, a major theme was the need to raise the ratio of revenue to GNP to some 20% to finance a minimum level of current expenditure and make provision for adequate capital formation. This is simply one illustration of the authors' willingness to make normative judgements and not confine discussion to the analysis of observed differences in revenue and expenditure patterns. A wide-angled approach of this kind can illuminate a lot of ground; for instance, the kernel of what has been variously described as the relative price effect of Baumol's disease (i.e. the consequences of divergences in productivity growth rates over time between the goods and services sectors) is to be found on pp. 206-8 of the paper. There are also dangers in an approach embodying both factual exposition and policy advice e.g. the advocacy of general sales taxes in developing countries on p. 227 has not found many Finance Ministers willing to introduce such taxes in a really comprehensive fashion.

The remainder of this paper will be what is best termed a lazy survey of the development of some of the more important topics covered in Martin and Lewis (1956). It will be a survey in the sense of picking out some of the main developments in the last quarter-century, drawing on inter alia another contribution by Sir Arthur Lewis (1967) and some previous papers by this author (1972, 1978(a), 1978(b), 1981). The exposition will be lazy in the double sense of not indulging in any new statistical exercises and in not giving a comprehensive list of references. The need for the latter is largely met by another recent publication (Afxentiou 1979) which lists the main contributions up to 1975 or so. Subsequent contributions will be referred to in this paper.

Section ll will outline the general developments of the various subjects covered in the Martin and Lewis paper. Section lll will concentrate on the details of that topic which has attracted and continues to attract most attention: the ratio of total revenue or expenditure to a national aggregate. In Section lV we review the criticisms which have been levelled against the methodology and conclusions of the studies

examined in Section 111. Finally, we say something
in Section V about the lessons to be learned from a
quarter-century's history of thought on this particular subject.

SECTION 11

It should be made clear at the outset that
this paper is being written at the beginning of 1981
and so any major findings which may appear around that
time or subsequently will not be taken into account.
Furthermore, we confine ourselves to published material or at least material which is widely available and
so do not pretend to touch on, for instance, surveys
which are internal to international organisations.

As we have seen, the original Martin and
Lewis article covered a number of separate topics :
ratio of total expenditure or revenue to GNP, the
composition of expenditure and revenue, the particular
features of local revenue and expenditure. The amount
of attention paid to these different topics in subsequent years has varied very considerably.

It seems fair to say that interest in
expenditure and revenue composition has been somewhat
fitful. If, for instance, we look at Musgrave's work,
we find a reasonably extensive coverage of these
subjects together with econometric results of varying
degrees of satisfactoriness in Musgrave (1969) but a
fairly attenuated treatment in Musgrave and Musgrave
(1980) with references to data which are a number of
years old (ibid, pp. 803 & 813). International
Monetary Fund authors, who dominate the field on the
taxation side, have given some attention to revenue
composition in the past (Chelliah, 1971 and Chelliah
et al, 1975) but the subject is not mentioned in the
most recent offering from that source (Tait et al,
1979). It should also be added that even when revenue
composition has been mentioned by this group of
writers it has received far less intensive discussion
than the subject of total tax revenue/ national
aggregate ratios. And although concentrated work is
to be found in recent examinations of expenditure
composition in individual countries (Meerman, 1979;
Solowsky, 1979) attempts at larger scale comparative
exercises are less frequent than they were a few years

age (see, for instance, Pryor 1968, and Enweze, 1973 as examples of earlier work).

Martin and Lewis also devoted a whole section of their paper to local finance problems. In this area developments have been very uneven. Little attempt has been made to follow the Martin and Lewis lead in examining expenditure patterns but, on the other hand, there have been a number of examinations of local revenue sources, especially in recent years. Lent (1978), Bahl (1979) and Prest (1981) are examples.

What is absolutely clear is that there has been much more interest over the years in the relationships of total revenue or expenditure to national aggregates than in the topics above. However, there is one major departure from the Martin and Lewis position in that they looked at these relationships for a wide range of countries at all levels of development. More recently, there have been two different streams of work, one relating to developing and the other to developed countries. In addition to the IMF authors mentioned earlier, other IMF contributions to comparative analysis of developing countries have been made by Lotz and Morss (1967), Bahl (1971) and Bahl (1972).

Typical of the developed country analysis is the annual publication of revenue data by OECD (1980) and the many articles based thereon. In emphasising this division of labor, we do not imply that an individual working in one field never mentions the other. It is rather that people have become wary of the meaning of econometric exercises applied across the board to such ratios. (See, for instance, Musgrave and Musgrave, 1980 pp. 149-51, for the argument that a good linear fit of total tax/GNP to income per head for all countries together may be very misleading).

To summarise, Martin and Lewis have been followed by a large and still very active set of discussions relating to the totality of taxes and expenditures, but work in the other fields of their enquiry has been more spasmodic.

SECTION 111

We now distinguish the main features of the

total tax or expenditure studies as they have evolved over the years.

The first proposition is that although there are still plenty of deficiencies in the data, they are at least readily available and no longer have to be dug out from the original sources. Data on revenue are now available in some detail from United Nations (1979b), IMF (1980) and OECD (1980) publications. And GNP and similar aggregate totals are to be found on a regular basis in the UN Yearbook of National Accounts Statistics (1979a) together with amplifications such as those in UN (1980). A prepared set of ingredients such as these was simply not available in the early 1950's.

A second feature of modern developments is the extensive use of econometric techniques. The pioneering work was by Hinrichs (1966) and Lotz and Morss (1967). Lotz and Morss regressed the ratio of tax yield to GNP on income per head and a measure of foreign trade, as likely indicators of ability to pay taxes. The particular format of these regressions has changed over the years, the latest IMF publication (Tait et. al., 1979) concentrating on non-export income per capita, the share of mining and oil in GNP and the ratio of exports (excluding minerals) to GNP. Whatever the precise format of the equation the aim has been to estimate a "standard" ratio so that comparisons might be made with the actual tax/GNP ratio. It might also be noted that the most recent exercise was noteworthy for its use of more sophisticated statistical techniques in the shape of two-stage least squares as well as ordinary least squares.

Before summarising the sorts of lessons which have been drawn from these exercises, another approach should also be noted. Bahl (1972) showed how the concept of the yield of a representative tax system (as given by the average of effective tax rates for all the countries in the sample, multiplied by the relevant base for an individual country) could be used, when compared with the yield of the actual tax system operating in a country, to deduce various lessons about relative tax performance of different countries. As the lessons drawn are of the same kind as those stemming from the more usual regression techniques, we shall not spend more time on this line of approach but simply note that it is an alternative way of proceeding.

Whichever of these approaches is taken three different calculations have to be made for each individual country. First, there is the straightforward ratio of tax yield to GNP. One can get a certain way with such figures by examining the differences between countries and searching for the explanations of the differences in much the same way as did Martin and Lewis, or as is often done today with the OECD data. But clearly one is very limited in the deductions which can legitimately be drawn from such summary statistics, there being many admissible explanations of such differences in most cases. Secondly, by use of regression (or representative tax systems) techniques it is possible to estimate the ratio which one might expect to find in any given country given its supply of such "tax handles" as a mining or oil sector. In other words, the tax/GNP ratio predicted from the regression equation can be thought of as corresponding to a measure of the taxable capacity of a country, slippery as that concept is (Prest, 1978b). Thirdly, once a measure such as that is available a comparison can then be made with the actual ratio, thereby deriving a measure of tax effort in any one country. In other words, tax effort is measured by dividing the actual ratio of taxation to GNP by the predicted ratio.

On the basis of such calculations, one can divide countries into four different groups at any one time:

(a)   high capacity and high effort
(b)   low capacity and high effort
(c)   high capacity and low effort
(d)   low capacity and low effort

Examples of countries falling in each category in 1975 were (a) Brazil; (b) Sudan; (c) Trinidad; and (d) Pakistan.

Alternatively, if comparable calculations for more than one year are available one can have a classification of tax effort into high and falling, high and rising, low and falling, and low and rising. Examples given by Tait et al (1979, p. 136) for each

of these categories in the 1970's are respectively
Senegal, Sudan, Paraguay and Bolivia. Comparisons
can also be made between changes over time in tax
ratios and in measures of tax effort. It is worth
noting that approximately half the 47 countries in
the 1979 sample were judged to have reduced tax effort
in the period considered even though some two-thirds
were characterised by increases in tax/GNP ratios.
And needless to say, there are plenty of ways in
which one can refine the analysis such as by distin-
guishing between large and small countries, high
population and low population densities, geographical
location and so on.

SECTION 1V
        In appraising data and the manipulation of
data relating to total revenue or expenditure and
national aggregates the first question is whether the
data commonly used are appropriate for the purpose in
hand.

        Clearly there are likely to be many techni-
cal deficiencies, especially in developing countries.
That goes without saying. It also goes without saying that many people will admit it, but promptly
proceed to argue as if they had never heard of such a
proposition. Not much can be done about that particular human frailty but it should be specifically noted
that the figures of local revenues are often incomplete and so overall tax data are likely to be
particularly deficient in that respect (Chelliah, 1971,
p. 257).

        Apart from, but in no sense neglecting,
technical deficiencies there is also the fundamental
question of what one is trying to measure when using
such data. The usual argument (Shoup 1969, Prest
1972) is that in the case of public expenditure one is
trying to measure the cost of the payments which it
has been decided to make on a non-market basis; and
with public revenue one is concerned with the flow of
income which is compulsorily deducted from individuals,
corporations and the like and so is not at their
direct disposal. Given that general objective, many
problems arise in computing both the tax and expenditure totals and the appropriate national aggregate.

231

In looking at tax or expenditure totals there is the familiar question whether some items are better included positively on one side of the accounts or negatively on the other. There are many manifestations of this alternative treatment and a good deal of illumination has been shed on it in the tax-expenditure literature of recent years (Surrey 1973; Willis and Hardwick 1978). Profits of public utilities and the like raise a series of questions and it can be debated whether the relevant entry in the taxation total is the totality of such profits or only the excess over some normal rate of return on capital employed. Social security is a long-standing conundrum, the answer being heavily dependant on whether one thinks of social security contributions as being nearer to a payment for a specific quid pro quo or nearer to the standard concept of a tax.

Other issues have also come to the surface in recent years. As governments are usually net debtors they tend to make capital gains in real terms when prices rise; this 'inflation tax' is just as much a diversion of purchasing power from the population at large as that due to, say, an income tax and so there is a strong case for including it in the revenue total. There are also some built-in mechanisms to take into account. Suppose the authorities raise tax rates in an attempt to raise the tax/GNP ratio; insofar as the result is more unrecorded activity and concealment of income that will pro tanto lead to a recorded tax/GNP ratio which is greater than the true one.

Leaving aside the inaccuracy of national aggregate data in developing countries (peasant agriculture and all that), there are also some issues of principle. Some are pretty hackneyed questions such as the choice between GNP and GDP, the market price v. factor cost controversy and so on. What is less often discussed is what sort of concept relates most closely to the stream of income from which tax payments are made. I have argued on a previous occasion (Prest, 1972) that the most appropriate concept is something like personal income (including personal capital gains) plus undistributed profits of companies (together with corporation taxes paid) and, in addition, the trading surpluses or net property income of public corporations. I do not propose to reiterate

232

all the arguments here but would simply assert that such a total comes much nearer to that which is relevant for these purposes than do the conventional national aggregates.

But, it might be said, does any of this matter? I think it does. In an earlier paper (Prest, 1978a) I showed that relatively small changes in the composition of the public expenditure total and the definition of a national aggregate would produce expenditure/national aggregate ratios ranging from 44% to 54% in the UK in 1974. And a recent paper on the operation of VAT in Italy (Pedone, 1980) suggests that concealment of taxable transactions is on a monumental scale in that country.

But suppose we leave on one side all these questions of defining and measuring revenue/expenditure totals and appropriate national aggregates, are there any problems to do with the inwardness of taxable capacity and tax effort calculations? An extremely important line of thought was opened up by Richard Bird (1976) in arguing that a statistical relationship between tax/GNP and income per head can have two entirely different meanings. It may on the one hand be an indicator of ability to pay, with the implication that countries with acutal tax/expenditure ratios below predicted ratios are making low tax efforts. This, as we have seen, is the usual interpretation. On the other hand, it can plausibly be argued that demand for public expenditure, whether on goods and services or transfer payments, is an increasing function of income per head. In other words, we have a relationship indicating willingness to pay tax to finance public expenditure; and on this interpretation divergences between actual and computed ratios reflect differences in attitudes towards the advantages of public and private provision rather than differential tax effort. Thus country A may have a higher income per head than country B but a lower ratio of tax (and expenditure) to GNP. This might be due to, say, a preference for leaving medical services, pensioner provision and the like in the private sector rather than to slackness in imposing or collecting taxes.

What is really at stake here is a modern manifestation of the very old econometric problem of identification - of not knowing whether a structural relation between prices and quantities, for instance, reflects a demand or a supply function. It may be that some formulations of the relationship between the tax/GNP ratio and other variables which have been explored to get round this difficulty. But the authors of these various exercises have not really paid the necessary amount of attention to this problem. And it is certainly not easy to see any line of escape in a number of cases (e.g. the inclusion of non-export per capita income as an explanatory variable can equally well be regarded as an indicator of low ability to pay tax or of low demand for government provision, associated with, say, a large rural population).

Now let us make another large flight of the imagination and assume that we know that the regression inform us unambiguously about ability or about willingness to pay tax. What inferences can then be drawn?

The first authority to quote is Sir Arthur Lewis himself, who wrote as follows (Lewis 1967 p.210):

> "Such comparisons (of revenue and expenditure in relation to GDP) are obviously of limited value. They are relevant only in cases where most countries have the same proportion or where differences can be clearly related to some measurable index. Even then they are merely suggestive; if your country's proportion is very different from what the index suggests, you do not conclude that it is wrong but merely start trying to discover what accounts for the difference."

One can also note a change in gear among the successive IMF writers on this subject. Whereas earlier authors all used the term 'tax effort' to characterise differences between actual and computed ratios, the latest version (Taitt et al, 1979) prefers to use the term "international tax comparison" on the grounds that "it eliminates the connotation that

234

countries with low tax indices could try harder to raise their tax revenues and that they are making insufficient "efforts" to raise them". (op. cit. p. 126)

But if the calculations are devoid of any implications about what countries could or should do, what exactly do they tell us? Obviously, there are a number of areas on which they do not shed any light; and, we must hasten to add, no one has ever seriously pretended that they did. The degree of government involvement in an economy cannot possibly be captured in this way. One might, for instance, have two countries, one with government financial provision for people injured in accidents at work and the other with legislation enabling injured workers to pursue claims against employers in the courts; both situations reflect government intervention in the working of the market but only the first would affect the tax/GNP ratio. A second illustration of the irrelevance of actual or predicted tax/GNP ratios is the determinants of upper limits to taxation in a country. This is a subject which has attracted a good deal of attention over the years from Colin Clark (1945) to Carl Shoup (1981). But no one could argue that actual or predicted tax/GNP ratios shed light on it.

Of course, one can always say that such calculations are of use when combined with various judgmental factors in taking views about tax levels and tax policy in particular countries. This is indeed a standard argument in much of the literature (Chelliah, 1971 pp. 298-300; Tait et al, 1979, p. 140). Even this argument, however, must be qualified in the light of some of the recent findings about the vulnerability of the statistical results to changes in the sample and data availability. Rank correlations do not fare too badly but nevertheless the most recent IMF authors do have to say (Tait et al, 1979, p. 142):

> "However, many countries' ITC (International Tax Comparison) indices are sufficiently sensitive to changes in sampling procedures that the degree of precision and stability provided by the rankings may be misleading."

One might be forgiven for thinking that such a

statement is more naturally associated with an
epitaph than a hymn of victory.

SECTION V

For our final topic we ask what lessons can
be learned from the economic analyses and statistical
exercises relating to this subject over the last
quarter-century.

The first is that the subject is no longer
easily amenable to one or two researchers using slide
rules or even pocket calculators. Although data about
individual countries are more plentiful and more readily available than formerly, it should be noted that
the latest IMF exercise (Tait et al 1979) explicitly
mentions that it had to draw on unpublished information (op. cit. p. 126). Investigations now tend to
relate to groups of 50-60 countries rather than 10-20.
And whatever the precise meanings of some of the
regressions which one finds, it would obviously be
unrealistic to think that one can tackle these issues
today without the use of such techniques.

Secondly, investigators have become much
more cautious and circumspect over the years. As we
have seen, examinations of developing country data
tend to be conducted separately from those relating to
developed countries. It is no longer fashionable to
think that there are some grand laws of motion explaining the fiscal history of all countries whatever their
stage of development; or that there is one road and
one road only along which all countries travel. These
more cautious attitudes also colour the approach taken
by most investigators. Although there may be recourse
to special information of one kind or another, the
personal experiences and predilections of the authors
are kept out of sight and maybe even out of mind.
Changes in terminology also reflect this change in
attitudes, with the phrase 'tax effort' being replaced
by 'international tax comparisons'.

Thirdly, most of the running has been made by
studies relating total revenue and expenditure to
national aggregates rather than those concerned with
revenue and expenditure composition. Whether one is
much nearer to agreed interpretations of the meaning

of actual or predicted ratios of tax or expenditure
to GNP is another question. I must confess to being
more sceptical of their usefulness than I was a few
years ago. And one might note that others have had
similar changes of mind (Bird, 1976). I would not
wish to condemn such studies as being devoid of any
useful content but it now seems to me that their role
is subordinate to that of detailed country studies
rather than the other way round. And there are certainly other calculations relating to aggregate data
such as income elasticities of tax yields, which
should not be thought of as poor relations of international tax comparisons, to use the most recent
euphemism again.

But when all is said and done there is one
very good reason for remaining vigilant about exercises involving aggregate revenue and expenditure data:
that uses may so easily become abuses. There are
dozens of examples which might be quoted but pride of
place (no mean honour) might be given to a UK
government Green Paper The Taxation of Husbands and
Wives (1980). Page 29 contains the following statement:

> " ..... substituting a cash benefit
> for existing tax allowances would mean
> increasing public expenditure. In the
> government's view more than accounting
> conventions are involved here: the
> distinction between cash benefits
> (which increase public expenditure) and
> tax allowances (which do not) is an
> important one."

It may be that the authors of this statement had the
idea that incentives to work, save and so on are less
adversely affected the smaller are the published
totals of revenue and expenditure. If so, that is a
singularly simple-minded view of the complex interactions between tax rates and allowances, expenditure
levels and components and incentives. Alternatively,
they may have felt that despite the usual arguments
against tax expenditures there is some great merit in
keeping the published expenditure total (and with it
the ratio of expenditure to GNP) as low as possible.
If so, why not add to the list of tax expenditures by

say, publishing interest payments on public debt or renumeration of civil servants on a net of tax basis? With sufficient ingenuity, we might get the ratio of tax and expenditure to GNP down to single figures!

All in all if, after two hundred years of systematic economic analysis the government of a major country can make a statement of this sort, there is still plenty of educative work to be done. So I would certainly endorse the continuation of work on tax and expenditure ratios for the non-trivial reason that it may help counteract nonsensical statements which might otherwise go unchallenged.

REFERENCES

Afxentiou, P.C. *Patterns of Government Revenue and Expenditure in Developing Countries and their Relevance to Policy*, Centre of Planning and Economic Research, Athens, No.35, 1979.

Bahl, R.W. 'A Regression Approach to Tax Effort and Tax Ratio Analysis' *International Monetary Fund Staff Papers*, Vol. XVlll, No. 3, November 1971.

Bahl, R.W. 'A Representative Tax System Approach to Measuring Tax Effort in Developing Countries', *International Monetary Fund Staff Papers*, Vol. XV, No. 1, March 1972.

Bahl, R.W. (ed). *The Taxation of Urban Property in Less Developed Countries*', University of Wisconsin Press, Madison 1979.

Bird, R.M. 'Assessing Tax Performance in Developing Countries : a Critical Review of the Literature', *Finanzarchiv*, Vol. 34, No. 2, 1976.

Chelliah, R.J. 'Trends in Taxation in Developing Countries' *International Monetary Fund Staff Papers*, Vol. XVlll, No. 2, July 1971.

Chelliah, R.J., Baas, H.J. & Kelly M.R. 'Tax Ratios and Tax Effort in Developing Countries, 1969-71, *International Monetary Fund Staff Papers*, Vol. XXll, No. 1, March 1975.

Clark, C. 'Public Finance and Changes in the Value of Money', *Economic Journal*, Vol. LV, December 1945.

Enweze, C. 'Structure of Public Expenditure in Selected Developing Countries : a Time Series Study' in *The Manchester School*, Vol. XLl, No. 4, 1973.

Hinrichs, H.L. *A General Theory of Tax Structure Change During Economic Development*, Harvard Law School, Cambridge, Mass. 1966.

International Monetary Fund *Government Finance Statistics Yearbook*, Vol. lV, 1980, Washington D.C.

239

Lent, G.E. 'Experience with Urban Land Value Tax in Developing Countries' *Bulletin for International Fiscal Documentation*, Vol XXX11, February 1978.

Lewis, W.A. "Planning Public Expenditure" in M.E. Millikan (ed.) *National Economic Planning*, National Bureau of Economic Research, Columbia University Press, New York 1967.

Lotz, J.R. and Morss, E.R. 'Measuring "Tax Effort" in Developing Countries' *International Monetary Fund Staff Papers*, Vol. X1V, No. 3, September 1956.

Martin, A. & Lewis, W.A. 'Patterns of Public Revenue and Expenditure' *The Manchester School*, Vol. XX1V, No. 3, September 1956.

Meerman, J. *Public Expenditure in Malaysia*, World Bank/ Oxford University Press, Oxford 1979.

Musgrave, R.A. *Fiscal Systems*, Yale University Press, New Haven 1969.

Musgrave, R.A. and P.B. *Public Finance in Theory and Practice*, Third Edition, McGraw Hill, New York 1980.

Organisation for Economic Co-operation and Development *Revenue Statistics of OECD Member Countries*, 1965-1979, Paris 1980.

Pedone, A. "Italy", Brookings Institution Conference on Value Added Tax, Washington D.C., October 1980 (processed).

Prest, A.R. 'Government Revenue, the national income and all that' in

Bird, R.M. and Head, J.G. (eds) *Modern Fiscal Systems*, University of Toronto Press, Toronto 1972.

Prest, A.R. 'Public Activities in Perspective : a Critical Survey' in International Institute of Public Finance (ed. H.C. Recktenwald) *Secular Trends of the Public Sector*, Cujas, Paris 1978(a).

Prest, A.R. 'The Taxable Capacity of a Country' in Toye J.F.J. (editor) *Taxation and Economic Development*,

Frank Cass, London 1978(b).

Prest, A.R. 'Land Taxation and Urban Finances in Less Developed Countries' in *Proceedings World Congress of Land Policy*, Cambridge, Mass. 1981.

Pryor, F.C. *Public Expenditures in Communist and Capitalist Nations*, George Allen and Unwin, London 1968.

Selowsky, M. *Who Benefits from Government Expenditure? A Case Study of Colombia*, World Bank/Oxford University Press, Oxford 1979.

Shoup, C.S. 'Economic Limits to Taxation', *Atlantic Economic Journal*, March 1981.

Surrey, S.S. *Pathways to Tax Reform*, Harvard University Press, Cambridge, Mass. 1973.

Tait, A.A., Gratz, W.L.M. and Eichengreen, B.J. 'International Comparisons of Taxation for Selected Developing Countries, 1972-76' *International Monetary Fund Staff Papers*, Vol. XXVl, No. 1, March 1979.

The Taxation of Husbands and Wives, Cmnd 8093, H.M. Stationery Office, London, December 1980.

United Nations 'Comparative GDP Levels' *Economic Bulletin for Europe*, Vol. XXXl, No. 2, New York 1980.

United Nations *Yearbook of National Accounts Statistics 1978*, New York 1979(a).

United Nations *Statistical Yearbook 1978*, New York 1979(b).

Willis, J.R.M. & Hardwick, P.J.W. *Tax Expenditures in the UK*, Institute for Fiscal Studies/Heinemann, London 1978.

THE TERMS OF TRADE AND DEVELOPMENT

by
W. W. Rostow*

INTRODUCTION

This essay concerns the interacting linkage between movements in the terms of trade and economic development. It argues not only that conventional neo-classical economic theory does not provide tools capable of usefully framing this problem but also that critical variables must be introduced from outside the terrain of economics.

SECTION 11

A good deal of Arthur Lewis' work has focused on the connections between the terms of trade and economic development: both the commodity (or net barter) terms of trade and the factoral terms of trade measuring relative physical productivity. His approach and method belong in a long tradition reaching back to Adam Smith and Robert Torrens, carried forward in counterpoint to orthodox foreign trade theory by Keynes, D.H. Robertson, Colin Clark, C.P. Kindleberger, and myself, among others.[1] It is a tradition of dynamic Marshallian long period analysis which takes its start historically with the perception that the course of productivity might differ as between agriculture and raw materials, on the one hand, manufactures, on the other. Thus, Adam Smith contrasts the "necessary rise on the real price of rude materials" with "the natural effect of improvement -- to diminish gradually the real price of almost all manufactures."[2] But economic history did not unfold in a simple and elegant way, reflecting the steady operation of diminishing and increasing returns to raw materials and manufactures, respectively. There were, it is true, recurrent fears that the old devil, diminishing returns, was at last, once and for all, about to force an industrializing world, in

*I wish to acknowledge with thanks the helpful comments on an earlier draft of this essay by David Kendrick, Charles P. Kindleberger, and Stephen P. Magee.

242

Stanley Jevons' phrase, 'to reduce its motion to rest.'[3] But the opening up of new areas and resources, multiple revolutions in transport, and the generation of new technologies relevant to agricultural and raw materials output have managed for two centuries to fend off diminishing returns to the sectors rooted in material resources, excepting timber where substitutes have had to suffice. Now, in the wake of the explosion of grain and energy prices in 1972-1973, it is once again to be proved, as on at least four occasions in the past, that human ingenuity and enterprise can continue to hold diminishing returns at bay.

The unfolding of this drama, since the late eighteenth century, has taken the form of erratic, more or less cyclical phases of relatively abundant and relatively scarce basic commodities yielding periods of relatively low and relatively high prices for Smith's "rude materials." The phases were not only erratic but, of course, the relative prices of such materials did not all move together. Nevertheless, the analytic literature to which much of Lewis' work belongs responded to such phase and, in some cases, looked back over the sweep of history in an effort to give order and sense to the contemporary scene. That was notably true of the period between the two world wars. A great deal of this literature was oriented towards Britain, a massive importer of basic commodities, coal excepted. It was, therefore, natural that analysis of this bent should examine the discomfiture experienced by a highly industrialized nation as it sought to adjust to large, often sudden, shifts in its commodity terms of trade; e.g., Keynes, Robertson, Clark, Alfred Kahn. Lewis belongs to a narrower group of analysts who have been at least equally concerned with the impact of such shifts on nations producing and exporting predominantly basic commodities.

The fact is that the major shifts in the terms of trade over the past two centuries can only be understood if one is prepared to examine the price dynamics of the major commodities entering into world trade; and then to examine the impact of their special vicissitudes on the terms of trade of particular countries in the light of the changing composition of their imports and exports, as they move -- or fail to move -- through the stages of economic growth. One must learn a good deal about wheat and cotton, wool and coal, meat and dairy products, timber, coffee, oil, etc. It is interesting, rich, often inelegant, work; but indispensable if one aims to account for the terms of trade movements that have actually occurred. Putting wars and the luck of weather aside, such analyses, however, are not shapeless, empirical exercises. As I have long argued, what we observe in economic history are dynamic, interacting national economies, trying rather clumsily to approximate optimum sectoral equilibrium paths -- Allyn Young's "moving equilibrium" -- tending successively to undershoot and overshoot these paths, like a drunk making his way home on Saturday night.

Take, for example, the British terms of trade set out in Chart 1 for the period 1796-1974.4

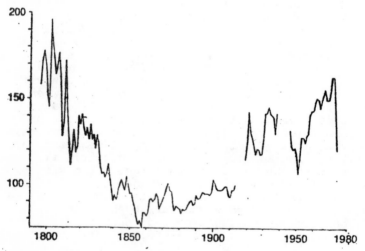

CHART 1. *British Terms of Trade, 1796–1974 (1913 = 100)*

Source: Albert H. Imlah, *Economic Elements in the Pax Britannica,* updated from Board of Trade data (*Statistical Abstract of the United Kingdom*).

Putting aside the complexities of the

pre-1815 years, much influenced by harvest fluctuations and the relative efficacy of blockades and embargoes, here, tersely summarized, are some of the major forces which determined movements in the British terms of trade.

The postwar rise: 1814-1821. Despite a few bad harvest years, the return of peace brings down the prices of basic commodities, notably cotton and wheat, more than export prices. This happened because sources of supply obstructed by war are reopened, while freight and insurance rates fall sharply.

The downward trend: 1821-1840. Down to 1830 this powerful movement is the outcome of an interacting race between the decline of both export and import prices; specifically, between the cheapening of raw cotton, as new areas were opened up, the cotton gin was diffused, and Atlantic freight rates fell, and the cheapening of cotton goods, as the technologies of modern manufacture unfolded. When the differing proportions raw cotton bore to total imports, cotton goods to total exports, and the proportion of raw cotton to total cost of manufacture are taken into account, it emerges that the net downward trend in the British terms of trade up to 1830 is mainly the consequence of the technological revolution in the cotton industry.[5]

Although technological progress in cotton manufacture continued at a decelerating rate beyond 1830, the sharp deterioration of the British terms of trade in the 1830's results from a different set of circumstances than those operating in the 1820's; the catching up of cotton demand with existing acreage by the end of the 1820's; the consequent transatlantic cotton boom down to 1836;and then a sharp decline in British export prices, after the cyclical peak of 1836, unmatched by an equivalent fall in import prices.

Easement in the 1840's. The relative supply of cotton and some other basic commodities generated by investments of the 1830's permits Britain a powerful cyclical expansion, with a double peak in 1845 and 1847, accompanied by a favorable shift in the terms of trade; but the Irish potato famine and parallel troubles on the Continent yield a rise in imported grain prices and a transient terms of trade deterioration in 1845-1847.

The terms of trade collapse of the 1850's. The British terms of trade worsened by 18% between 1848 and 1857. At the heart of this shift was a turning point in the relative price of grain. The international wheat price just about doubled in 1852-1854 and, in the United States, fluctuated thereafter in a relatively high range. The raw cotton price also rose substantially, as demand caught up with the over-supply induced during the boom of the 1830's. These relative price movements led to a major expansion into new wheat and cotton lands in the United States, accompanied by large capital imports (as in the 1830's) and massive immigration. The inflationary forces at work from these causes were heightened by the Crimean War and the Indian Mutiny.

The quiet 1860's, the transient energy crisis of 1871-1873 and its subsidence to 1877. Despite the effect of the American Civil War on the raw cotton price, the British terms of trade oscillated in a higher range during most of the 1860's than in the previous decade: higher prices for textile exports (including wool and linen) and some years of abundant, cheap grain (notably, 1863-1866) countered the quadrupling of the cotton price from 1860 to 1864. In the great boom leading up to 1873, centered in Germany and the United States, the British coal export price doubled, in the face of an intense, transient supply bottleneck, as did the price of pig iron, yielding a sharp peak in the British terms of trade which subsided to a trough in 1877 as the first phase of the Great Depression struck harder at British export than import prices. This happened, in part, because a building boom in Britain was sustained down to 1877, despite the cyclical peak in 1873. Between 1873 and 1877 coal prices fell by more than a half; timber prices by only 14%.

Improvements and reversal, 1877-1913. After moving irregularly in the phase of acute depression (1878-1879) and the "profitless" expansion of 1880-1881, a new phase begins. From the early 1880's to the famous reversal of price trends in the mid-1890's, powerful supply-side forces, including enlarged U.S. wheat exports from the late 1870's and a rapid fall in freight rates, drove down British import more rapidly than export prices; and in the subsequent boom another major coal shortage, induced in part by shipping requirements during the Boer War, imparted a second-stage booster to the British terms of trade, lifting them to a level 19% higher than their 1881 low. A 6% deterioration followed, down to the eve of the First World War, as the United States reached the end of its frontier and a rise in prices for imported raw materials (notably cotton and wheat) lifted import prices even more rapidly than rather ebullient export prices,the latter responding to rapid expansions in Canada, Australia, Argentina, New Zealand, and other areas producing and exporting foodstuffs and raw materials.

There is an evident parallel between the basic commodity price turnarounds of the mid-1890's and the early 1850's and their aftermaths in enlarged capital exports from Britain to overseas agricultural regions; but the large British coal export position cushioned the impact on the British terms of trade in the latter case.

Inter-war pathology, 1919-1938. The British terms of trade index was about 25% more favorable in 1920 than in 1913, the product of a brief export boom; but the underlying over-supply of basic commodities, in the face of relatively sluggish European growth, asserted itself with the recession of 1920-1921, maintaining favorable terms of trade for the balance of the decade as compared to the pre-1914 years, although below the 1920 peak. The terms of trade improve 24% between 1929 and 1933 during the deep global depression, but they trend downward thereafter (excepting the sharp recession year 1938) as the demand for raw materials expands and policies of supply constraint in agricultural and raw material production have some success. As we all know, this phase of extraordinarily favorable British terms of trade was largely dissipated by its depressing effects in British overseas markets, compounded by the 1925 return of the pound to its pre-war gold value, leading to chronic high unemployment in British export

industries, diminished earnings in shipping, loss of
investment income, etc.

Post-1945 strain and two decades of easement: 1946-1972. The terms of trade in immediate
post-war Britain were substantially less favorable
than in 1938 as agricultural and raw material production revived less rapidly than industrial output; and
the trend continued down to 1951, exacerbated by the
effect on raw material prices of the Korean War.
This imposed strain on the British standard of living
but rendered possible a rapid expansion of exports to
overseas markets and a reduction in the sterling
balances built up during the war -- a process compensated for, in part, by Marshall Plan aid. From
1951, however, the terms of trade for Britain and
other advanced industrial countries improved down to
1972 underpinning the great boom in consumers durables
and services of that generation. The improvement
decelerated as the 1960's wore on. Unlike the inter-
war years, the marked improvement in the terms of
trade was not dissipated in unemployment: the proportion of British trade with primary producers was
less; and the primary producers were better sustained
by their own development efforts, the strength of the
boom in the North, and, to a degree, by a flow of
inter-governmental loans and grants.

The inter-war years in reverse: 1972-   .
Foreshadowed in the 1960's by attenuating grain stocks
in relation to global consumption and by the peaking
out of U.S. oil and natural gas production around
1970, Britain and the advanced industrial countries
experienced as sharp an unfavorable shift in the terms
of trade in 1972-1973, with the explosions in grain
and oil prices, as they did a favorable shift after
the First World War. And they have done almost as
poor a job in gearing their policies to the new
realities in the world economy, notably the high and
rising real price of energy -- a subject to which we
shall return.

This brisk and evidently incomplete summary
of the major forces operating over some 180 years on
the British terms of trade is meant to drive home a
simple point: terms of trade movements reflect an
extraordinary melange of forces, including the supply-

demand history of particular commodities; industrial, agricultural, and transport innovations; business cycles: wars; in fact, the whole range of factors which have shaped the world economy over the past two centuries. If one is concerned to explain terms of trade movements, there is no way to escape the kind of laborious historical analysis of an erratically expanding world economy the inherent complexity of the problem demands.

SECTION 111

In a majestic, parochial tour de force, conventional expositions of the theory of international trade, rooted in Ricardo and the more static propositions of Torrens, have managed down to the present day virtually to set aside the variables required to understand movements in the terms of trade. This is all the more remarkable because Frank Taussig induced an impressive array of his inter-war students to test the adequacy of classical foreign trade theory as it related to the role of the terms of trade in the transfer mechanism.[6] The results differed, of course, country by country; but John Williams' conclusion is a fair summary of what these exercises demonstrated:[7] "The classical theory assumes as fixed, for purposes of reasoning, the very things which, in my view, should be the chief objects of study if what we wish to know is the effects and causes of international trade, so broadly regarded that nothing of importance in the facts shall fail to find its place in the analysis."

Nevertheless, in Frank Graham's phrase, mainstream analyses of international trade have "done nothing but tread the same old Mill;"[8] although they have done so with refinements of increasing elegance to which diminishing returns have sharply applied.

Put less polemically, the conventional theory of international trade continues to address itself to a set of questions quite different from Williams' "effects and causes of international trade.. broadly regarded...." Those questions are set out lucidly, for example, in Chacholiades' textbook:[9]

"The pure theory of trade...is mainly

249

concerned with the following three questions:

> "1. Which goods are exported or imported...?
>
> "2. Which are the terms of trade...?
>
> "3. Which are the gains from trade...?"

In expositions in this tradition, the terms of trade begin as the factoral terms of trade; that is, they derive from the relation between the quantity of factors of production required to produce a unit of the same commodities in different countries. Conventionally, only two countries and two commodities are assumed to exist. From assumptions relating to relative labor productivity and, later, the relative productivity of the various factors of production, a range is established within which it is of advantage for the two countries to trade with one another. The exact "terms of interchange," within this productivity range, on which trade will take place, is determined by the relative "strength of the demand" of the two countries for the two commodities in question. The possible outcomes are compared, in the fundamental propositions of theory, by assuming constant returns to scale; that is, by rigorously excluding either short or long-period changes in real costs.

This assumption, along with the others within which classical trade doctrine was framed, permitted the transition from a fundamental productivity and real value consideration of international trade to a monetary and, then, income analysis approach which isolated the effects of demand shifts on the scale and composition of trade as well as on the commodity terms of trade. Short-period cost changes and supply as well as demand elasticities were introduced into the structure of classical analysis, but long-period changes were mainly ruled out. As Haberler wrote:[10]

> "A reduction of costs of this dynamic and historical nature has no place in our analysis, since it represents a change of data not to be explained by economic theory."

As neo-classical price and, then, growth theory evolved, they were also woven into conventional expositions of trade theory. With respect to price theory, Haberler's dictum continued to apply; that is, radical changes in the supply of basic commodities were excluded from the analysis. The mechanics of indifference and production possibility curves were introduced; but, as noted above, the bulk of the exposition of international trade theory is still conducted within the framework of constant returns to scale, with given factor endowments and technology.[11] It is, essentially, a static theory.

The elaboration of neo-classical growth theory, from its base in the Harrod-Domar model, has led to formal expositions of the effects of economic growth on trade. Those models were controlled by three characteristics which drastically limited their capacity to illuminate terms of trade movements in the real world:

The availability of resource-bearing land for the production of food and raw materials is either aggregated out of such models or implicitly assumed to appear as an automatic function of the level or rate of growth of demand. This casualness about the supply of basic commodities is, perhaps, an understandable reflection of the fact that most such models were designed by economists in the advanced industrial world during a period of falling or relatively low prices of basic commodities (1951-1972).

The two sectors isolated in neo-classical growth models were generally capital goods and consumption goods, produced by varying proportions of capital and labor. Therefore, the problem of relative prices and income distribution emerged as the question of the relative marginal return to capital and labor. There was no awareness that, historically, major shifts in income distribution within nations and among nations were mainly brought about by periods of relative abundance or scarcity of foodstuffs and raw materials, consequent changes in the relative prices of basic commodities, and the movements of capital and people that flowed from them.

Changes in the capital stock were viewed as incremental: no variations in periods of gestation were envisaged, if, indeed, such lags were introduced at all.

The negative outcome was not surprising. Economists working this terrain were not exploring the dynamics of relative price movements. They were, mainly, trying to define the conditions for a dynamic, full-employment equilibrium, assuming a fixed, over-all rate of technological change, with varying capital-labor (and capital-output) ratios.

With a variable for progress in technology inserted, with a stable consumption function, and with entrepreneurs assumed to choose their technologies in ways which kept inventions Harrod-neutral, such models yield a balanced equilibrium path with per capita GNP growing steadily at the rate of technical progress.

Thus, when the apparatus of neo-classical growth models is introduced into international trade theory, a process pioneered by Harry Johnson, it yields outcomes in which shifts in the terms of trade are the result of the growth process for a given country, depending on: (i) whether or not growth is concentrated in the export sector; (ii) the international price elasticity of demand for the export product; (iii) the extent to which growth is shared in the international economy; (iv) the income elasticity of demand for the export product; and (v) whether technical change is neutral, labor-saving, or capital-saving. These manipulations have permitted international trade theorists to elaborate a range of cases, including the paradoxical case of "immiserizing growth" in which excessive export-based growth by a country whose role in the world market is substantial can under certain conditions, so tip the terms of trade against it as to counter the effects of growth, yielding a net decline in real income.12

In general, one can say of this literature what Kindleberger said of the behavior of the terms of trade in the case of capital transfer:13 "Most readers will mop their brows as this point and conclude that one cannot say much about the terms of trade under capital transfer. Sad but true." In both cases -- capital transfer and growth -- the number of variables determining the upshot for the terms of trade is so great that the results are either indeterminate or can be made determinate only under strong, simplifying assumptions which render the conclusions of interest only to fellow theorists engaged in the same sport.

Basically, what is wrong with the conventional literature on the terms of trade in relation to both the transfer problem and the process of growth is that it treats changes in the terms of trade as a dependent variable. A more useful sequence is to begin with a shift in the terms of trade, with its roots in the dynamics of the world economy, and then examine the impact of that shift on trade, capital movements, population movements, and growth — including, quite possibly, playback effects of the process on the terms of trade themselves.

SECTION lV

Arthur Lewis' analysis of relative price movements in the period 1870-1913 is, in my view, a model of how one must proceed if the intent is to understand and explain the terms of trade movements that actually occur.[14] The problem is, broadly, to explain the shift in the terms of trade against agricultural products down to the mid-1890's, the subsequent improvement down to 1913 and the consequences of this relative price turnaround in both core and periphery. Lewis proceeded at both highly aggregated and disaggregated levels. In a laborious and original statistical exercise he established the aggregate rate of growth of industrial production for the major industrial countries (the core), the major cyclical fluctuations and their intensity, and the rate of population growth. He thus had in hand a rough index of demand for food and raw materials. This index is then applied to the supply of four major commodities moving in international trade -- cotton, wool, wheat, and coffee -- and equations established to yield estimated prices which can be compared to actual prices. He is then in a position to demonstrate his central proposition: the upward movement in the relative prices of agricultural prices after the mid-1890's is the result of a "decline in the rate of growth of wheat, wool, and cotton, with

the price of substitutes acting in sympathy." Lewis
was strengthened in this exercise by finding that his
method of estimation approximated the actual coffee
price which did not follow the U-shaped trend path
of the other three commodities.

Putting Lewis' further exposition of his
theme aside for a moment,it is clear that a favorable
shift in the terms of trade for agricultural products
or raw materials will have three probable and one
possible effect in the producing country or region.

1. A direct real income effect. By permitting a larger quantity of imports to be acquired
with a fixed quantum of exports a favorable shift in
the terms of trade directly raises real income.

2. An increase of immigration. Population
is likely to flow to the country or region experiencing the lift in real income brought about by a
favorable shift in the terms of trade, a lift heightened with the passage of time, by the forces delineat-
ed in elements 3 and 4.

3. An expansion of investment and acceleration of growth. The investment rate in the country or region experiencing favorable terms of trade
is likely to rise for three distinct reasons: to
supply infrastructure and other capital to expand output of the commodities whose relative rise in price
has caused the favorable shift in the terms of trade;
to supply housing and urban infrastructure for the
migrants; and to exploit disproportionately high
profit possibilities through increased capital imports.

4. A possible acceleration of industrialization. If the society experiencing the expansionary
impulses set out in elements 1-3 is otherwise prepared
to absorb new technologies efficiently, the forces
set in motion by a favorable shift in the terms of
trade can yield a surge of industrialization. This
happened, for example, in pre-1914 Canada, Australia,
and Southern Brazil. It is happening now in some
OPEC countries as well as in the western mountain
region of the United States. It did not happen in
pre-1914 Argentina, nor the tropical countries, which

benefitted to a degree from the increased real income provided by their expanding plantation sectors but did not move on, at that time, into sustained industrialization.

Returning to international trade theory, capital imports are, from this perspective, not a cause for the shift in the terms of trade but a consequence. In the 1896-1913 period it is quite clear that accelerated expansion in the peripheral areas had proceeded for some time before large capital imports arrived. This happened, in part, because the financing of the Boer War constrained the London capital market until 1903. Canadian wheat production averaged, for example, 46 million bushels in 1894-1896, 86 million in 1901-1903. Captial exports to Canada, in fact, move up only modestly until 1905 when, after a brief setback, a truly extraordinary expansion begins.[15] The pattern is general. British net investment abroad averaged £40 million per annum for the period 1896-1900; £45 million, 1901-1905; £150 million, 1906-1910; £214 million, 1911-1913.[16] The secondary role of capital imports -- reinforcing rather than initiating the process -- is suggested by the case of New Zealand. It enjoyed from the mid-1890's to 1913 a period of great expansion, including increased immigration, based on favorable terms of trade and the potentialities of refrigeration, with only a modest increase in capital imports towards the end of the period.[17]

The flow of capital abroad to the prosperous periphery enjoying favorable terms of trade did, of course, have important consequences. It permitted domestic expansion to proceed at a higher rate and/or for longer than if capital imports were not cushioning the balance of payments; and these typically disproportionate booms, backed by capital imports, had the effect of shifting the terms of trade still further in favor of the peripheral country -- a kind of second-stage booster effect. This process can also be observed in the United States during the 1830's and 1850's. But a good many cases of increased international (and interregional) capital flows cannot be understood in the first place unless one is prepared to begin where Lewis begins; that is, with the global supply-demand balance for particular commodities.

International capital flows, however, could also be induced by at least two other forces: major technological change and public policy. And the two were sometimes interwoven.

Argentina, Canada, Australia, and New Zealand, for example, imported a good deal of capital from Britain at various intervals during the period of declining basic commodity prices, say, 1873-1896.[18]

The circumstances of each country differed; but their development during an apparently unpropitious period has certain common characteristics.[19] As of 1870 these regions all suffered from transport systems inadequate for the full development of their resources; and their resources were sufficiently productive to justify economic exploitation at current, even falling, prices, given the economies in transport the railroad and the unfolding revolution in ocean shipping, based on steel, could provide. Other technical developments helped: refrigeration, barbed wire, new seed strains, agricultural machinery, and mining techniques to exploit non-agricultural resources the railroads also made accessible. Political changes in Argentina and new public policies in Canada, Australia, and New Zealand converged with these economic possibilities to draw large flows of foreign capital. Their years of golden prsoperity and massive immigration come only after the price turnaround of the mid-1890's; but the 1870's and 1880's were creative decades and a necessary prelude; and they saw considerable, if erratic, inflows of foreign capital.

In Australia, railroad mileage open more than doubled in the 1880's, a period when net capital inflow was about half of gross domestic capital formation. This occurred at a time when wool dominated Australian exports, as gold production tapered off. In the 1880's Australia turned to domestic development and found the rather depressed London capital market in a mood to finance its enterprises. There was no immediate expansion of Australian exports. But from 1884 Australian land policy changed in ways to encourage agricultural rather than pastoral activity.

The Argentine case bears a family resem-
blance to that of Australia. The initiation impulse
in this process was political: the consolidation of
a firm central government by Julio Roca in 1880. At
the time, Argentina, like Australia, was primarily
an exporter of wool. The pampas were, however,
obviously an area capable of profitable grain exploitation even at low world prices, if immigrants could
be attracted and efficient transport provided. A
massive inflow of British capital in the late 1880's
provided the latter. Unlike the case of Australia,
immigrants came to Argentina in large numbers in the
1880's. As the railways moved out over the pampas
and barbed wire permitted the segregation of pastoral
areas, the immigrants put increased acreage into production. There was a spectacular surge of output and
exports in the early 1890's, helping stabilize the
Argentine economy after the Baring Crisis in the face
of falling export prices which otherwise would have
had disastrous consequences; and then the price increase, from the mid-1890's, induced a tripling in output and a period of golden prosperity.

As in the case of Australia and Argentina,
a prior period of creative preparation was necessary
for Canada fully to exploit the possibilities of the
price increase from the mid-1890's. From the Land
Act of 1868 and the Homestead Act of 1872, the
Dominion government had been trying to bring the
western acreage, with its palpable potential for low-
cost wheat, effectively into production. But the
railroads had to be built, the population expanded by
substantial net immigration, the competition of
American extension of the frontier overcome. In addition, there was something of a lag in the adoption
and full understanding of the dry-farming techniques
pioneered in the United States. All this was framed
by an acute political awareness that a Free Trade
Britain had left Canada to fend for itself in North
America and that the dynamism of post-Civil War
United States might absorb Canada on north-south lines
unless an east-west transport axis could be established and the resources of the country developed. There
were surges of immigration and capital imports (in
support of railway building) in the early 1870's and

and 1880's; and some expansion of new homesteads, responding to transient wheat price increases in the early 1880's and a decade later; but only from the mid-1890's did the great expansion in western Canada take hold and net immigration rapidly increase.

After surviving in the 1860's the Maori rebellions and experiencing a brief gold mining boom and bust, the government of New Zealand turned in 1870 to long term policies designed to exploit its "permanent resources:"[20] "The great barrier to further progress was the lack of an adequate system of internal transport; settlement was still largely confined to coastal districts, a national system of roads had hardly been begun, and there were less than fifty miles of railway in the whole country." Over 1000 miles of railway line were open for traffic by 1877, almost 2000 by 1893. Roads and ports, telegraph, telephone, and postal communications similarly expanded. The proportion of the working force engaged in industry expanded substantially; modern farm machinery was imported and used on the wheat lands; and, above all, refrigeration was gradually introduced, changing the structure of agriculture and exports. It was in the period 1870-1882 that capital imports played their largest reinforcing role. The decline of the wool price bore down heavily; but when prices lifted New Zealand was in a position to make the most of it:[21] "After 1895 the years of meagre return for strenuous effort gave way to a period of widely diffused and increasing prosperity...solidly based upon the development of the new industries opened up by refrigeration."

The point here is simple enough: international capital movements could be set in motion by cost-cutting new technologies in transport and production -- and by public policies designed to exploit them -- as well as by relative price movements rendering the exploitation of basic commodities more profitable through the supply-demand dynamics of the world economy.

An international trade theory that excludes technological change and treats the terms of trade as the outcome of a two-country, two-commodity trading world is, thus, of extremely limited relevance.

SECTION V

We turn, finally, to an aspect of the linkage between the terms of trade and development which transcends economics; that is, the character of the response of a society to the potentialities, for good or ill, of a sharp shift in its terms of trade. Here we are dealing with a distinction I sought to make central im my Process of Economic Growth by viewing economic decisions as a result of the interaction of economic yields, representing objective economic potentialities, and a range of propensities, reflecting the effective response of a society to the yields.[22] The propensities incorporated the cultural, social, and political factors that bear on a society's economic decisions and which may dilute or, even, reinforce an outcome calculated simply in terms of profit maximization.

So far as the terms of trade in general are concerned, Kindleberger has dealt with this linkage most explicitly and systematically.[23] His central proposition is that the cost to a society of an adverse shift in its terms of trade (or of any other adverse change in demand or supply from abroad) depends on its "capacity to transform"; that the "reasons for incapacity to adjust are social in developed countries as well as underdeveloped;" and that "economics is able to tell us very little about the conditions under which given societies will respond in one way or another to the same stimulus."[24]

Arthur Lewis deals with this problem in both Growth and Fluctuations, 1870-1913 and The Evolution of the International Economic Order.[25] In the former his central concern is to explain the differential response to favorable terms of trade from the mid-1890's to 1913 of the temperate and tropical peripheral countries. In general, they all experienced the first three consequences of a favorable shift in the terms of trade listed above (pg. 254); i.e., a rise in real income, increased immigration; and expanded investment, including foreign investment; but only in Canada, Australia, New Zealand, and Southern Brazil was there a movement, on the basis of these stimuli, into sustained modern industrialization.

He prefaces this enquiry with the following observation:26

> "To explain why some countries do
> better than others within the same
> category is a formidable task,
> which needs to be approached from
> two directions simultaneously.
> One approach deals in generalisa-
> tions, in theories of what stimu-
> lates and what retards industrial-
> isation; the other deals in case
> studies of individual countries.
> Without simultaneous movement from
> both directions understanding is
> impossible. Valid generalisations
> cannot be formulated without deep
> knowledge of many (preferably all)
> individual cases; while the indivi-
> dual case cannot be understood
> without sound general theory."

This is not the occasion to paraphrase what Lewis had to say about the unique circumstances determining the outcome in each case. The point here is simply that he combines flexibly his basic general analysis of the nature of underdevelopment with social and political factors (including colonial policies, where relevant) to explain particular outcomes. As we all know, his technical explanation for underdevelopment lies in his view of the factoral terms of trade; that is, the low productivity of food production per acre (and, in some cases, per man) relative to Western Europe -- a low-level trap sustained and reinforced by acute population pressure. Thus, poor factoral terms of trade and unlimited supplies of labor decree low per capita real income and prevent a large domestic market for manufactures from emerging. The temperate countries of the periphery (including the United States) enjoyed, in general, even higher per man yields in agriculture than Europe and higher per capita real income. Under the stimulus of the favorable terms of trade of the pre-1914 generation, the latter (excepting Argentina) not only expanded their production and exports of basic

260

commodities but also moved into take-off; while the
tropical countries (excepting Southern Brazil) moved
forward no further than the higher per capita incomes
permitted by expanded production and export of tropical plantation products under favorable market circumstances.

Lewis is quite aware that there is more to
the story than low productivity in agriculture with
all its far-reaching consequences; and so he contrasts
the urban politics of Australia with the dominance of
the landed aristocracy in Argentina; clashes between
the vested interests of entrepreneurs oriented towards the import as well as export trades and those
who aimed to produce manufactures for the domestic
market; and he examines a spectrum of colonial
policies in a discriminating, subtle and dispassion-
ate way. Lewis judges their impact being in general,
not directly to frustrate economic development but
"to hinder the development of a native modernizing
cadre," in part, because of a neglect of education.[27]

Lewis describes his essay in weaving together the economic and non-economic factors as they
bore on the response to a phase of favorable terms of
trade as a limited effort "to identify contributing
factors which were common to many countries."[28] To
undertake a definitive analysis would require in each
case the kind of well-focused multi-disciplinary
approach used for example, in Cyril Black et al., The
Modernization of Japan and Russia.[29] And, indeed,
the comparative approach might work well in exploring,
for example, why a pre-1914 coffee boom (plus railroads) in Southern Brazil triggered a quite distinct
regional take-off into sustained industrialization
whereas the concurrent beef and wheat boom (plus
railroads) in Argentina failed to do so.[30]

Moving beyond the period on which Lewis
focuses his analysis, there are three final observations to be made.

First, a negative as well as a positive
shift in the terms of trade can yield a constructive
outcome if a society commands Kindleberger's

"capacity to transform" and exercises it. The best known constructive response to an almost catastrophic economic event is, of course, the successful movement of a number of Latin American countries and Turkey into their first sustained phase of industrialization during the 1930's in response to the collapse of their export markets and export prices.

Second, terms of trade shifts, positive and negative (including wartime attenuation in the supply of imports), have played a role in helping bring about a substantial proportion of the take-offs into self-sustained growth that have been analyzed. By way of a rough arbitrary sampling, I took the twenty take-offs dealt with in Part V of The World Economy: History and Prospect, plus the three regional take-offs identified (New England, Southern Brazil, and Manchuria). Of these, twenty-three cases, 11 are related to sharp terms of trade movements: 6 to favorable shifts (United States (1850's), Sweden, Canada, Australia, Southern Brazil, Russia); 5 to unfavorable shifts (New England, Argentina, Brazil, Turkey, and Mexico).

In addition, there is the pre-take-off stimulus afforded industrialization in France, Belgium, and elsewhere on the Continent by the restriction of British manufactured imports during the Napoleonic wars and the parallel process in the United States, during the Embargo and War of 1812, until Francis Cabot Lowell's success gave the New England take-off a solid foundation.

It should be noted that the United States take-off from, say, 1843 to 1860 is a rather special case: its first decade was marked by relatively low agricultural prices and unfavorable terms of trade, with investment flowing into the railroadization of the North-east and the build-up of heavy industry in the Middle Atlantic states; its second decade, by relatively high agricultural prices and favorable terms of trade, with investment, including high capital imports, flowing into the railroadization of the Middle West.

The terms of trade in relation to development is, then, a quite serious aspect of the story of how one country after another moved, finally, into sustained industrial growth; but in no case do terms of trade movements constitute a sufficient explanation for the transition; the non-economic elements at work are of critical importance; and, above all, as the early portion of this essay argued, terms of trade movements themselves can only be understood as a by-product of the dynamics of the world economy; that is, a by-product of the development process itself.

Third, the interaction between the terms of trade and development is a subject highly germane to our disconcerting experiences of the 1970's and the challenges ahead in the 1980's.

With relatively few exceptions, the nations which make up the world economy -- developed or developing, capitalist, socialist, or mixed -- have exhibited a low "capacity to transform" in the face of the massive shift in the relative price of energy, the considerable relative shift in the price of agricultural products.[31]

So far as energy is concerned, the scale and urgency of the problem of creating a new energy base in substitution for expensive and waning oil supplies has not yet been translated into effective policies. For different reasons, both the United States and the Soviet Union, each well endowed with alternative energy resources, have been extremely sluggish in adjusting to the transition ahead: the United States because of political pressures from consumer interests intent on decreeing continued cheap energy and extremist environmental groups intent on sabotaging the generation of additional energy production; in the Soviet Union because of the implication for other resource commitments of the extremely large, long period of gestation investments required to bring alternative energy resources into production. All but a few current oil exporters also confront the need to develop alternative energy resources promptly if they are to maintain the momentum of their development; but they have been content to postpone such decisions, relying implicitly on a continuing rise in the real price of oil to see them through. Meanwhile, in a profligate way, some of these nations are becoming dependent on food imports on a scale which will cost them dearly in the future. In different degree, the

oil importing developing nations are being throttled
back as the proportion of the foreign exchange they
earn allocated to oil imports continues to rise,
reaching, in some cases (e.g., India and Brazil),
close to 50%; while North-South cooperation, which
will be required to build a new energy base in the
developing regions, is deflected by rather sterile
debate about the New International Economic Order.
Some of the oil importing developing nations have
done relatively well by disciplining inflation at home
via explicit or implicit social contracts and pressing
successfully to expand exports abroad. And Brazil,
at least, is going about the business of generating an
oil substitute with the war-production mentality the
problem justifies. But the failure "to transform" at
a pace and on a scale required to maintain economic
and social momentum is endemic. Chronic stagflation
in the North and decelerated growth in the developing
regions, at a critical juncture in their evolution,
have been the predominant method for balancing our
energy books.

So far as the themes of this essay are concerned, there are two observations to be made on this
rather undistinguished performance. First, in part it
stems from the fact that, as compared to the world before 1914, price and investment decisions are much
more nearly in the hands of governments and the political process, in the wider sense. With respect to
energy, we are simply not getting the prompt diversion
of capital flows in the world economy responding to
relative price movements that occurred, for example,
in the 1830's (cotton, 1850's (wheat and cotton),
1896-1913 (agricultural products generally). (The
fact that economic decisions had become more politici-
zed also helps explain the sluggishness of Britain's
un-satisfactory response to excessively favorable
inter-war terms of trade).

Second, behind these generally inadequate
performances in the face of the challenge posed by the
relative rise in the price of energy lie, of course,
deeper social forces. All analysts agree that the
resources and technologies exist to cope with the
transitional period when oil supplies wane while we
await the emergence of essentially infinite and hopefully less polluting sources for the longer future;

e.g., solar, breeder, fusion. If we went about the task seriously, a ceiling could quite soon be imposed on the OPEC oil price by a sharp reduction in demand for oil imports and the large scale production of alternatives at prices lower than the current OPEC price. Technically and economically, these are quite attainable objectives in a reasonable period of time; say, less than a decade.

Putting exhortation aside, the lesson is, as Charles Kindleberger and Arthur Lewis have emphasized, that the response to challenges posed by shifts in the terms of trade are determined by forces which transcend economics, even when economics is broken out of its neo-classical straight-jacket to embrace the Marshallian long period.

FOOTNOTES

1. For a discussion of various approaches to the analysis of the terms of trade, see, for example. W.W. Rostow, "The Terms of Trade in Theory," Chapter 8 in The Process of Economic Growth, Oxford: At the Clarendon Press, 1953, 1960.

2. Adam Smith, The Wealth of Nations, Book 1, Chapter Xl, "Effects of the Progress of Improvement upon the real Price of Manufactures" (p. 196 in Routledge edition, London, 1890).

3. W.S. Jevons, The Coal Question, second edition, London: Macmillan, 1866, p. vii.

4. The major movements in the British terms of trade are analyzed in W.W. Rostow, The World Economy: History and Prospect, Austin: University of Texas Press (London: Macmillan), 1978, pp. 91-99 and at greater length in the course of Part Three, "Trend Periods."

5. See W.W. Rostow, Process of Economic Growth, pp. 201-205.

6. Ibid, pp. 175-181. For an interesting return to the transfer problem, see Thomas Balogh and Andrew Graham, "The Transfer Problem Revisited: Analyses Between the Reparations Payments of the 1920's and the Problems of the OPEC Surpluses," Oxford Bulletin of Economics and Statistics, Vol. 41, No. 3, August 1979, pp. 183-191.

7. John H. Williams, "The Theory of International Trade Reconsidered," Economic Journal, Vol. 39, 1929, pp. 195-209.

8. Frank D. Graham, The Theory of International Values, Princeton: Princeton University Press, 1948, pp. 5-6.

9. Miltiades Chacholiades, The Pure Theory of International Trade, Chicago: Aldine, 1973, p. 13. I use Chacholiades' study here as a serious and representative effort to incorporate refinements in neoclassical price and growth theory into the received

body of classical international trade theory.

10. G. Haberler, The Theory of International Trade, Clifton, New Jersey: Augustus M. Kelley, 1936, p. 202.

11. Occasionally efforts are made to deal with the inherently awkward case of increasing returns to scale. See, for example, M. Chacholiades, op. cit., pp. 170-185, with a selected bibliography on p. 185. He observes (p. 170): "The analysis so far has been based on the assumption of constant returns to scale. When this assumption is dropped, several difficulties arise, in particular, the problems created by the phenomenon of increasing returns to scale.

        "Increasing returns to scale are an indisputable fact of life. However, the treatment of increasing returns in the field of international trade theory has been scanty and unsatisfactory, because of the enormous difficulties encountered in incorporating the phenomenon of increasing returns in a general-equilibrium model." Chacholiades' formal resolution of this problem is achieved, as he acknowledges, only at the cost of extreme simplifying assumptions. C.P. Kindleberger, in dealing more pragmatically with this case, argues persuasively that it helps explain in the large scale trade among highly industrialized countries in "like, but not quite identical, goods" induced by specialization (International Economics, Homewood, Illinois: Richard D. Irwin, 1953, pp. 91-94). It should be noted that increasing returns through economies of scale are to be distinguished from increasing returns brought about by substantial discontinuities in supply via major innovations or the opening up of new sources for foodstuffs or raw materials. Conventional economic theory has, essentially, failed to deal with the latter problem. For an extended discussion of this failure, see W.W. Rostow, "Technology and the Price System," Chapter 4 in Why the Poor Get Richer and the Rich Slow Down, Austin: University of Texas Press, 1980, pp. 154-188. For an interesting effort to introduce one Marshallian long period factor into foreign trade analysis -- research and development and the Vernon product cycle -- see Stephen P. Magee, International Trade, Reading, Mass.: Addison-Wesley, 1980, pp. 28-38.

12. For a good example of Johnson's work in the field,

see "Economic Development and International Trade" in
Harry G. Johnson, Money, Trade and Economic Growth,
Cambridge, Mass.: Harvard University Press, 1963,
pp. 75-103, including a useful, eclectic bibliographi-
cal appendix. For a later analytic review of the
propositions emerging from the linking of international trade and neo-classical growth theory, with certain
original features, see Jagdish Bhagwati, Trade,
Tariffs, and Growth, Cambridge, Mass.: M.I.T. Press,
1969, pp. 311-338. The formal literature linking
modern growth analysis to foreign trade theory is only
rarely related to concrete situations. Richard Caves
and Ronald Jones (World Trade and Payments, Boston:
Little, Brown, 1973, p. 536) do refer to the possibly
perverse effects on the Brazilian terms of trade of a
bumper coffee crop; but one would have thought
analysts interested in this problem would have paused
to contemplate the story of the British terms of trade
during the cotton textile revolution: a powerful
technological advance in industry so increases demand
for a basic raw material (cotton) as to induce in the
United States a major technological innovation (the
cotton gin) and three major phases of acreage expansion (1816-1820, 1828-1836, the 1850's), yielding a
trend decline in the raw cotton price which would
have tipped the British terms of trade favorably if
the proportions cited earlier (see above, p. 4) did
not operate. To introduce this case, which is by no
means unique (e.g., petroleum production down to 1972)
the analyst must, it is true, leave the world of two
commodities; but that should prove manageable.

13. International Economics, pp. 316-317.

14. W. Arthur Lewis, Growth and Fluctuations, 1870-
1913, London: George Allen and Unwin, 1978. In dealing with the much debated fluctuations of the pre-1860
cotton price, two dynamic supply-demand exercises have
been conducted similar to Lewis'. See Jeffrey G.
Williamson, American Growth and Balance of Payments,
1820-1843, Chapel Hill: University of North Carolina
Press, 1964, pp. 38-43; and Robert William Fogel and
Stanley L. Engerman, Time on the Cross, Vol. 1, The
Economics of American Negro Slavery, Boston: Little,
Brown, 1974, pp. 86-94.

15. See, for example, A.K. Cairncross, Home and
Foreign Investment, 1870-1913, Cambridge: At the

University Press, 1953, p. 53.

16. C.H. Feinstein, Statistical Tables of National Income Expenditure, and Output of the U.K., 1855-1964, Cambridge: Cambridge University Press, 1976, Table 15 T37-38, col. 16.

17. C.G.F. Sinkin, The Instability of a Dependent Economy, Economic Fluctuations in New Zealand, 1840-1914, Oxford: Oxford University Press, pp. 40-48, 182-187.

18. I take a different view of this phenomenon than Arthur Lewis who attributes these counter-terms of trade capital flows mainly to "the band-wagon effect" created by large capital flows to the United States in the 1880's (Growth and Fluctuations, 1870-1913, pp. 180-181).

19. The cases of Australia, Argentina, and Canada in this period are treated at greater length and documented in W.W. Rostow, The World Economy: History and Prospect, pp. 169-172, with further references on pp. 448-455, 456-462, and 466-474.

20. C.F.G. Sinkin, op. cit., pp. 145-146.

21. Ibid, p. 169.

22. On the propensities, see, especially, The Process of Economic Growth, Chapters 1-3.

23. See C.P. Kindleberger, Foreign Trade and the National Economy, New Haven: Yale University Press, 1962, especially section 7, Capacity to Transform," pp. 99-115. See also Kindleberger's The Terms of Trade: A European Case Study, Cambridge, Mass.: Technology Press, 1966, especially pp. 303-313.

24. Ibid., pp. 109-110 and 115. The final sentence from Kindleberger quoted here is a precise statement of why, in The Process of Economic Growth, I insisted on the introduction of the propensities.

25. In Growth and Fluctuations, 1870-1913, see, especially, Chapter 8, "Response," pp. 194-224; in The Evolution of the International Economic Order,

Princeton: Princeton University Press, 1978, see, especially, pp. 10-11.

26. Growth and Fluctuations, 1870-1913, p. 195.

27. Ibid., pp. 214-218.

28. Ibid., p. 196.

29. New York: The Free Press, 1975.

30. A clue to the answer runs counter to one of Lewis' generalizations; that is, that importers in developing countries generally opposed local industrialization. In pre-1914 Southern Brazil importers led the way in industrialization. See, notably, Warren Dean, The Industrialization of Sao Paulo, 1880-1945, Austin: University of Texas Press, 1969, especially Chapter 11, pp. 19-33.

31. On the latter less familiar phenomenon, see Economic Report of the President, Washington, D.C.: G.P.O., January 1981, Chart 6, p. 116 (ratio of implicit price deflator for food to implicit price deflator for all personal consumption expenditures, 1947-1980). Typical of a Kondratieff upswing, this index moves sharply upwards, over a relatively short period of time (1972-1973), and then oscillates in a substantially higher range than that which obtained in most of the prior downswing (1951-1972).

A NOTE ON THE RATIONALE AND
MECHANISMS OF ECONOMIC INTEGRATION

by
William G. Demas [1]

Economic integration in the Caribbean is in our view nothing more or less than a process whereby more effective use is made of existing resources in the very broadest sense of the term through their voluntary and co-ordinated use so that additional opportunities to national economic development are made available. In the process stronger national economies and a stronger "regional economy" could generally emerge over time. To use the terminology of economic analysis, properly designed and implemented co-ordinated efforts at development within an economic integration framework can promote over time the continuing shifting outwards of the "production frontier" of each national economy and of the regional economy. In other words, the kind of integration which pursues co-ordinated development can produce benefits which are greater than the arithmetical sum of individual benefits which would accrue to the constituent national economies action in isolation.

If we may use the language and concepts of Systems Analysis, we see an economic integration system as an ordered grouping of neighbouring nations economic sub-systems in which certain key economic activities are co-ordinated through common strategies so that the whole (system) is greater than the sum of the parts (sub-systems) thereby further strengthening the parts (sub-systems).

---

1. This note was prepared as a background paper for a group of Caribbean Experts (including Sir Arthur Lewis) appointed by the Caribbean Common Market Council of Ministers to propose strategy for Caribbean Integration in the 1980s. I must acknowledge critical suggestions from Rupert Mullings, Marius St. Rose, Arnhin Eustace and Nigel Baseley of the Caribbean Development Bank and Kurleigh King and Byron Blake of the Caribbean Community Secretariat.

On this view regional integration is a process which difuses elements of strength and reduces elements of weakness of the separate national economies (sub-systems) throughout the entire regional economy (the system) and therefore maximises strengths and minimises weaknesses of both the parts and the whole.

The point of departure in the discussion of this issue must be the fundamental consideration that the pooling of resources and the co-ordination of efforts can lead to a situation in which the benefits of pooling and co-ordination are greater than the sum of the benefits to the parts acting individually and that consequently new opportunities for strengthening of all the national economies are brought into being.

But this view of the beneficial effects of integration rests on the crucial assumption that each participating country has a coherent and well conceived development policy and a well-managed national economy. This assumption is made throughout this note.

The argument has to be developed to deal with two types of interaction within the system:

    (a)   interaction between the national economies of more or less equal strength; and

    (b)   interaction between the national economies of unequal strength.

As between economies of approximately equal economic strength, co-ordinated development strategies and measures (which include but go beyond market integration) can bring about mutual benefits through the various mechanisms of interaction - trade in goods and services; combination and pooling in specific activities of human, financial and natural resources; and the creation of production linkages both intra-sectorally and intersectorally. This dynamic interaction and its resultant more effective use of resources and economies of large-scale production and specialisation have positive effects on the rate of economic growth and structural transformation of the economy at both the national and regional level.

(This analysis holds true only of "normal" situations and has to be qualified, but not set aside, if one or more of the stronger countries is experiencing serious short-term difficulties - for example, Guyana and Jamaica at the moment).

As between economies of unequal strength, if the markets are simply integrated and no other integration instruments are used, the strong will most likely gain at the expense of the weak. This is the well-known "polarisation" effect. The "spread" effects of the economic strength of the stronger to the weak will be more than offset by the "backward" effects - especially where the weaker countries have to pay more for goods imported from the stronger countries than for goods previously imported from the outside world ("trade diversion", brought about by interregional Free Trade and a protective Common External Tariff). In principle, the cost of trade diversion to the weaker countries could be compensated either by permitting workers from the weaker countries to move freely to the stronger countries or by moving resources from the stronger countries to the weaker countries. The movement of resources can be seen as the "functional equivalent" of freedom of movement of labor which seeks to "bring development" to the weaker countries rather than "taking the people to development". This alternative is favored by most integration movements among developing countries. More is said on this below. Accordingly, the growing strength of the strong will be at the expense of the weak if everything is left to market forces.

In this situation the instruments of integration will have to go beyond market integration and include as well instruments for co-ordinated development and for providing special development opportunities for the weaker countries within the integration movement. However, in making available these special development opportunities and concessions to the weaker countries, the stronger countries must not themselves be weakened; they must not experience economic debilitation in net terms.

The stronger economies will have to agree to certain special arrangements in favor of the weaker countries on a continuing long-term basis under the

integration Treaty, partly to compensate them for the
short-run cost involved in "trade diversion", partly
to provide them with special development opportunities
and partly to enable them to undertake their obliga-
tions under the Treaty at a cost that is not too
burdensome to them.

Such special development opportunities can
be made available to the weaker countries in the areas
of trade, technical assistance, finance and other
direct actions in order to stimulate increased production so that, provided always that the weaker countries pursue coherent and effective national development policies and have good national economic management, the economies of the weaker countries could be
strengthened in the long-run. In this way, the
elements of strength throughout the regional system
can in the long-run be maximised and the elements of
weakness minimised.

The case for the provision of such special
development opportunities and concessions is further
strengthened by the consideration that in the short-
run the stronger economies can have certain immediate
benefits. One obvious source of such benefit is the
increase of their exports to the markets of the weaker
countries with whom they can quickly develop (or increase) export surpluses since the weaker ones, almost
by definition, cannot increase their exports to the
stronger because in the short-run they have very little
or no production to sell.

We should also recognise that the Integration
Treaty might, in some cases, provide short-run benefits
to the weaker countries in one or two areas - for example, in the case of CARICOM, the Agricultural Marketing Protocol (AMP), the Guaranteed Market Scheme (GMS),
Oils and Fats Conference and certain bilateral and
multilateral capital inflows from the stronger countries can gain in the short-term if the integration
process goes beyond a Common Market and also provides,
as does the Treaty of Chaguaramas, for Co-operation
and Common Services in non-economic fields (single
systems of University Education, Secondary School
Examinations, Sea and Air Transport) and in joint
external policies and actions in the external field -
both political and economic. Nevertheless, while both

groups are likely to gain more than they lose, the balance of advantage in the short-run is still likely to be in favor of the stronger countries and is likely to remain so until in the medium - and longer-term when agricultural and industrial production increases significantly in the weaker countries.

Another fairly obvious way in which the stronger countries could gain in the short-run is through certain "perverse" flows of investment funds either to the stronger from the weaker or to the stronger from outside the grouping when extraregional entities show preference for the stronger. The latter type of flow cannot be avoided. All that one can realistically hope is that, in the long-run, relative investor preference as between the strong and the weak may not be so marked in favor of the strong. However, the former type of "perverse" flow from the weak to the strong could be avoided or minimised if the Integration Treaty is appropriately structured, as the Treaty of Chaguaramas is in this regard.

The burden on the stronger countries of providing these special development opportunities and concessions to the weaker countries is offset by the fact that:

(a)   the integration instruments
      expand the economic potential
      of all the Member Countries
      and of the grouping as a
      whole, as we have seen; and

(b)   they can derive immediate
      benefits from market inte-
      gration to a greater extent
      than the weaker countries.

In addition, the burden on the stronger countries would be less:

(a)   the smaller is the combined
      size of the weaker countries
      in relation to the combined
      size of the stronger countries.
      (In the case of CARICOM the
      total combined size of the
      population and Gross Domestic

275

Product of the LDCs amount
to 14% and 7% as a proportion of the total CARICOM
population and Gross
Domestic Product, respec-
tively); and

(b) the greater the likelihood
of joint external action on
the part of all countries
in the grouping being able
to result in the inflow of
additional financial and
technical assistance resources.

Thus, both in the short-run and long-run net
benefits could accrue to both the weaker and stronger
economies - even though in the short-run, while both
could gain, the balance of advantage would still be in
favor of the latter. But to the extent that the weaker countries could in the medium - and long-term take
advantage of the special development opportunities and
special concessions embodies in the instruments of
integration and improve their national development
policies and economic management, to that extent would
their economies grow stronger. To the extent that
this occurs, the interaction between them and the
stronger economies will bring about mutually reinforcing and beneficial processes of growth and structural change, accompanied by greater trade, financial
and structural interdependence among them.

It remains to discuss a final point relating
to the interaction between strong and weak countries
in the integration process. Indeed, a central issue
in integration concerns the criterion by which the
justification for the participation of any country
(but particularly a weaker one) in an integration
grouping should be assessed. As Alister McIntyre
pointed out a decade and a half ago, the logical
criterion is not that every participating country
should achieve the same level of development within a
reasonable time period or that rates of economic growth should be identical for all countries. It is
rather that every country should be better off (in
terms of a stronger and more diversified economy) inside the grouping than it would be outside. This

appears to be the case in CARICOM. In our judgement, the LDCs are certainly better off (in both economic and non-economic terms) by being participants in the Community and Common Market than by remaining outside of it.

The foregoing implies that the health and strength of each national economy in an integration grouping must be the concern of all. This means that in such a grouping there must be prior and continuing consensus on the need for the highest possible standards of competence and effectiveness of long-term national development policies and short-term national economic management. There must therefore be regional machinery for joint regional reviews of development policy and economic management of each Member State.

In concluding this section, we wish to emphasise that, particularly among developing countries such as those in the Caribbean, market integration which is very useful - should not be relied upon as the sole set of instruments of integration. For the fundamental problem, unlike the case with developed countries, is not so much to expand trade in existing production capacity as to expand, through joint and co-ordinated actions, productive capacity and to achieve more structural transformation of the economies of all the countries.

The approach to economic integration in terms of pooling resources and co-ordinated efforts should lead to the provision in a formal integration Treaty not only for Market Integration (that is, Free Trade and a Common External Tariff) but also, and more importantly, for more direct actions involving Co-ordination and Co-operation in Production and Development and a Special Regime for the Less Developed Countries. In addition, the Treaty should also provide, as the Treaty of Chaguaramas does, for Common Services and Functional Co-operation as well as the "Externalisation" of Integration through co-ordinated external actions with a view to increasing the bargaining-power of the countries forming the integration grouping with outside countries, blocs of countries and other external entities. Finally, there should be periodic review and re-examination of the formal instruments of integration with a view to examining their relevance to the necessarily changing internal and external environments of the participating countries and making any amendments or changes in priority and emphasis which may appear to be called for in the light of such review and re-examination. Such a "feedback" mechanism can provide useful "lessons" from experience.

We attempt to illustrate the foregoing conceptual framework of integration in a necessarily approximate and oversimplified manner in the Diagram contained in the Appendix.

THE FIVE SETS OF ECONIMIC INTEGRATION
INSTRUMENTS IN THE TREATY OF CHAGUARAMAS

Let us now see in more concrete terms how the strengthening of national economies through the voluntary pooling of resources and co-ordinated national efforts could be fostered through five sets of instruments of integration provided by the Treaty of Chaguaramas. These are:

(a) Functional Co-operation
     (including Common Services);

(b) Market Integration;

(c) Co-ordination and Co-operation
     in Production and Development;

(d) A Special Regime for the LDCs; and

(e) the "Externalisation" of the
     integration effort (that is,
     developing a common front
     vis-a-vis outside countries,
     groups of countries and other
     external entities).

(i) FUNCTIONAL CO-OPERATION
     (INCLUDING COMMON SERVICES)

Let us look first at simple forms of non-economic functional co-operation (including, where appropriate, common services) among the Caribbean countries. Here we can easily see that the whole is greater than the sum of its parts.

No high level of abstraction is necessary to demonstrate that, in most cases, such forms of co-operation (University Education; Caribbean Examinations Council; Technology Development and Adaptation; certain regional Health Programmes; Shared External Trade and Investment and even Diplomatic Services; Rationalised and Co-ordinated Systems of Sea and Air Transport; and, in the economic field, the pooling of foreign exchange reserves by the participation of the East Caribbean LDCs in a Common Currency through ECCA) yield benefits from the pooling of resources and therefore additional opportunities for development to the participating Member States. Shared or rationalised services in the small and very small and, for the most part, financially and economically weak English-speaking Caribbean countries have the effect of either reducing costs for each country or making available a service that, on an individual country basis, could not exist at all or could fail to achieve its purpose by functioning most inadequately because of lack of the necessary minimum "critical mass".

The provision of valuable exchanges of information, experience and cross-fertilisation of ideas in other forms of functional co-operation not involving Common Services is also of great assistance in many areas of economic, social and technological development.

(ii)   MARKET INTEGRATION

Among resources which national economies can pool are their national markets. By having a single combined market for goods, Caribbean economic integration can help (albeit to a limited extent) to provide "critical mass" for specialisation and an economic scale of production of some manufactured goods. In this way, the creation of a single regional market by pooling of national markets brings about a result greater than the results that would follow from the mere arithmetical sum of national markets so that the whole is greater than the sum of its parts. But mere market integration can do this only to a limited extent since it is only a necessary, but not a sufficient condition, for bringing about specialisation and structural interdependence among the national economies. Deliberate and positive action to avoid uneconomic duplication of production and to achieve specialisation, and hence economies of large-scale production, are needed. Such actions are also required if the LDCs are to be provided with special opportunities to benefit from integration.

However, we should recognise that even market integration by itself could assist in the process of increasing exports of manufactures to extra-regional markets, which is a generally agreed objective of policy in all the countries of the region. For it is often the case that exporting to regional markets is a means whereby manufacturers in the countries of the region "learn" how to export to the rest of the world.

(iii)   CO-ORDINATION AND CO-OPERATION IN PRODUCTION AND DEVELOPMENT

As we have mentioned earlier, market integration among developing countries has serious limitations. Indeed, by itself it cannot do very much to strengthen the national economies and the regional economy. This can be achieved only by combining the instruments of market integration with those of Co-operation in Production to develop new productive capacity and achieve specialisation and the benefits of economies of large-scale production by joint, co-ordinated actions such as programming for investment and increased production in the industrial, agricultural and natural resource fields and mutual assistance in the implementation of specific, concrete, joint (and sometimes even national) projects in the case of the weaker countries. The result of this approach will be an increase in intraregional trade. But compared with the situation where market integration is the only set of instruments employed, the type of trade will be different, using more local and regional raw materials and other inputs, and less subject to product differentiation and to the "swapping" of brand-names.

Programming for new investment and increased

production in Agriculture, Industry and Natural Resources needs to be effected through the "combination" or integration of the use of regional resources (natural, human and financial) at the sectoral or intersectoral level and through the formation of joint venture projects for the national, sub-regional or extraregional markets. It is particularly through such actions that productive structures of national economies are strengthened and structural inter-dependence between them is effectively brought about. Benefits that are greater than the sum of benefits to individual countries acting in isolation are likely to result from activities based on this set of instruments to a greater extent than from any other set of integration instruments. Such activities lie at the core of the economic integration process. What is more, it is in large part through such measures and actions that special opportunities can be effectively provided for the LDCs to benefit from integration.

It is also important to note that actions falling under the category of Co-ordination and Co-operation in Production can be undertaken to assist in achieving greater levels of production of both manufactured and non-traditional agricultural products for export to extraregional markets. Here, as we have shown in the body of our Report, direct actions involving the formation of a Regional Export Company and a joint export promotion service would be of great assistance.

It should be stressed that this approach of Co-ordination and Co-operation in Production and Development involves, not only the formulation of general, regional and national policies and guidelines; but the designing of machinery to secure speedy and efficient carrying out of a number of co-ordinated specific and concrete tasks by the public and private sectors of the several Member Countries.

(iv)   SPECIAL REGIME FOR THE LDCs

From our earlier discussion, it should be clear that the relatively more developed Member Countries should have a direct interest in the strengthening of the national economies of the relatively less developed countries since strengthening the latter will have a feedback effect on the further strengthening of the former.

Direct action in the field of Co-ordination and Co-operation in Production and Development, while of crucial importance to all participating countries, has a direct relevance to the problems of the relatively less developed participating countries.

For co-ordinated efforts at economic growth and structural change, and hence the strengthening of national economies, yield their major results not immediately but in the medium - and long-term. And the time element is of great importance to accruals of benefits and costs to individual Member Countries of the grouping. This is one reason, among others, why market integration alone is insufficient. For, as we have seen, market integration can confer fairly immediate benefits on the relatively more industralised Member Countries who can very quickly increase their exports of both agricultural and industrial products to the relatively less developed countries. Hence in all integration groupings of developing countries, including CARICOM, it is necessary to provide a special set of additional opportunities for the LDCs to benefit in both the short - and long-run, both by structuring market integration in their favor and, more important, by using direct methods of co-ordination and co-operation to increase their productive capacity in the shortest possible time. If this is done both sets of countries could have an excess of benefit over cost in the short-run. But while the advantage of net benefit in the short-run will be greater for the relatively more developed countries than for the LDCs, in the medium - and long-run this excess of advantage for the former could be reduced significantly, even if not totally eliminated. And, what is more, the relatively less developed countries would be better off inside the integration movement than outside it. It is also relevant here to point out once again that the relatively less developed countries could gain from integration instruments other than the Common Market - for example, Functional Co-operation and Common Services and the "Externalisation" of the integration movement. It is to the latter that we now turn.

(v)   THE "EXTERNALISATION" OF INTERACTION

        Bargaining-power, in relation to the rest of
the world, is also a resource that can be regionally
pooled. The adoption of a common front vis-a-vis outside countries, blocs of countries and other entities
is of very great importance to our small and very
small countries with highly dependent and fragile
economies and can clearly produce a greater collective
bargaining-power than the sum of the bargaining-power
of the individual States acting in isolation. This
has been proved time and time again by the recent
experience of the countries of the region in international negotiations and actions.

        Economic gains to individual countries from
this form of pooling of resources can take the form of
better access on improved terms to external markets;
to increased flows of aid and technical assistance on
improved terms; to the inflow of foreign private investment and the "transfer" of technology on more
favorable terms; and to better deals with regard to
Civil Aviation, etc. This is the simple explanation
of why the Treaty of Chaguaramas makes provision,
inter alia, for the co-ordination of foreign policies
of the Member States; the "progressive co-ordination
of their trade relations with Third Countries or groups
of Third Countries"; the harmonisation of fiscal incentives to industry; the negotiation by individual
Member States of double-taxation treaties with Third
Countries on the basis of a common set of agreed
principles; and a common policy on foreign investment
and the transfer of technology.

        In addition - and this is a separate point -
regional co-operation could, under certain circumstances, attract external financial and technical
resources for the countries of the region additional
to what might become available in the absence of such
co-operation. The classic case in point is the additional resources that have flowed into the region
through the Caribbean Development Bank (CDB) and
through regional projects financed under the Lome
Convention. International financial institutions and
donor countries have themselves made this claim of
additionality of resource transfers to regional institutions and regional projects. This is of specific

relevance to most countries of the region today,
facing, as they are, severe fiscal, financial and
balance-of-payments difficulties.

CLARIFICATION OF FIVE OTHER
INTEGRATION ISSUES

Before we end, we try to clarify five issues
which have given rise to considerable misunderstanding
in the Member States of CARICOM:

    (i)   freedom of movement of
             factors of production and
             rights of establishment
             and to provide services;

    (ii)   the issue of a common
             independent currency;

    (iii)   inward-looking <u>versus</u>
             outward-looking strategies;

    (iv)   the respective roles of
             the public and private
             sectors in national and
             regional development; and

    (v)   ideological differences
             and economic integration.

(i)   THE ISSUE OF FREEDOM OF
       MOVEMENT OF FACTORS OF
       PRODUCTION AND RIGHTS OF
       ESTABLISHMENT AND TO
       PROVIDE SERVICES

In a "classical" common market among
developed countries, as in the EEC, there is provision - usually after the end of a fairly long
transitional period - for free movement of capital and
labor and for nationals of each Member State to have
the absolute Right of Establishment and to provide
services in any other Member State.

The Treaty of Chaguaramas provides for the

Right of Establishment but in a form so watered down and so qualified as to be virtually meaningless. Similarly, the Right to Provide Services confers a right on a national of a Member State to provide (self-employed) services in any other Member State; but he is not placed on par with a national of the Member State Concerned. Instead, all that he is entitled to is to receive preferential treatment over nationals of Third Countries.

The Treaty also does not obligate in any way, any Member State to admit persons (employees or otherwise) who are nationals of other Member States to work or to seek employment in that Member State. And on movement of capital, it merely provides that "the Council shall examine ways and means for the introduction of a scheme for the regulated movement of capital within the Common Market, giving particular attention to the development needs of the LDCs and shall recommend to Member States proposals for the establishment of such a scheme".

The philosophy behind the Caribbean Common Market, as far as rights of establishment and to provide services and movement of labor and capital are concerned, is not to provide compensation for countries which gain less than others from market integration by having a "free-for-all" which might lead to "perverse" movement of capital, enterprise and skills from relatively less to more developed countries and from the less prosperous MDCs to the more prosperous MDCs. Instead, there is provision for a "planned" regime of factor movements and pooling of skills and resources on a case-by-case basis, as is illustrated by the CARICOM Enterprise Regime. It is also possible, in the context of the obligation imposed upon Council by the Treaty to "examine ways and means of introducing a regime of regulated movement of capital", to develop general guidelines for more liberal treatment of CARICOM nationals regarding Establishment, Provision of Services and the Movement of Capital and Labor on the basis of which administrative decisions could be made by individual Governments on a case-by-case basis.

All of this is very much in keeping with the approach which we have termed Co-ordination and Co-operation in Production and Development.

(ii)   THE ISSUE OF A COMMON
        INDEPENDENT CURRENCY

        From a strictly analytical point of view, a
common independent currency (as distinct from a
Currency Board arrangement, as in the East Caribbean
LDCs or Belize) is possible only with full Monetary
Union which is an extremely advanced form of economic
integration, virtually amounting to a Political Union.
A common independent currency is in effect one of the
final consequences of integration rather than a
promoter of integration. It is possible to achieve a
high level of economic integration without the participating countries sharing a common independent currency.
All that they need to have is a reasonable degree of
monetary co-operation, not monetary integration. The
EEC, in spite of the high level of economic integration
it has achieved, is still a long way from a common
currency.

(iii)   INWARD-LOOKING VERSUS OUTWARD-LOOKING
        DEVELOPMENT STRATEGIES AND ECONOMIC
        INTEGRATION

        This issue will be discussed in relation to:

        (a)   The General Issue;

        (b)   Highly Dependent Integration
              into a bigger Extraregional
              Country or Bloc;

        (c)   The widening of the Caribbean
              Integration Movement; and

        (d)   Economic Co-operation with
              mainland countries of Latin
              America.

(a)   THE GENERAL ISSUE

        For most groups of developing countries
integration is not and cannot be exclusively a turning
inwards on each other. Some element of collective
turning inwards is certainly needed but must be com-
plemented by a policy of looking outwards beyond the
boundaries of the particular grouping. What is more,

the relative extent of "looking inwards regionally"
and of "looking outwards extraregionally" must depend
on the size of the total regional market (population
multiplied by per capita income) and the richness and
variety of the natural resource base of the countries
of the particular integration grouping.

In the specific case of the Caribbean, we
need to exploit opportunities for both national and
regional import substitution, while vigorously promoting exports of both agricultural and manufactured
goods to extraregional markets. The former does not
preclude the latter, unless extraregional and regional
import substitution take place behind excessively high
protective barriers.

But even in promoting exports extraregionally, joint actions and common policies within the
framework of the integration movement can be of
assistance - for example, in bargaining with Third
Countries and trade blocs on access to their markets;
harmonisation of fiscal incentives to export-oriented
industries; joint export promotion; and even the
establishment of a regionally owned export company for
the purpose of pooling production from different
Member Countries to enable large export orders from
abroad to be met. There is also scope for joint ventures which "combine" the human, financial and natural
resources of the Member Countries for production either
for the regional and the extraregional export markets
or for the extraregional export market alone.

Such co-operation and joint actions and
common policies within the framework of economic integration would still be essential, even if the main
thrust of economic strategy were to be directed towards
penetrating extraregional export markets. Further,
whatever the inward-looking/outward-looking balance,
the rationale for a regional approach to food production, to functional co-operation and common services,
and joint external bargaining and co-ordination of
both political and economic external policies would
remain strong.

(b)   HIGHLY DEPENDENT INTEGRATION
       INTO A BIGGER INTRAREGIONAL
       COUNTRY OR BLOC

To some people in the region (but hopefully to only a very small minority), the "pseudo-solution" of linking up with a bigger extraregional country or bloc in this hemisphere or in others in a highly dependent way might appear to be a seductive prospect. But in all probability, this "get rich quick" approach would offer little prospect of structural transformation of the economy and would almost certainly do nothing but create a lopsided unbalanced economy with greatly diminished political and economic sovereignty for the country. Admittedly, the argument here is not entirely economic but has to rest on intangible and complex issues of sovereignty, identity, dignity and self-reliance. Even if short-run prosperity were to be gained from this strategy, it is doubtful whether in the long-run it would be viable in the sense of all its implications being acceptable to the people of the country, particularly the younger generation. The fact that we have inherited economies that are highly externally dependent does not mean that we should seek to accentuate such dependence. Instead, most people in the region would probably share the view that the CARICOM countries should try to develop economic links with as many countries as possible, irrespective of ideology, economic size or geographical location and so avoid becoming in the long-term unduly dependent on any single one of them. The criteria for such external trade and economic relations should be:

-    short-term and long-term advantages to our countries;

-    the preservation and, if possible, enchantment of Caribbean political and economic sovereignty;

-    greater Caribbean inter-dependence; and

-    self-reliance and self-respect.

As argued elsewhere, the Caribbean countries

have a better combined natural resource base and a
stronger joint external bargaining-power than is
generally realised and accordingly, they have no reason to sell themselves short by adopting, either
singly or collectively, a strategy of highly dependent integration into a bigger country or bloc of
countries.

(c)   THE WIDENING OF THE
        INTEGRATION MOVEMENT

        The case for strengthening an integration
grouping by "widening" it to include other neighbouring countries at roughly similar levels of development
and economic size is very straightforward in principle.
Such widening makes available for pooling and co-
ordinated use a larger volume of resources (markets;
human, financial and natural resources; areas for
functional co-operation and common services; and
external bargaining-power).

        Nevertheless, practical difficulties could
arise, stemming from the existence in potentially new
Member Countries of such factors as lack of proper
national development policies and effective economic
management; much lower levels of economic development
and relatively large populations living in great
poverty; totally different systems of economic organisation;lack of sufficient constitutional and economic
autonomy; and a much lower level of administrative
capability. In the case of the widening of the
Caribbean Community to include many of the non-English-
speaking countries, territories and overseas depart-
ments of the Caribbean Archipelago, many of these
practical difficulties could arise and economic
integration, as distinct from looser forms of economic
co-operation, may not in the near future be possible
with some of these countries.

(d)   ECONOMIC CO-OPERATION WITH
        MAINLAND COUNTRIES OF
        LATIN AMERICA

        Given the fact that all or nearly all of the
CARICOM countries belong to various Latin American
organisations - ECLA, SELA, OLADE, GEPLACEA - and

Inter-American organisations - OAS and IDB - all of
which stress Latin American economic co-operation, and
given the proximity of the Caribbean Archipelago
countries to mainland Latin America, it is both desirable and feasible to seek to forge links of closer
economic co-operation with the mainland countries.
Already such links are being developed with Colombia,
Mexico and Venezuela. Accordingly, the CARICOM
countries, acting as a group through the Caribbean
Community, should seek to develop such links of
economic co-operation with other mainland countries,
particularly the Andean Group as a group and Brazil.
The new organisation to be established to replace
LAFTA has made it possible for relatively less developed countries such as CARICOM countries to obtain
tariff concessions from the mainland countries of
South America and Mexico on a non-reciprocal basis.

(iv)   RESPECTIVE ROLES OF THE
         PUBLIC AND PRIVATE
         SECTORS IN NATIONAL AND
         REGIONAL DEVELOPMENT

         The respective roles of the public and
private sectors in both national and regional development is a subject that has gained much attention in
recent years. On this we can be very brief. In the
two activities of national and regional development,
the State must both encourage and regulate private
economic activities and sometimes itself play a direct
role in production. And in both activities, there is
considerable scope for a dynamic and vigorous national
private sector. It is more than time that all concerned accept the fact of the mixed economy (with
expanding opportunities for popular participation in
various forms) and its continuation for as far ahead
as one can see. And it is time to bring an end to the
sterile, time-consuming and ultimately futile debate
on "free enterprise" versus "State ownership and control". In the Caribbean, the main actors on both the
national and the economic integration stage must be
Governments and their institutions and the private
sectors and their institutions. Both sets of actors
(as well as actors representing popular interests such
as Trade Unions, Youth Groups and Village Councils)
must be involved at both the planning and implementation stages in both national and regional development.

(v)   IDEOLOGICAL DIFFERENCES

In strict economic logic the benefits to be derived from economic integration, functional co-operation and common services and the co-ordination of external policies and actions through a process of pooling of resources and co-ordinated development exist quite independently of the ideological complexions of the Governments of the States participating in the integration grouping. Economies of large scale and of specialisation; gains from the combination in specific projects of the human, financial and natural resources of Member Countries, economies and gains from participation in common services and functional co-operation; and increased bargaining strength with the outside world through common policies and joint actions are certainly not a function of ideology. Where ideological differences between the countries in an integration group are not extremely wide and the political will to integrate is strong enough, meaningful economic integration is certainly possible. It is really a question of degree. If the ideological differences between States become too wide - in terms of the organisation of the internal economic system, in terms of pursuit of fundamentally different strategies and planning approaches and in terms of fundamental differences in the orientation of foreign policies, then the integration effort becomes very difficult to organise and implement. Under these circumstances, it would be preferable to have a looser form of economic co-operation rather than a more ambitious scheme of economic integration. In our view, the ideological differences among the Caribbean countries have so far never got to the point where economic integration would have to give way to mere economic co-operation.

Editors' Note: The Caribbean Community (CARICOM) was established in 1972 under the Treaty of Chauguarams signed at Chauguarams, Trinidad and Tobago. Member states designed 'Less Developed Countries', are Antigua, Belize, Dominica, Grenada, Montserrat, St. Kitts-Nevis-Anguilla, St. Lucia and St. Vincent. The 'More Developed Countries' are Barbados, Guyana, Jamaica and Trinidad and Tobago.

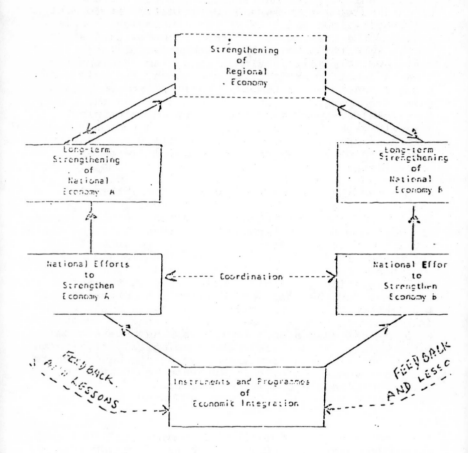

LIST OF THE WORKS OF W. ARTHUR LEWIS

A. BOOKS, MONOGRAPHS, PAMPLETS AND
   OFFICIAL DOCUMENTS

The Evolution of Peasantry in the West Indies -
1936.

Labour in the West Indies - Fabian Society,
London, 1939.

Economic Problems of Today - London, 1940.

Monopoly in British Industry - Fabian Society,
1945.

Economic Survey 1919-39 - London and New York,
1949.

Overhead Costs - London and New York, 1949.

Industrial Development in the Caribbean -
Caribbean Commission, 1949.

The Principles of Economic Planning -
London, 1950.

Land Settlement Policy - Caribbean Commission,
1950.

Attitude to Africa - (with others) Penguin,
1951.

*Measures for the Economic Development of
Underdeveloped Countries* - (with others)
United Nations Department of Economic
Affairs, 1951.

Report of National Fuel Policy - U.K.
Government, 1952.

Industrialisation and the Gold Coast - Gold
Coast Government, 1953.

Aspects of Industrialization - National Bank of Egypt, 1953.

The Theory of Economic Growth - London and Homewood, Ill., 1955.

Why a University of the West Indies - Address of 1960 Matriculation Ceremony at University College of the West Indies, Jamaica, 1960.

Eastern Caribbean Federation - Report to the Prime Minister   Federal Government of the West Indies, Trinidad, 1961.

Eastern Caribbean Federation : Further Notes - 1962.

Proposals for Eastern Caribbean Federation of Eight Territories - Federal Government of the West Indies, Trinidad, 1962.

Economic Problems of Jamaica - Daily Gleaner, Kingston, 1964.

The Agony of the Eight - Barbados Advocate, Bridgetown, 1965.

Politics in West Africa - (The Whidden Lectures) Allen and Unwin, London, 1965.

Development Planning : The Essentials of Economic Policy - London, 1966.

Reflections on Nigeria's Economic Growth - O.E.C.D. Paris, 1967.

Some Aspects of Economic Development - (The Aggey Memorial Lectures) London, 1969.

Aspects of Tropical Trade - (The Wichsell Lectures) Stockholm, 1969.

Partners in Progress - Pearson Commission
(with others)   Report to the World
Bank, Washington, 1969.

The Development Process - United Nations,
New York, 1970.

Socialism and Economic Growth - (The Annual
Oration) L.S.E. London, 1971.

Tropical Development 1880-1913
Studies in Economic Progress, London,
1971.

Presidential Address to Board of
Governors, 1st Annual General Meeting,
Caribbean Development Bank, Bridgetown,
1971.

Presidential Address to Board of
Governors, 2nd Annual General Meeting,
Caribbean Development Bank, Bridgetown,
1972.

Some Constraints on International Banking -
Caribbean Development Bank, Bridgetown,
1972.

The Evolution of Foreign Aid - (The David
Owen Memorial Lecture) University of
Wales, Cardiff, 1972.

Presidential Address to Board of
Governors, 3rd Annual General Meeting,
Caribbean Development Bank, Bridgetown,
1973.

Development Economics : An Outline - General
Learning Corporation Modules, Morristown
N.J., 1973.

Dynamic Factors in Economic Growth - (Tata
Memorial Lectures) Orient Longman,
New Delhi, 1974.

The University in Less Developed Countries -
International Council for Educational
Development, New York, 1974.

The LDC's and Exchange Stability - (1977 Per
Jacobsson Lecture) I.M.F. Washington,
1978.

*The Evolution of the International Economic
Order* - (Janeway Lectures) Princeton
University Press, Princeton, N.J.,
1978.

Growth and Fluctuations - Allen and Unwin,
London, 1978.

The West Indies - London, Shelton Press
(undated).

B.   ARTICLES IN BOOKS

"Nationalization as an alternative to
Monopoly Control : the British experience"in - *Monopoly and Competition and
their Regulation*, (ed.) E.H. Chamberlin,
London, 1954.

"The Economic Development of Africa"
in *Africa in the Modern World*, (ed.)
C.W. Stillman, Chicago, 1955.

"The Economic and Social Council" in
The United Nations, (ed.) E.A. Wortley,
Manchester, 1957.

"The Shifting Fortunes of Agriculture"
in *Report of the Tenth International
Conference of Agricultural Economics*, London,
1959.

"Sponsored Growth : Challenge to
Democracy" in *Problems of Economic Growth*,
(ed.) M.K. Haldar and E. Ghosh, Delhi,
1959.

296

"Economic Conditions for Greater Agricultural Output" - *Report of the Annual Meeting of the British Association for the Advancement of Science*, 1960.

"Depreciation and Obselescence as Factors in Costing" in *Depreciation and Replacement Policy*, (ed.) J.L. Meij, Amsterdam, 1961.

"The Emergence of West Africa" in *The Promise of World Tensions*, (ed.) H. Cleveland, New York, 1961.

"Science, Man and Money" in *Science and the New Nations*, (ed.) R. Gruber, New York, 1961.

"Competition and Regulation in the West Indies" in *Economic Systems of the Commonwealth*, (ed.) C.B. Hoover, Durham, N.C., 1962.

"Tension in Economic Development" in *Restless Nations*, (ed.) L.B. Pearson, New York, 1962.

"Social Services in Development Planning" in *Planning for Economic Development in the Caribbean*, Report of a Caribbean Organisation Conference, Puerto Rico, 1963.

"Industrialisation and Social Peace" in *Conference Across a Nation*, Report of H.R.H. The Duke of Edinburgh's Study Conference, Macmillans of Canada, 1963.

"Closing Remarks" in *Inflation and Growth in Latin America*, (ed.) W. Baer and I. Kerstenetzky, New Haven, 1964.

"Economic Development and World Trade"
in *Problems in Economic Development*, (ed.)
E.A.G. Robinson, London, 1965.

"Africa Economic Development" in
Africa : Progress Through Co-operation,
(ed.) J. Karefa-Smart, New York, 1966.

"Planning Public Expenditure" in
National Economic Planning, (ed.)
M.F. Millikan, New York, 1967.

"Unemployment in Developing Areas"
in *A Reappraisal of Economic Development*,
(ed.) A.M. Whiteford, Chicago, 1967.

"International Trade and Economic
Growth" in *Fiscal and Monetary Problems
in Developing States*, (ed.) D. Krivine,
New York, 1967.

"Development Planning" in *International
Encyclopedia of the Social Sciences*, 1968.

"Epilogue" in *The West Indies : The
Federal Negotiations*, J. Mordecai, London,
1968.

"Economic Aspects of Quality in
Education" in *Qualitative Aspects of
Educational Planning*, (ed.) C.E. Beeby,
Paris, 1969.

"On Assessing a Development Plan", in
Leading Issues in Economic Development, (ed.)
G.M. Meier, New York, 1970.

"On being Different" in Speeches made
at the 1971 Graduation Ceremony of the
University of the West Indies, Kingston,
1971 (Reprinted in D. Lowenthal &
L. Lomaters (ed.) : Aftermath of
Sovereignity : West Indian Perspectives,
Anchor, 1973.

"Report on the Industrialisation and the Gold Coast" in *Economic Development and Social Change*, (ed.) G. Dalton, New York, 1971.

"Objectives and Prognostications" in *The Gap Between Rich and Poor Nations*, (ed.) G. Ranis, London, 1972.

"Reflections on Unlimited Labour" in *International Economics and Development (Essays in Honour of Raoul Prebisch)*, (ed.) L.E. DiMarco, New York, 1972.

"The Development Process" in *The Case for Development : Six Studies*, United Nations, New York, 1973.

"Development and Distribution" in *Employment, Income Distribution and Development Strategy*, (ed.) A. Cairncross and Y. Puri, London, 1976.

"Prospects for World Development" in *Financing of Long Term Development*, Institute of Bankers, London, 1979.

"The Diffusion of Development" in *The Market and the State*, (ed.) T. Wilson, Oxford, 1976.

"Development Strategy in Limping World Economy" in *Proceedings of the 17th International Conference of Agricultural Economists*, 1979, Oxford Institute of International Economics.

C.   ARTICLES IN JOURNALS

"The Inter-relations of Shipping Freights" - *Economica*, 1941.

"The Two Part Tariff" - *Economica*, 1941.

"Notes on The Economics of Loyalty" - *Economica*, 1942.

"Monopoly and the Law" - *Modern Law Review*, 1943.

"An Economic Plan for Jamaica" - *Agenda*, 1944.

"Competition in Retailing" - *Economica*, 1945.

"Spare Time Activities of Employees" - *Modern Law Review*, 1946.

"Fixed Costs" - *Economica*, 1946.

"The Prospects before Us" - *The Manchester School*, 1948.

"Colonial Development" - *Transactions of the Manchester Statistical Society*, 1949.

"Whither Prices" - *District Bank Review*, 1949.

"The British Monopolies Act" - *The Manchester School*, 1949.

"Industrial Development in Puerto Rico" - *Caribbean Economic Review*, 1949.

"The Effects of an Overseas slump on the British Economy" - (with F.V. Meyer), *The Manchester School*, 1949.

"Developing Colonial Agriculture" - *The Three Bank Review*, 1949.

"Sur Quelques Tendances Seculaires" - *Economic Appliquee*, 1949.

"The Price Policy of Public Corporations" - *The Political Quarterly*, 1950.

"Industrialisation of the British West Indies" - *Caribbean Economic Review*, 1950.

"Issues in land settlement Policy" - *Caribbean Economic Review*, 1951.

"Food and Raw Materials" - *District Bank Review*, 1951.

"World Production, Prices and Trade 1870-1960" - *The Manchester School*, 1952.

"Reflections on South East Asia" - *District Bank Review*, 1952.

"United Nations Primer for Development : A Comment" - *Quarterly Journal of Economics*, 1953.

"Thoughts on Land Settlement" - *Journals of Agricultural Economics*, 1954.

"Economic Development with Unlimited Supplies of Labour" - *The Manchester School*, 1954.

"Trade Drives" - *District Bank Review*, 1954.

"Secular Swings in Production and Trade 1870-1913" - (with P.J. O'Leary), *The Manchester School*, 1955.

"Investment Policy" - *Bulletin of the Oxford Institute of Statistics*, 1955.

"Patterns of Public Revenue and Expenditure" - (with A. Martin), *The Manchester School*, 1956.

"International Competition in Manufactures" - *American Economic Review*, 1957.

"Employment Policy in an Underdeveloped Area" - *Social and Economic Studies*, 1958.

"Unlimited Labour : Further Notes" -
The Manchester School, 1958.

"Recent Controversies over Economic
Policy in the British Labour Party" -
World Politics, 1958.

"On Assessing a Development Plan" -
Ghana Economic Bulletin, 1959.

"Education and Economic Development" -
Social and Economic Studies, 1961.

"Education for Scientific Professions" -
Daedalus, 1962.

"Secondary Education and Economic
Structures" - *Socail and Economic
Studies*, 1964.

"A Review of Economic Development" -
(Richard T. Ely lecture), *American
Economic Review*, 1965.

"Beyond African Dictatorship : the
Crisis of a one-party state" -
Encounter, 1965.

"Unemployment in Developing Countries" -
(Stephenson Memorial Lecture), *World
Today*, 1967.

"World Trade since the War" - *Proceedings
of the American Philosophical Society*, 1968.

"Black Power and the American University" -
University : A Princeton Magazine, 1967.

"The Economic Profile of the American
Black" - *Journal of Religion and Health*, 1970.

"Summary : The causes of Unemployment in
Less Developed Countries" - *International
Labour Review*, 1970.

"The Caribbean Development Bank" -
*Proceedings of the 7th West Indies
Agricultural Economics Conference,*
Trinidad, 1972.

"The Shortage of Entrepreneunship" -
Journal of the Barbados Chamber of Commerce,
1973.

"Profits Do Work" - *Developed Forum,*
1976.

"The Dual Economy Revisited" - *The
Manchester School,* 1979.

"The Less Developed Countries and
Stable Exchange Rates" - *Third World
Quarterly,* 1979.

"The Slowing down of the Engine of
Growth" - *American Economic Review,* 1980.

W. Baer is Professor in the Department of Economics
   at the University of Illinois at Urbana-
   Champaign, U.S.A.

A.K. Blomqvist is Associate Professor in the Department of Economics University of Western Ontario,
   Canada.

W. Demas, formerly Head of the CARICOM Secretariat
   in Guyana, is now President of the Caribbean
   Development Bank, Barbados.

J. Harewood is Associate Director, Institute of
   Social and Economic Research, University of the
   West Indies, Trinidad.

B. Johnston is Professor and Economist at the Food
   Research Institute at Stanford University, U.S.A.

P.F. Leeson is Senior Lecturer, Department of Economics
   at the University of Manchester, U.K.

F. Long is currently Research Fellow at Queen Elizabeth
   House, Oxford University, U.K.

A.R. Prest is Professor in the Department of Economics,
   London School of Economics, U.K., formerly Stanley
   Jevons Professor of Political Economy at the
   University of Manchester, U.K.

W. Rostow is Professor in the Department of Economics,
   University of Texas at Austin, U.S.A.

P. Streeten is Director, Centre for Asian Development
   Studies at Boston University, U.S.A.